A Century of Change in a Chinese Village

A Century of Change in a Chinese Village

The Crisis of the Countryside

Lin Juren and Xie Yuxi
Edited by Linda Grove
Translated by Linda Grove, Li Dan,
and Marcella Siqueria Cassiano

ROWMAN & LITTLEFIELD
Lanham • Boulder • New York • London

Translation of this book was supported by the Chinese Fund for the Humanities and Social Sciences.

Published by Rowman & Littlefield
A wholly owned subsidiary of The Rowman & Littlefield Publishing Group, Inc.
4501 Forbes Boulevard, Suite 200, Lanham, Maryland 20706
www.rowman.com

Unit A, Whitacre Mews, 26-34 Stannary Street, London SE11 4AB

British Library Cataloguing in Publication Information Available

Library of Congress Cataloging-in-Publication Data

Names: Lin, Juren, author. | Grove, Linda, 1944- editor, translator.
Title: A century of change in a Chinese village : the crisis of the countryside / by Juren Lin ; edited and translated by Linda Grove.
Description: Lanham : Rowman & LIttlefield, 2018. | Series: Asia/Pacific/perspectives | Includes bibliographical references and index.
Identifiers: LCCN 2017060295 (print) | LCCN 2018017942 (ebook) | ISBN 9781538112366 (Electronic) | ISBN 9781538112359 (cloth) ISBN 9781538158319 (pbk)
Subjects: LCSH: Rural development—China—History. | Urbanization—China—History. | Social change—China—History.
Classification: LCC HN740.Z9 (ebook) | LCC HN740.Z9 C6217 2018 (print) | DDC 307.1/4120951—dc23
LC record available at https://lccn.loc.gov/2017060295

Contents

List of Measures

Pinyin	Chinese	Equivalences
Measures of Area		
Mu	亩	666.67 square meters
Fen	分	66.67 square meters
Gongqing (15 *mu*)	公顷	2.5 acres or 10,000 square meters
Qing (100 *mu*)	顷	16.4 acres or 66,667 square meters
Measures of Length		
Chi (Chinese foot)	尺	0.33 meter
Cun (Chinese inch)	寸	33 millimeters
Li	里	500 meters
Zhang	丈	3.33 meters or 10 feet
Measures of Weight		
Gongjin	公斤	1 kilogram
Jin (Chinese pound)	斤	0.5 kilogram or 1.1 pound
Liang (Chinese ounce)	两	50 grams

List of Figures and Tables

Tables

Chronology

1899–1900	Boxer Rebellion.
1905	End of imperial exams.
1906	Establishment of the South Manchurian Railway Co.
1901–1910	New government reforms.
1911	Fall of Qing Dynasty.
	Jinpu Railway Station in Licheng County opened.
1912	Founding of the Republic of China.
1913	Establishment of Lengshuigou's primary school.
1919	May Fourth Movement.
1921	Founding of the Communist Party of China (CPC).
1926–1928	Northern Expedition War.
1928	Establishment of the Kuomintang (KMT) government in Nanjing.
1937	Japanese forces occupied Licheng County in December.
	The "Three Saint Hall" was rebuilt in Lengshuigou.
1940	Lengshuigou faced severe drought in the summer.
1940–1942	Japanese *Kankō Chōsa* Survey Team studied Lengshuigou (November–December 1940; May–June 1941; February–March 1942).
1943	"Agricultural supplementary classes" were launched in Lengshuigou. Enrollment began in the spring of 1944.
1945	Japanese surrendered.
1948	The Liberation Army entered Lengshuigou before the Mid-Autumn Festival.
	The Office of the Communist Party of China for Licheng District was moved from Zhonggong to Lengshuigou.

1949	Founding of the People's Republic of China. A new administrative structure was established in Lengshuigou at the beginning of 1949, with Li Yuquan serving as village head and Li Xingfu as the vice-chairman of the Peasant Association.
1950	National government promulgated Agrarian Law (May 1950). Land Reform completed in Lengshuigou, fall of 1950. National government promulgated Marriage Law.
1951–1952	"Three-Anti," "Five-Anti," and "Thought Reform" campaigns were launched.
1952	Lengshuigou set up "agricultural producer's mutual-aid teams" in the spring.
1953	The local government began collection of grain in Lengshuigou, assuring the state monopoly over the purchase and marketing of grain. Marketing cooperatives were established in Lengshuigou.
1953–1957	Beginning of the collectivization movement through the setup of cooperatives. The "Anti-Rightist" campaign was launched.
1954	Lengshuigou established eight "lower level agricultural producer's cooperatives."
1955	The higher level agricultural producers' cooperative—"Red East"—was established in Lengshuigou in the fall.
1956	Licheng County's first small-scale electric-power generation station was constructed in Lengshuigou.
1958	Beginning of the Great Leap Forward. Household Registration System implemented. Establishment of the Dongjiao People's Commune in Licheng County, with jurisdiction over the people's commune of Lengyang (including villages of Lengshuigou, Shuipo, Yangjiatun, and Lijiazhuang). Establishment of the Lengyang Batallion. 300 *mu* of Lengshuigou land expropriated.
1959	End of the commune of Lengyang and of the military camp organizational system.
1963	Lengshuigou Brigade established.
1964	Establishment of Lengshuigou bristle-processing factory.
1966	Beginning of the Cultural Revolution. The "Four Old" and the "Four New" campaigns were launched.

1967 Establishment of the "Revolutionary Committee" in Lengshuigou.

1972 Lengshuigou village expanded its bristle factory, with the number of workers reaching 200; the factory's annual revenue marked 200,000 *yuan*.

1974 Establishment of Lengshuigou's village clinic and beginning of the cooperative medical service.

1976 Death of Chairman Mao Zedong.

1978 "Opening Up Policy" was launched.

Beginning of the "Household Contract Responsibility System."

The National People's Congress passed a new constitution.

Lengshuigou built water supply pipelines and set up tap water in the village.

1979 End of the system of discriminatory labels–based "class" statuses assigned at time of land reform.

"One Child Policy" was launched.

1980 Water supply pipelines were rebuilt, and an 8,000-meter-long asphalt road was constructed in Lengshuigou.

1983 The "Household Contract Responsibility System" was implemented in Lengshuigou.

1984 Lengshuigou middle school was rebuilt.

Establishment of a fertilizer factory in Lengshuigou.

The commune system was abolished in Lengshuigou, and a "dual organization" formed by the Village Committee and the Village Group was set up.

The Village Committee adopted a self-government organization with villagers democratically electing their representatives.

1986 The Lengshuigou dairy farm started operations.

1987 A farmer's market was established in Lengshuigou in the fall.

1990 Establishment of a chemical plant in Lengshuigou.

1994 The village spent more than 200,000 *yuan* repairing dilapidated houses into the Lengshuigou Primary School.

1995 Lengshuigou Senior Association was restored in the spring.

1999 A cow-breeding demonstration base was built in July on an area of 80 *mu*, employing 17 families.

2002 Lengshuigou invested more than 800,000 *yuan* to build the village office. The village gave about 100 *mu* of land to build the Kaiyuan Road and 200 *mu* to expand the Baicai Road.

	Cheng Kehong rents 400 *mu* to build the first industrial park in Lengshuigou.
	Beginning of the second phase of the cow-breeding demonstration base, covering an area of more than 300 *mu*.
2003	The current policy ruling the "New Rural Cooperative Medical Care System" was issued, and Lengshuigou began to gradually implement this medical care system.
2003	Lengshuigou spent 220,000 *yuan* to build a sports park, covering 9,800 square meters.
	Lengshuigou allocated 205 *mu* of land to build the Wangsheren Experimental Middle School.
2005	The original Lengshuigou Middle School merged with the Wangsheren Experimental Middle School.
2010	Wangsheren town was reclassified as a "sub-district" of Jinan (*jiedao*) in May, and Lengshuigou village has its administrative classification upgraded to "town" (*chengzhen*).
2010	Shandong University Team conducted a survey in Lengshuigou.
2011	Jinan's municipal government confirmed the plan to build Jinan's East Train Station in the area where Lengshuigou was located.

Preface

Linda Grove

The transformation of China from a poor rural country to an economic and geopolitical powerhouse is one of the great stories of our contemporary world. One of the central features of that transformation has been rapid urbanization: today more than half of the Chinese population live in cities, and China has more cities over one million in population than either the United States or Europe, including approximately fifteen megacities with populations exceeding ten million. The flip side of the story of rapid urbanization is the crisis of the countryside. As migrant laborers have flooded out of rural villages, what has happened in the rural communities that were once the center of Chinese economic, social, and cultural life? That is the question that the Chinese authors of *A Century of Change in a Chinese Village* set out to answer. Their study takes up some of the classical issues of social analysis: family and lineage; social stratification, personal networks and patterns of interaction; annual and life style rituals; village politics and elite formation; and social and market relations between countryside and cities. The authors focus on major structural changes that have transformed patterns of interaction among families, lineages, and individuals and their reflections in the economic, political, and ritual lives of villagers across seven decades, from the 1940s to the 2010s.

The village of Lengshuigou, the site for this intensive examination of rural change, is located on the North China plain, just south of the Yellow River, in the suburbs of Jinan, the provincial capital of Shandong province, which has a population of more than six million. Lengshuigou villagers, like those in other rapidly urbanizing areas in China, have been on the cutting edge of China's contemporary social revolution. Their village is being transformed from a farming community into an urban bed town: every morning office and factory workers leave the village to commute to work—some in the nearby industrial parks, but others in the nearby town of Wangsheren or in the slightly more distant city of Jinan. While older women and some men continue to farm tiny plots on the village's shrinking agriculture land, in most families at least one member now works in non-agricultural activities and most families earn most of their income from non-farm work.

The impact of urbanization, particularly of increasingly large numbers of former peasants leaving their home villages to seek employment in the factories and commercial and service sectors in cities and towns, is experienced in different ways in different parts of rural China. In villages that are more distant from the cities, men and women of prime working age leave the village for work outside, sending their children back to be raised by their rural grandparents. Lengshuigou represents a different pattern of urbanization. While some Lengshuigou villagers have left the village and taken up permanent residence in more distant places, most have been able to find jobs nearby, allowing them to continue to live in the village. Thus, in contrast to the pattern in more remote villages, families in Lengshuigou tend to remain intact, with a much lower percentage of families comprised exclusively of grandparents and small children while parents live and work far from home. While family relations are changing even in a village like Lengshuigou, they have changed in ways that are different from those in more remote villages where those in their prime working years may only be able to return to their homes and their "left behind children" once or twice a year.

As readers will see, changes in the patterns of work have led to changes in individual lives, but equally importantly, to transformations in the nature and significance of the village community in the lives of its members.

A Century of Change in a Chinese Village analyzes the changes in one village as a way to understand the fundamental changes that are transforming the lives of Chinese peasants since the initiation of the reform policies in the late 1970s. Lengshuigou is an ideal site for such a study for several reasons. First, there is a long history of earlier studies of the village, which have left a rich record of materials for comparison. The earliest social-science study of the village was conducted by Japanese researchers as part of a major early 1940s research project on Chinese customary law (*kankō chōsa*). Follow-up studies were carried out by other scholars in the mid-1980s, early 1990s, the first decade of the 2000s, and this study conducted in 2010 (Grove 2014). Second, the village's long tradition of emphasis on education nurtured a group of village intellectuals who have taken the initiative in recording facts about the village's history and cultural practices. Finally, researchers at Shandong University have, over several decades, developed close connections with the village, creating a network of relationships that culminated in the large-scale survey that provides significant data on patterns of inter-personal interaction and attitudes.

The village of Lenshuiguo also may be familiar to some readers since several of the theoretically most important studies of rural China by foreign scholars used the wartime *kankō chōsa* materials as core materials shaping their understandings of the nature of the Chinese village. Philip Huang's (1985) arguments about "involution" in the agricultural economy and Prasenjit Duara's (1988) theory of the "cultural nexus of power" both drew on close readings of the wartime Japanese surveys, including the survey of Lengshuigou. Huang used the *kankô chôsa* reports and other Japanese survey materials to explore the agrarian economy, arguing that the rural Chinese economy in the early twentieth century experienced growth without development, so while there was an overall increase in output (= growth) this was realized by an intensification of farming, resulting in no improvement in per capita production (= development). Duara, on the other hand, was interested in the self-government processes within Chinese villages; his theory of the "cultural nexus of power" focused on the roles of lineage and religious organizations in the village in local politics, as well as in shaping interactions with the formal institutions of government at the county level.

The same wartime survey materials have also been central to Japanese academic debates about the nature of "community" (*kyōdōtai*) in rural Chinese society. Japanese scholars, beginning with the original Mantetsu researchers, were interested in the level of communal cohesion and action within the Chinese village. Starting from their assumptions based on the experience of Japanese villages, they searched for communal institutions in rural China, focusing on such questions as village boundaries, cooperative activities for crop watching, and labor exchanges during the busiest agricultural seasons. Chinese scholars, most prominently the anthropologist Lan Linyou, have also used evidence from Lengshuigou in formulating theories about Chinese rural society. Lan's major contributions to the debates on the Chinese village have focused on lineage, and his contention that not all of those in a village who shared a common surname belonged to the same lineage. As we will see, this was clearly true of Lengshuigou, where the largest surname group, the Li, were divided among a number of lineages in which members shared a common ancestor.

A Century of Change in a Chinese Village, published in Chinese in 2013, is the result of a large project designed and supervised by Lin Juren, professor of sociology at Shandong University, with the collaboration of Yang Shanmin and Xie Yuxi of the sociology department, Tao Ye of the department of anthropology, and Li Shanfeng of the Shandong Academy of Social Sciences. The book combines materials from earlier studies of the village with a wealth of documentary evidence, interviews with village informants, and a large survey that drew respondents from 540 of the village's 1,143 households. Sociology students at Shandong University actively participated in the study, conducting interviews and gathering the survey data.

Each chapter of the book focuses on a specific aspect of village society—village politics, family and lineage, social networks, etc.—across four time periods: early twentieth century to 1949; the period of socialist construction (1949–1977); the early reform period (1978 to the mid-1990s), which saw the dissolution of the commune and the development of village-based industries; and the later reform period (late 1990s to 2010), a period in which village families became increasingly incorporated into non-agricultural employment and life styles. The authors use a diachronic approach, with parallel descriptions and analysis of each of the subjects for each era, as a way to present the dramatic changes in village society, the changing patterns of personal interaction among villagers, and shifts in perceptions and attitudes. Using this method, the authors delineate the changes in power relations and patterns of interaction as a result of war and socialist revolution, including the collective transformation of rural economy and society, the revival of certain "traditional" elements in the early reform period, and the gradual realignment of lives and patterns of interactions and attitudes that have reshaped individuals, families, rural society, and rural-urban relations as a result of the penetration of markets and the spread of what they refer to as "instrumental rationality," that is, the pursuit of goals primarily based on individual interests.

Lengshuigou is, of course, only one of almost a million Chinese villages, each with its own history and its own stories of successes and failures, advances and declines, and social transformations. The heart of this book is the story our Chinese authors tell, so here I only want to provide a very brief profile of Lengshuigou and how it compares with other villages. The Japanese researchers who conducted the first study described Lengshuigou as a large—over three hundred households, where an average North China village was closer to one hundred households—and relatively prosperous village, most of whose households, as in many North China villages, were owner-farmers. Like most villages across the North China plain, Lengshuigou was home to families who belonged to different lineages, and village self-rule was mediated by a council with representatives of the major lineages. Although the region came under Japanese occupation in 1937, there are no reports of fighting in the village, nor did the village have an active Communist Party-led resistance movement. Land reform was carried out in Lengshuigou after the establishment of the People's Republic of China in 1949. By that time, regulations for implementing land reform had been clearly specified and the movement was carried out in what might be described as an almost administrative process, avoiding the kind of class conflict that occurred in some areas of North China where work teams incited peasants to engage in mutual denunciations that often led to violent clashes.[1]

Beginning in the early 1950s, leadership roles in the village passed from an older elite who were economically better off, to new revolutionary leaders drawn from poor and lower-middle peasants. In many villages in China, 1950s revolutionary leaders were not only poor, but also men who had little or no education. Lengshuigou's long tradition of education—both traditional Chinese schools as well as a modern elementary school—meant that most of the poor who were chosen for leadership positions were literate and better prepared to deal with the new socialist economic and political systems. I have chosen the word "men" here to describe the early leaders since, as we will see in the book, education in village schools in the period before 1949 was exclusively for boys. As a result, most of the leadership roles in the village in the early socialist period were held by men. *A Century of Change in a Chinese Village* does, however, consider gender issues, since one of the greatest changes in village social life was the change in the status of women during the socialist era and in the subsequent period of reform.

Economically, the Maoist years were difficult. In earlier times Lengshuigou villagers had grown rice as a cash crop on about a third of their fields. When the state established a monopoly over the grain trade and set low compulsory purchasing prices, the extra income that had been earned from the cash crop disappeared. Then the Great Leap Forward and resulting famine dealt another blow to the village economy. During the famine years, the death rate rose, the birth rate declined, and a small number of people died of starvation or of diseases brought on by malnutrition. While Lengshuigou villagers suffered during those years, the number of deaths was small in comparison with other areas in the province.[2] The village's first non-agricultural enterprise—a bristle factory—was set up by one of the teams in 1964 in collaboration with a brush factory in Jinan. At its peak in the 1980s, the factory employed 280 villagers and provided not only income but also managerial experience to many villagers.

In the reform era, Lengshuigou has been quite successful in leveraging its location in the nearby suburbs of Jinan, utilizing connections with a village native who had become an entrepreneur, to set up a successful industrial park that has brought both jobs and income to the village. At the same time, some villagers have developed dairy farming, and the Lengshuigou dairy farm—with more than 7,000 cows—is the largest supplier of milk to the Jinan market. Improved infrastructure, including construction of highways giving easy access to the nearby town of Wangsheren and to Jinan city, opened up other commercial opportunities; many village households have set up restaurants and shops to serve the workers in the industrial parks, while others rent spare rooms to workers and their families. While those with education, special skills, or entrepreneurial initiative are doing quite well in reform era China, those without these advantages have fallen behind, as is evidenced in the growing income gap within the village.

The physical transformations of the village are easy for a casual visitor to see: a broad road through the middle of the village, paved lanes, new housing, apartment blocks, wifi-connected computers and smartphones in many households, cars and trucks parking along the village lanes, and uniformed sanitation workers cleaning village streets. It is much harder to see the transformations in relationships within families and groups in the village, and the changes in attitudes that stand behind those transformed relationships. *A Century of Change in a Chinese Village* provides a guide to and analysis of these deeper structural changes in contemporary rural China. The authors have asked about and listened carefully to what the villagers have told them about contemporary social transformations; data collected in their survey provides a solid basis for delineating the reactions of different segments and age groups of village society to those changes. Perhaps the most striking of those changes is the reversal of authority within families. Generational ordering, in which older males—fathers and grandfathers—controlled family decision making, was for centuries a fundamental principle of order within Chinese families and lineages. However, the results of the survey revealed that in the twenty-first century, members of the younger generation, who are much better attuned to media and the Internet, are now taking the lead in family decision making, based on their greater access to information on economic and social trends.

The survey also explores the nature of individual networks—who did an individual rely on for assistance when facing difficulties. In both pre-1949 and socialist Lengshuigou, networks were almost all within the village. In the pre-1949 village, networks privileged family and lineage; in the socialist era, membership in the same work team was added on as an additional basis for building networks. In the reform era, especially in the most recent two decades as villagers have found employment outside the village, non-related friends, as well as relatives through marriage, have come to supplant relationships that were based on the patrilineal lineage. While the patrilineal lineage survives as a focus for certain ritual activities, younger villagers much prefer to call on those outside of the patrilineal line, where they have more freedom in choosing their associates.

This translation involved a collaborative effort between the Chinese authors, Chinese translators, and the editor of the English edition. We have made some changes in the ordering of material, shortening and combining several of the chapters to highlight material that we believed would be of particular interest to an English reading audience interested in comparative study of rural China.

A Century of Change in a Chinese Village was written for a Chinese audience that shares with the authors certain vocabulary and concepts that may at first seem strange to English readers. Our authors, for example, often refer to the rural land-holding system before land reform as a "feudal landholding system." Readers used to a relatively strict definition of "feudal" may find this puzzling, since there is no question that the Chinese system of landholding had for many centuries been grounded in private ownership of land, and that political institutions were rooted in a centralized state. Chinese scholars conventionally describe this system, which in many parts of China included high levels of tenancy, as "feudal," based on the view that the relationship between landlords and tenants was an exploitative one. The use of "feudal" is not meant to suggest that the overall political system resembled Western notions of a feudal political system. Our authors also frequently refer to elements of pre-1949 society as "traditional." The use of this term does not imply that the elements referred to are in some way "unchanging" cultural patterns that remained intact for centuries, but rather is simply used as shorthand to describe what was common practice in the period before the 1949 revolution.

NOTES

1. See for example the account, drawn from Anti-Japanese Base Area Archives, on land reform in the Shandong Base Area, which describes a very bloody process in which villagers turned against their neighbors, and large numbers of people—including some CPC cadre—were declared to be class enemies and killed (Zhang 2006) [Zhang Xueqiang, *Xiangcun bianqian yu nongmin jiyi: Shandong laoqu Junanxian tudi gaige yanjiu* Village Transition and Peasant Memory: A Case Study of Land Reform in the Shandong Base Area, 1941-1951]. Beijing: Shehui Kexue Wenxian Chubanshe, 2006.] The classic work in English on Chinese land reform is William Hinton's *Fan Shen: A Documentary of Revolution in a Chinese Village* (New York: Vintage, 1966). Another account, based on extensive field work in neighboring Hebei province by Edward Friedman, Paul Pickowicz, and Mark Selden with Kay Ann Johnson, *Chinese Village, Socialist State* (New Haven: Yale University Press, 1991) provides an account of land reform in a village where there was more class struggle than in Lengshuigou, but certainly less than in places like the Shandong Base Area.

2. For example, in one of the other *kankō chōsa* villages where I participated in a follow-up study (Houxiazhai in northwest Shandong Province), 200 out of a village population of 700 died of starvation during the famine years. In Houxiazhai and the surrounding region in Northwest Shandong province, the high death rates were the

result of both leadership problems and the consequences of decisions with regard to an irrigation scheme that had created channels to bring Yellow River water to irrigate the fields. The planners had neglected to plan for drainage: heavy rains led to waterlogging, the rise of alkaline residues to the land surface, and a sharp decline in agricultural productivity. There have been a number of studies trying to understand why some villages and regions were harder hit in the famine. Village leadership clearly played a role: in villages or counties where local leaders followed directions from higher authorities and inflated crop output figures, excessive grain expropriations by the state left little for villagers to eat, resulting in starvation.

Acknowledgments

The authors, translators, and editor would like to thank the Chinese Fund for the Humanities and Social Sciences for its support for the translation and publication of this book, and the reviewers for the Fund and the Fund's committee. The Chinese edition of this book was selected for inclusion in the series "100 Chinese Villages" (Zhongguo Baicun Diaocha Congshu), and the authors thank the late Lu Xueyi and Xu Jingze for their support. The research project and publication of the Chinese edition of the book received support from colleagues and students of Shandong University who participated in the gathering of materials, carrying out the survey, interviewing, and selection of materials. We would particularly like to thank: Yang Shanmin, Tao Ye, Liu Cuixia, Qin Tong, Wang Furui, Wu Yu, Zhou Wenjing, Li Xiao, Wang Fengqiu, Liang Zhen, Wei Ya'ni, Zhang Xiaoli, Xing Yan, Zhang Ying, Dong Hongzhan, and Chen Xiaobin.

Li Dan and Marcella Siqueira Cassiano did much of the work in producing the draft translation and Marcella Cassiano made great contributions in assisting with the final editing of the manuscript. Dr. Li Miao checked for consistency between the English manuscript and the Chinese original, and Xiang Wei and Xu Youjun assisted with editing.

Finally, we would like to offer our warmest thanks to Mark Selden, who has played a major role in shaping the final manuscript, repeatedly reading and offering advice on the manuscript. We also thank him for his assistance in arranging for publication.

Acknowledgments

Introduction

For several thousand years, most Chinese have lived in agricultural communities dominated by farming, creating a cultural system in which the small-scale peasant style of production and way of life shaped both the social structure and rural culture. This led Fei Xiaotong, China's greatest twentieth-century anthropologist, to argue that "China is fundamentally a rural society" with the village as its basic unit (Fei 1992 [1948]). For this reason, the study of the village and its development can serve as an entry point to understanding Chinese society.

This book looks at the transformation of one of China's almost one million villages over the last hundred years. Our focus is on Lengshuigou, a large North China village, located just south of the Yellow River and some ten kilometers east of the Shandong provincial capital of Jinan. First studied by Japanese researchers in the early 1940s, the detailed records of their study of Lengshuigou and five other North China villages have been one of the most important sources for understanding rural life in China before 1949 and one of the chief sources for theories about the structure and organization of Chinese rural society. In the last three decades, scholars associated with Shandong University have carried out a number of follow-up studies on Lengshuigou, making it one of the best-studied villages in China. When we undertook to do a re-study of Lengshuigou in 2010, we chose this village because this long history of study offered us an opportunity to look at long-term structural changes over the twentieth and twenty-first centuries.

Our approach is to look at the village of Lengshuigou from a number of perspectives incorporating methodology from several disciplines. Before setting out our own approach to the study of Lengshuigou, we would like to briefly reflect on what the French philosopher Michel Foucault called the "archaeology of knowledge," a process that involves a reflexive examination of the ways in which scholarly discourse shapes thinking about a subject—in this case rural China and the "Chinese village." Throughout the twentieth century, both foreign and domestic Chinese scholars have been interested in studying the village as a way to understand the fundamental logics and building blocks of Chinese civilization—and for many of us, also as a way to devise policies that might lead to its transformation. While many of the early works on rural China were written by international scholars, the dramatic changes in China beginning in the 1980s have led a new generation of Chinese scholars working in China to turn their attention to the study of villages. Anthropologists, sociologists, and political scientists, using the analytical tools of their own disciplines, have produced a large number of studies on different localities.[1] The multidisciplinary approach used in this book draws on much of that work and is grounded in perspectives from three disciplines: anthropology, political science, and sociology.

Anthropology is well known for its research focus on foreign cultures and efforts to understand "the other," as well as for its stress on "reflexivity," a methodological stance that is deeply conscious of the interplay between different elements of a small community. At the beginning of the development of anthropology as a discipline, anthropologists particularly focused on what they categorized as primitive societies. Through fieldwork, the researcher tried to dig out and understand the existence and meaning of the cultural world of the village through thick description of village customs, beliefs, kinship, human relationships, lineage, folk rituals, production, ways of life, and the symbolic system.

One of the classic studies in this tradition is Fei Xiaotong's *Peasant Life in China,* which focuses on the use of land in the reproductive process of a peasant family, describing the economic and social life of peasants and showing how the Chinese social scene was reflected in the community life of one small village. He thus established an experimental paradigm showing how the observation of a small village community could reveal much about the larger Chinese society. Fei's research, which was the first major work by a non-Western anthropologist working in his own culture, is regarded as a milestone in anthropological field research. For us as rural sociologists, the studies of Fei and of many contemporary Chinese anthropologists have shown how the combination of fieldwork research methods with ethnographic thick description can provide deep understanding and analysis of micro societies. Some question, however, whether such anthropological research, with its thick description focused on a single "point" can get beyond the culture and life of a single village to offer clues to the large macro picture of Chinese society.

Political science provides the second disciplinary approach, especially what is usually termed the "state-society analytic framework." Village studies from the perspective of political science focus on the distribution and mechanisms of village power, examining questions about village autonomy, the election of village committees, and the political behavior of village people. Fundamentally, both Chinese and foreign researchers have tried to answer the question, "How far down does the power of the state reach?" From this perspective, village study is usually carried out under the state-society analytic framework, that is, focusing on questions related to how the state's power reaches the village and functions there. Political scientists consider the nature of village leaders: To what extent are they representatives of their communities, to what extent agents of the state? How does the village implement and adapt state policies, and how do villagers communicate their own wishes to higher levels of government? These questions were an important focus of pre-1949 village studies and are even more so in the studies of villages during the Maoist era and our own studies of post-reform contemporary Chinese society. Studies have taken up the interaction between village and state, with a special focus on village power structures and village management gaining increasing attention. In recent years the acceleration of urbanization and the transformation of the village management system have led to conflicts between villages and the outside world and frequent mass protests. The academic world has responded by studying such issues and pondering how peasants can best express their interests and what kind of public service provision is most appropriate.

Sociology provides the third disciplinary approach. Contemporary Chinese society is in a period of intense transformation, and scholars have struggled to understand the very complicated impacts of that transformation. Sociological studies, which have focused on changes in village economic structures and the resulting diversification of behavior and patterns of interaction, have created a new style of research, based on a structural change approach. This approach provides a fresh perspective to examine the transition in village society under the framework of a dualistic structure of rural-urban society and a dualistic analysis of tradition-modernity in time and space. These studies focus on the series of social transitions, beginning in the mid-twentieth century, which have dramatically impacted fundamental organizational principles in the villages: land reform, collectivization under the People's Commune system, dissolution of the commune, and the shift to the family-contract system under the reform policies.

When we compare the contributions of the different disciplinary fields to village studies, we might say that anthropologists usually study the village as discoverers of "the other," seeking to understand a society that is different from their own, while sociologists study the village as observers or participant-observers. One of the key issues in sociological village studies is how the village and its inhabitants are being transformed from membership in a traditional social community into one in a modern urban society. The sociological research method is based on empirical study designed to grasp the development of rural Chinese society from a macro perspective. While sociologists and anthropologists are both interested in understanding the fundamental building blocks of society, our approaches to the use of micro case studies differ. To borrow the words of Zhuang Kongshao on the contrasting approaches to the study of village society, sociologists specialize in the "locust" method, which involves covering a large area, while the anthropologists specialize in the "mole" method of thick description of a particular spot (Zhuang 2007). So for example, in this micro study of Lengshuigou, our investigation is directed to understanding how the grand narratives of change at a regional or national level can be seen in the experience of villagers.

The above summary of perspectives is intended to provide us with a rough map of approaches to studying the Chinese village. Needless to say, the distinctions between the perspectives are not clear-cut, and most scholars use a combination of research methods. In addition, research done from the perspectives of history, economics, law, and even geography, architecture, rural justice, and rural land system and employment patterns of village people, and their income may shed some light on our comprehensive understanding of rural society. In this book, we will use all of these different perspectives to gain a greater understanding of rural China, and also—as Chinese scholars—suggest ways to reform rural society to provide better and more fulfilling lives to those who continue to live in rural communities.

RESEARCH ON LENGSHUIGOU

Lengshuigou is one of the most studied villages in all of rural China. The first study of Lengshuigou was done by a Japanese research team, which selected Lengshuigou as one of six villages for intensive study as part of a wartime project, commonly referred to as the *Kankō Chōsa*. This was a large and well-funded project designed to investigate what the researchers called "customary law." The term "customary law" referred to common practices used in negotiating daily life that had been developed before the adoption of modern legal codes. To understand this kind of customary law, the Japanese researchers queried various aspects of rural life—family and family organization; lineage organization and function; economic activities; landholding and customs related to buying, selling, renting and mortgaging land; taxation; markets and market practices; religious activities; annual ceremonies; births and deaths; marriages and funerals; village leadership; village governance; village relations with township and county government; and so on. After the war, the results of the research project were published in six large volumes, presented in question-and-answer style, which allow us even today to "hear" the voices of individuals in a village—village heads and councilors as well as ordinary villagers, landlords, tenants, and owner cultivators, and so forth. These volumes became the main source for a number of well-known English-language works on North China rural society, including books by Ramon Myers (1970), Philip Huang (1985), and Prasenjit Duara (1988), as well as many books and articles by Japanese scholars (Hatada 1973, Uchiyama 2009, Uchiyama 2003). Translated into Chinese, works based on the *Kankō Chōsa* have had a major impact on stimulating Chinese interest in the study of rural society, and are now a major source for study of pre-Liberation Chinese rural society.

Japanese *Kankō Chōsa* Study of Lengshuigou

The first major study of Lengshuigou village was undertaken in the early 1940s as part of the study of customary law in rural North China, based on collaboration between the research bureau of the South Manchurian Railway Company and legal scholars based at Tokyo and Kyoto Universities. The South Manchurian Railway Company was founded in 1906 and became the biggest Japanese monopoly enterprise in China. In addition to running the South Manchurian railway and affiliated companies, it also established a large research bureau to provide military, political, economic, and social intelligence to support Japanese aggression in China.

In the early 1940s, during the Anti-Japanese War, legal scholars from the Academic Committee of the Sixth Research Committee of the East Asian Institute and scholars from the North China Branch Research Bureau of the South Manchurian Railway Research Bureau undertook a large-scale investigation of North China villages. A leading legal scholar from Tokyo University, Suehiro Izutarō, provided the intellectual leadership for the project, which was originally planned to cover Hebei, Shandong, Shanxi, the Suicha area, Jiangsu, and Zhejiang provinces. The first phase of the project, estimated to take about ten years with an estimated cost of 557 million Japanese yen (old yen), was to employ nineteen to thirty-four professional researchers per year.

Later, with the drastic turn of the war and victories of Chinese resistance forces, this massive project was suspended after completing studies of North China villages in four counties in Hebei province and two in Shandong province, between November 1940 and August 1944. The *Kankō Chōsa* surveys were based on interviews, and it was the publication of the verbatim interviews that has attracted so much interest from foreign and Chinese scholars.

Researchers, following a detailed research outline, held long conversations with all kinds of village people and recorded the contents of those conversations. The major results of this project were transcriptions of the interviews, which were compiled in 123 volumes as Research Materials on Customary Behavior in Rural North China. Based on these reports, a six-volume series, *Chūgoku Nōson Kankō Chōsa* (Survey of Chinese Village Customs) (1952–1958), was published by Iwanami Shoten. These six volumes, with a total of 3,200 pages covering several villages in six Chinese counties, are regarded as the most comprehensive material on early-twentieth-century rural Chinese economy and society. Volume 4 of the series includes the transcripts of fieldwork in Shandong, in Lengshuigou in Licheng County and in Houxiazhai in En County.

The Japanese researchers paid three visits to Lengshuigou in November–December 1940, May–June 1941, and November–December 1941, and the records of their interviews cover 351 pages in the published volumes. Editors of the volume divided the interviews into six major categories: village (1–54), lineage (55–146), tenancy (147–90), land purchases and sales (191–229), rural credit and transactions (230–68), and taxes and finance (269–351). From these figures, we can see that in the records from Lengshuigou, sections on lineage occupy 26.2 percent of the space, followed by taxes and finance at 23.7 percent. As for the subjects of the interviews, researchers selected township heads, village heads, and leaders of the *baojia*, a mutual-responsibility system in the village that had been a part of state-imposed efforts to control villages under the last imperial dynasty, reorganized under the Republic and again under the Japanese occupation. They also conducted a small number of interviews with ordinary peasants. Researchers worked from a long and detailed research plan, adjusting the questions they asked to fit with the informant's status and role in the village. Thus, the same questions appear many times: sometimes the answers are similar, but we can also discover different answers to the same question, reflecting the differing views of people as a result of their different positions in the village.

For example, in the section on village organization, most of the interviews were with leaders of the *baojia*. The *baojia* system divided the village population into decimal units, with ten households forming a *jia,* and ten of the *jia* units forming a *bao*. The researchers interviewed twelve heads of the smaller *jia* units, and six heads of the large *bao* units. Among the items on the interview protocol were such issues as the general situation of the village, that is, how the village name came into being and legends about this, the size of the village, its location, its climate and type of soil, village people's residences, transportation, crops, marketplace and transactions, migrant labor among village people, long-term and short-term hired hands, beliefs, folk customs, festivals, land ownership, tenancy, livestock, sidelines, administrative organization in the village, public order maintenance, justice system, village fees, common wealth of the village (property, schools, and temples), relationships among the villagers and arrangements for mutual assistance, and relationships with other villages.

By late 1941, changes in the security situation made it difficult to continue the research, and researchers reported that among the six surveyed villages, Lengshuigou was the most difficult. According to the preface to volume 4 of *Chūgoku Nōson Kankō Chōsa*, with the beginning of the Pacific War, the Chinese resistance forces strengthened their power, and the Japanese forces started to weaken; at the same time, there was a noticeable change in the peasants' willingness to participate in the interviews. This presented a situation very different from that encountered in Shajing village, Shunyi County, Hebei Province, where the research work had proceeded much more smoothly. In their initial investigation of Lengshuigou done in 1940, the investigators had been able to visit the village; but as a result of growing hostility from the villagers, subsequent interviews took place in the county town, and many of the respondents gave only "Yes" or "No" answers. As a result of these difficulties, the research team switched their focus to a smaller village, Lujiazhuang.

Let us now briefly consider questions related to the use of these surveys by later scholars. Although the first volume of the *Chūgoku Nōson Kankō Chōsa* won the Asahi Culture Award, the sales were terrible, and the next few volumes all faced the same fate.[2] The volumes were also controversial within the Japanese academic world. Some saw them as making important contributions to knowledge, while others were critical, believing that the work was tainted by its connections to Japanese imperialist activities in China. Let us briefly review some of those arguments.

All participants in the debates agreed that there was no question that the fieldwork had been undertaken under the protection of the Japanese occupation forces at a time when they were engaged in an aggressive war in China. On one side of the debate were those who believed that in spite of that, the *Chūgoku Nōson Kankō Chōsa* should be considered as precious historical materials that could be used by different disciplines. Included in this group are those who undertook efforts to revisit the villages to verify the original work. The most impressive project of this category was the resurvey project on North China villages and historical change in rural society, a team project headed by Mitani Takashi (Mitani 1999, 2000) and the anthropological research on Lengshuigou done by Nakao Katsumi (Nakao 1990).

Another group of Japanese scholars believed that because of their association with Japanese aggression in China, these investigation results were tainted, and to make use of them was tantamount to committing crimes and represented ignorance of contemporary Japanese history. This view was in line with the Japanese left wing after World War II. The best known representative of this group is Kobayashi Kazumi (Lu and Sasaki 1993, 3).

The third position differed from the first view, which had recognized the role of South Manchurian Railroad investigations in supporting colonial rule. It viewed the *Chūgoku Nōson Kankō Chōsa* as valuable raw material in studying and describing Chinese society, believing that the materials could be used to make up for deficiencies in the research on the living conditions of the peasants. The most prominent figures in this group were the legal historian Niida Noboru and the historian Furushima Toshio (KC 1955, 1 and 3–7).

As Chinese scholars interested in long-term change in rural China, we believe that despite deficiencies in the investigation done by the South Manchurian Railway Company on Lengshuigou village, it still includes precious research materials. The contents are rich, quite useful for sociology, history, demography, and folklore studies and the study of rural finance. The investigation data is comprehensive, and the survey questions are detailed. In comparison, similar research done by scholars at home and abroad or by the government in pre-Liberation China just provided vague figures. The projects on peasant households done by the South Manchurian Railway Company are detailed as well, peerless among the many researches on "old China." Hence, American scholar Ramon H. Myers praised these research materials and noted, "It is precisely because these surveys provide us with a picture of rural change since 1890 that they are so valuable. It is thus possible to compare conditions in the countryside for different periods, particularly the periods before and after 1937" (Myers 1970, 38). We should note, however, that most of the researchers did not speak Chinese and worked through interpreters, so answers may have been filtered as a result.

Although scholars differ on their evaluation of the *Chūgoku Nōson Kankō Chōsa*, the abundant research materials accumulated on this basis are of great historical and academic value, providing important reference for later research on rural North China villages. The historian Philip C. C. Huang commented that

> the Mantetsu surveys stand as the most precise and detailed body of information available to us on pre-Revolution Hebei-Shandong villages. If, when the materials from the many oral-history projects undertaken in China in the 1950's and early 1960's become available, they prove to be more substantial than the few pieces that have been published or have otherwise found their way into collections outside China, perhaps the Mantetsu surveys can be superseded. If not, with all their imperfections, they will remain our primary source for a close up examination of the Hebei-Shandong villages in the 1930's." (Huang 1985, 43)

Lengshuigou in Western Studies

Three American scholars—the economist Ramon Myers, and Philip Huang and Prasenjit Duara, who are both historians—published important books using the *Kankō Chōsa* materials. We would like to briefly look at what they had to say about Lengshuigou. Myers was the pioneer in using the *Kankō Chōsa* materials to study the economy of pre-Liberation North China, publishing *The Chinese Peasant Economy: Agricultural Development in Hopei and Shantung, 1890–1949* in 1970. The book used material on four of the surveyed villages to study the nature of the peasant economy. Myers treated the village as a unit of production and exchange, examining land, labor, capital, and production techniques in an effort to determine to what degree each of the villages was able to support itself through agricultural and nonagricultural activities. Myers examined changes in these factors of production, analyzed the organizational processes and forms of village and peasant economy, the role of village leaders, and the financial relationship between the villages and local government. Myers summed up his view of Lengshuigou, concluding that it was "probably the village with the highest living standard of the four. In this village there were shops and artisans; only a small percentage of the village's households dispatched workers outside to earn nonfarm income; most debt was held within the village; and many households possessed some consumer durables such as bicycles" (Myers 1970, 123).

Philip Huang's work *The Peasant Economy and Social Change in North China* (1985) was published fifteen years after Myers's work and played a major role in focusing attention on the *Kankō Chōsa* materials as a source for village study. After spending ten years reading the Japanese survey materials, he also visited some of the villages. Using a neoclassical economics approach, Huang focused on peasant economic relations to try to answer the important historical question of why the peasant economy in modern China did not transit into a modern capitalist economy. Huang's study used not only the *Kankō Chōsa* materials but also materials on a total of thirty-three North China villages, moving from the individual villages to a consideration of regional development patterns (Deng 2010, 134).

Huang's study, like that of Myers, placed Lengshuigou village in a comparative framework that explored the relationship between village organization and economic structure. Key elements in his analytical framework were economic involution and social differentiation. Within this comparative framework, he saw Lengshuigou village as a "closed" community featuring landholding peasants, distinct from other villages that were comparatively more open with higher levels of commercialization. "The villages that were relatively stable communities of mainly owner-cultivators tended to deal with external threat as solidary units. The villages in which a large proportion of the peasants had become partly proletarianized tended to fall apart in the face of external threat and to become vulnerable to abuse by aberrant elements" (Huang 1985, 274).

Prasenjit Duara's *Culture, Power and the State: Rural North China, 1900–1942* (1988), offered a very different take on the North China village, shifting the focus from economic relations to the question of state power and village organization. He demonstrated in detail how state power penetrated the basic level of society through many channels including commercial groups, agents, temple organizations, religion, myths, and symbolic resources. Duara termed the resulting complex of relations a "cultural nexus of power," a formulation that provided a new perspective and method for understanding rural society in North China.

Duara's study was based on a close reading of the *Kankō Chōsa* materials and visits to two of the villages—Shajing in the suburbs of Beijing and Lengshuigou—in the summer of 1986. Like Myers and Huang, Duara compared the six villages that he studied. In Duara's case, the division was based on three standards: whether the village was wealthy or poor, the degree to which lineage and religious organizations played a role in rural life, and distance from cities. He saw Lengshuigou village as a comparatively wealthy village, with religious organizations playing an important role, and close to a major city. Duara described Lengshuigou village as follows:

> Cold Water Ditch (Lengshuigou) is located in Licheng County in Shandong, not far from the provincial capital of Jinan. Now, as in the 1940s, it is an enormous and prosperous village. Before the end of the war it had a population of 370 households—far greater than the average North China village of approximately 100 households. Until the early Republic, Cold Water Ditch had a flourishing religious life, eloquently testified to by the 25 or so temple stele from the Qing period." (Duara 1988, 12)

Follow-Up Studies on Lengshuigou

Nakao Katsumi's Follow-Up Study on Lengshuigou

Japanese anthropologist Nakao Katsumi undertook systematic field study in Lengshuigou village from September 1984 to April 1986 when he was an international student at Shandong University, publishing the results in Japanese in *The Structure of Power and Social Change in a Chinese Village* in 1990. Nakao's ethnography described the physical and geographical setting, population, economy, power, and social life of Lengshuigou village. The book's seven chapters include a general introduction and history of Lengshuigou, a discussion of the bases of power in the village, changes in social groups, changes in social life and customs, and so on. He explored changes in village political organization and power before and after the revolution, kinship and changes in social groups, and changes in customs, particularly life-cycle rituals.

Nakao's study represented one of the first anthropological follow-up studies based on field research by a non-Chinese scholar on an ethnically Han village in rural North China. Before the launching of the policies for reform and opening-up, field research on Chinese "traditional social culture" and ethnic Han village society communities by non-Chinese scholars had focused on Taiwan, Hong Kong, and Southeast Asian Chinese society. Nakao's fieldwork extended over a reasonably long period of time, and in addition to studying Lengshuigou, he was able to visit nearby villages, which allowed him to place the experiences of Lengshuigou in a comparative context.

Nakao chose Lengshuigou because he could use the *Kankō Chōsa* materials to provide historical context and a baseline against which to measure change after 1949. Comparison with nearby villages and the broader North China region allowed for an extended general analysis. In a sense, his work can be seen as an attempt to combine diachronic and synchronic perspectives. Nakao's book placed social change at the center of the analysis, as he sought to explain "the static and dynamic characteristics of the structure of rural China" (Nakao 1990, 4).

Nakao's analysis attributed the change in social structure of rural mainland China after 1949 to the change in the power structure in village society and further pointed out that it was the change in the power structure that led to the struggle for more political resources in lineage social groups and finally led to the changes in the structure of relations (Nakao 1990, 169). Nakao's analysis and conclusions were based on three major factors. The first involved the form of political power. One of the features of Chinese society after the revolution was the extension of state power over individual villagers through new social authorities, reflected in the administration of power, the ability to make political decisions, and the redistribution of interests through grassroots organizations and leaders. The second focus was the relationship between power struggles and lineage relationships. The book argued that although the lineage was relatively weak in North China before the revolution, the unity of lineage organizations as actors in the political power game strengthened after the revolution due to internal political conflicts, which had led to a pattern in which different lineage groups' control over village power structures ebbed and flowed. In other words, while the lineage had existed only as a potential focus for organization in the pre-revolutionary period, after the revolution it became a major source of "strategic alliances." Nakao's third major contribution was his analysis of daily life. The book noted that the shift to public ownership of land and the collectivization of labor led to changes in the fundamental functions of the household in economic production, and that this in turn led to major changes in ideas about the role of the family. Moreover, the rapid improvement in women's status in production following land reform gave women an almost equal position with men, which weakened both ideas about and expressions of the patriarchal system. The older patriarchal system was replaced by a new system with greater equality between patriarchal and matriarchal relations in social life. As a result of these changes, as well as a result of various political movements, customary rituals and practices labeled as "superstitious" were banned.

Although the title of Nakao's book was *Power Structure and Social Change in Rural China*, his analysis was broader than the title suggests. Analyzing the complex relationships between economy, society, and political power, it represented an important break from other studies by foreign scholars at that time, which either focused exclusively on political analysis or which had put too much stress on literary works interpreting peasant life in the liberated areas. The book was an important step forward in anthropological study as one of the first anthropological studies of a post-revolutionary Chinese village, and one of the first anthropological studies of a Han-nationality village outside of southern China.

Follow-Up Studies by Shandong University

Scholars in the Department of Sociology of Shandong University have had a long-term interest in the study of Lengshuigou village, and have undertaken a number of research projects with the support of the local government and village leaders. In the early 1990s, a comprehensive survey was done in Lengshuigou village under the direction of Xu Jingze and Yang Shanmin. This project was the result of collaboration between Shandong University sociologists and Kim Kwang-ok, a prominent anthropologist from Seoul National University, who had used the *Kankō Chōsa* materials to write his MA thesis at Oxford University. Kim helped to design the research plan, with Shandong professors supervising the fieldwork. The final product was *Modernization: Village Choices—A Comprehensive Study of One Rural Social Community*, published in Chinese in 1994. The study used a combination of methods including participant observation, survey of archival and documentary records, and survey questionnaires to describe economic activities, social structure, social life, religion, customs, and beliefs. On the basis of the description, the authors made a systematic analysis of new developments in Lengshuigou village after Reform and opening up. In the conclusion, they argued, "Lengshuigou village is an independent rural community located in the suburbs of Jinan; agriculture is still the main industry; industry, commerce and services are beginning to develop; the community is opening up gradually; it is becoming a center for the surrounding villages and has close connections with Wangsheren Town and the city of Jinan" (Xu and Yang 1994, 23).

The research for *Modernization: Village Choices* was done in the early 1990s, about a decade after the beginning of the Reform and Opening Up Policies. In the twenty-first century, the pace of change in Chinese society has intensified, radically changing the relationship between rural and urban areas. Growing gaps in wealth and the distribution of resources, and the problems of rural migrants—both those who have left the countryside and in the villages they have left behind—have become a major focus of new academic research. At Shandong University, students and faculty have continued to investigate these changes through ongoing research in Lengshuigou, and several graduate students have written theses based on fieldwork in the village.[3]

RESEARCH METHOD AND CONTENTS OF THIS BOOK

Research Approach and Method

This volume builds on the rich research records on Lengshuigou to provide a systematic and comprehensive analysis of a century of change, using a method that we have called "re-research." This approach, which involves returning to a previously studied research site, has been an important approach to social research. For example, Fei Xiaotong repeatedly revisited "Jiang village" and "three villages in Yunnan" where he had first conducted research in the 1930s, and many other anthropologists have also undertaken follow-up studies on well-known villages.[4] There has been much academic interest in follow-up studies because they provide an opportunity to reexamine the same research subject and extend the significance of earlier research. They allow us to combine intensive study of a particular community with data from broader regional studies, deepening our knowledge and providing the basis for more convincing theoretical arguments. As Zhuang Kongshao notes, "Follow-up studies revive our interest in earlier studies, bringing together our emotional interest in a community with academic analysis and understanding" (Zhuang 2004, 491). Despite the attractions of such follow-up studies, few Chinese sociologists have undertaken this work.

Follow-up studies can take many forms. The method we are using, which we call "re-research," is more than simply an updating of earlier research. Our study on Lengshuigou is not a simple repetition of anthropological research on the village, but a new research project that builds on the rich records from earlier studies. Wang Mingming once noted that follow-up research should not just repeat arguments on the "past" and the "present," but should combine with academic reflection of "re-studies," that is, "reflective inheritance" (Wang 2005). Xu Bin and Hu Hongbao argued that "distinctions should be made between follow-up studies and re-studies. For those using ethnography, in essence, there are no so-called follow-up studies, but just re-studies. This is determined by the nature of the special text in ethnography" (Xu and Hu 2005, 44). Of course, our research is not a re-study in an ethnographic sense since our aim is not to provide a chronological discussion of changes in Lengshuigou over one hundred years, but rather involves a new analytical approach in both its research framework and the issues it discusses.

Our focus in this study of Lengshuigou is on social change, using a diachronic approach. To achieve that goal in each of the substantive chapters of the book, we present parallel analyses of the given subject at four time periods: at the time of the *Kankō Chōsa* study in the early 1940s; in the period of socialist construction, from 1949 to 1978; during the early reform period, 1978 to the 1990s; and in the later period of reform, late 1990s to 2010. In each stage, we focus on important transitions in Lengshuigou village during that historical period, explaining the changes from the perspective of structural social change. Our approach differs from that of social history, which is more concerned with presenting historical changes. Our sociological approach emphasizes explanations of social change. We are thus following in a long-standing sociological tradition that focuses on social change, especially structural social change. We have been inspired by the work of the Polish sociologist Piotr Sztompka, who noted, "Perhaps the reason for emphasizing structural change is that, more often than other types, it leads to changes of, rather than merely changes in, society. Social structure makes up a sort of skeleton on which society and its operations are founded. When it changes, all else is apt to change as well" (Sztompka 2003, 6). During the last hundred years, changes in rural China have been closely connected with the grand narrative of revolution in the Chinese social structure. Before the founding of the People's Republic of China, most Chinese lived in villages that were relatively closed small communities. However, after the establishment of the People's Republic of China, the processes of collectivization and socialist transformation turned the village into a state-controlled production unit and living unit, and activities of the villagers displayed high collectivity and homogeneity. In more recent years, the dissolution of the communes and introduction of the household contract responsibility system have brought significant structural change. While these structural changes have led to significant social and economic development, they have been accompanied by changes in villagers' social activities and their own understandings of social relations.

We are now in an era when the waves of rapid urbanization and incorporation into the market economy are having a dramatic impact on Lengshuigou life: almost every family gains a significant part of its household income from non-agricultural work, and villagers increasingly are incorporated in work and social networks that transcend family, lineage, and village borders.

When scholars study structural social change, they usually do so from a macro-societal perspective. In this book, however, our subject is only one village—a very micro-societal unit. Methodologically, the question is how to combine macro-level analysis with micro-level analysis. Our strategy is to regard Lengshuigou village as a case study—but not merely a case study. We are using the rich studies of Lengshuigou as a vehicle to illustrate important changes in Chinese rural society. Thus, our approach to this study is significantly different from ethnographic studies that focus on a single village.

This study aims to analyze comprehensively and systematically the history and development of Lengshuigou village over the last century. Our research combines documentary research and fieldwork. The documentary aspects of our study make use of materials from local gazetteers, archival records that provide annual statistical and social data, and historical materials on the social and cultural transition of Lengshuigou village. These materials provide a general picture of the background and historical and cultural evolution of the region. Building on those records, we then undertake an analysis of the population, economy, society, politics, culture, and family in Lengshuigou village, based on our own survey data gathered from questionnaires, interviews, and observation.

Documentary records used in this study include: (1) county gazetteers and village annals of Licheng County, (2) archive files on the transition of Lengshuigou village and Wangsheren town, and (3) other statistics and historical materials and visual materials.

Our field studies focused on: (1) overall development of Lengshuigou village (population, economy, society, politics, culture, and social relations, etc.); (2) changes in the life of villagers and customs (materials on living tradition, customs, and habits); (3) materials reflecting the changes in household and lineage life (family genealogy, family archives, and pictures); and (4) other materials and pictures reflecting the village conditions and new developments.

Beginning in November 2009, we gathered documentary materials and drew up a preliminary research plan. We tested our research plan in January–February 2010, and then moved on to concentrated field research. Supplementary research was finished in the summer of 2011. Our fieldwork collected data through questionnaires and interviews.

Survey Questionnaires

One of the special features of our fieldwork is a large survey, "Social Transition," that was designed to collect data on family conditions, economic structure and social development, social structure and social life, political organization and village elites, social relations and social communications, as well as attitudes toward changing society. We wanted a large sample. At the end of 2008, there were 1,143 households in Lengshuigou. We divided the village into six sub-divisions and collected 90 responses from each sub-division for a total of 540 households, or just under half of the village households.

The second step was sampling within the household. We took as an informant the first adult (who was not a student), who we encountered when we entered the family compound. If the first person we encountered was a minor, we took the second person or the parent. According to this principle, one person was sampled from every household, and altogether there were 540 people, which constituted the total number of the research sample. In the actual sampling process, if we were met with an empty household or an informant unable or unwilling to answer, we continued until we had 540 respondents.

We believe our sample represents the village population. The respondents were almost evenly divided between men and women, with 264 men and 276 women. In terms of age, 104 (19.3 percent) were under the age of 30, 60.7 percent were between 31 and 60, and 108 (20.2 percent) were above 61. Our respondents reflected the general population in terms of literacy level: 182 (33.7 percent) had received only primary school education; 185 (34.3 percent) had middle school education; 132 (24.2 percent) were high school graduates; and 41 (7.6 percent) had postsecondary education.

When we look at family structure, we see that 182 informants (33.8 percent) had 3 or fewer family members; 290 (53.9 percent) had 4 to 5 family members; and 66 informants (12.3 percent) had 6 or more family members.

When we look at the household registration status of our sample, we can see that those who answered our survey were overwhelmingly in the category of rural residents (*nongye hukou*): 430 (79.95 percent) of our sample had rural registration, while 91 (16.9 percent) had city or town resident status, and 17 (3.2 percent) had a limited local town residence status (*dangdi youxiao chengzhen hukou*).

Among the sample were 33 (5.1 percent) Communist Party members and 50 (9.3 percent) Youth League members; 455 (84.6 percent) were non–party members. Marital status: 33 (6.1 percent) were single; 469 (86.9) were married; there were 3 divorcees and 5 remarried informants; altogether, 28 widowers and widows; and 2 remarried people after the loss of a spouse.

Occupational distribution included 302 farmers, composing 56.6 percent; 159 (29.8 percent) half-farmer-half-worker; 40 (7.5 percent) enterprise employees; 17 (3.2 percent) in the professions of education, science, and health; and 16 people (3.0 percent) in other professions.

Household income and expenditure: the average household income was 35,794 *yuan* in the previous year and the mean was 20,000 *yuan*; average expenditures were 23,489 *yuan* and the mean was 15,000 *yuan*.

Main sources of household income: income from agriculture occupied 6.7 percent; income from outside work occupied 70.6 percent; income from running a business occupied 12.6 percent; income provided by the village committee occupied 4.1 percent; money from offspring and relatives occupied 2.0 percent; other forms of income occupied 3.9 percent.

Religion: 513 (95 percent) said they had no religion; 18 (3.3 percent) reported that they were Protestants; 2 (0.4 percent) that they were Roman Catholics; 5 (0.9 percent) said they were Buddhists; 2 (0.4 percent) reported that they were members of other religions.

Data from the survey is used in all of the subsequent chapters to provide a firmly based description of general trends in the early and later reform periods. In addition to providing the data described above, the survey questionnaire collected data about family and family relations and attitudes, which we present and analyze in later chapters.

In-Depth Interviews

Interviews were an important part of our survey work. Before entering the village for field research, researchers of each group designed interview protocols. In selecting informants, we adopted the snowball sampling approach, taking into consideration the gender, age, profession, and position of informants, all the time trying to get as representative a group as possible. We did major interviews with about fifty villagers, including present and former village leaders, teachers, doctors, educated elderly people, and ordinary villagers. Excerpts from the interviews are used in subsequent chapters to help us put a "face" on our quantitative data.

Through the interviews and the large-scale survey, we paint a comprehensive picture of the changing community of Lengshuigou, a community in which the strong collective elements of the socialist period are steadily being replaced by new forms of affiliation, forms in which individuals, who are no longer compelled to work together with their family and neighbors in the fields, are making personal choices about employment and constructing much more complex personal networks. This new world is one in which the younger generation often takes the lead in thinking about family strategies since they are the ones with up-to-date knowledge and skills that give them greater access, through friends and through social media, to the world outside the village.

Outline of the Book

Description and analysis in the book is divided into eight chapters. Chapter 1, "Lengshuigou in Time and Space," provides background information to help readers situate the village geographically and historically. It includes a survey of population growth and discussion of the role of education in development of the modern village.

Chapter 2 focuses on village politics and village elites. The Chinese state has for centuries tried to find ways to extend its control into the villages. This chapter looks at the efforts of successive governments in the first half of the twentieth century as a prelude to the analysis of efforts of the PRC government, which led to the establishment of the people's communes in the late 1950s. The latter part of the section on institutions looks at efforts since the Reform and Opening Up Policies to establish self-governance in the village, and the difficulties those efforts face in a rapidly urbanizing society. The second half of the chapter looks at the nature of the local elite, focusing on individuals who have played major leadership roles.

Lineage and family relations—the fundamental building blocks of Chinese society—are the subjects of chapter 3. Using the detailed records from the *Kankō Chōsa* surveys, we first analyze their roles is pre-1949 society, and then look at the major changes that collectivization brought to these fundamental units of Chinese society. Our analyses show how the production team came to displace many of the functions of the family and lineage during the collective period, and how both have been revitalized in the Reform era, although in ways that are significantly different from the pre-1949 forms.

Chapter 4 shifts the focus from an analysis of kinship-based structures to an analysis of social stratification and social life. In this chapter, we focus on social strata, looking at occupational divisions across the four time periods. Conceptually, we use this analysis based on changes in the occupational structure to show how different strata were able to use resources based on their economic status, political status, and cultural status. The chapter also examines changing patterns of social mobility, drawing on both statistical data and individual cases. The second half of the chapter turns to changes in material life, painting a portrait of daily life across the four time periods.

Chapter 5 shifts the focus from institutions to cultural values and the representations of cultural traditions and practices in the annual festivals and life-cycle festivals that play central roles establishing the rhythm of rural life. The first part of the chapter looks at the Confucian ethical tradition and the challenges to it after 1949, focusing on the PRC state's efforts to create a new socialist man. With the end of the collective era, some of the older ethical values reemerged, while new ideas coming from the cities contributed to the development of a more diverse cultural tradition. The second half of the chapter looks at changes in ritual activities, including the annual cycle of celebrations as well as important life-cycle rituals including weddings and funerals.

Chapter 6 examines social relations and social networks, focusing on the ways in which individuals in the village interact with others and the principles for construction of networks. This chapter uses data from our survey of almost half of the village households, as well as individual-interview data, to show changes over time and to provide a detailed analysis of contemporary interpersonal relations and the growing complexity of personal networks.

Chapter 7 looks at economic structure and development, focusing particularly on changes under the collective economy and the dramatic changes that have occurred under the Reform and Opening Up Policies. The chapter shows how, under the reforms, village leaders have been able to leverage Lengshuigou's position in the distant suburbs of Jinan to enrich the village, providing improved economic infrastructure and new job opportunities.

Chapter 8 draws together our conclusions on the changes in Lengshuigou, linking our understanding of this one village to the broader trends in contemporary Chinese society and economy.

NOTES

1. Our Chinese book on Lengshuigou has a long history and review of Western and Chinese literature on the Chinese village. We include an abbreviated version in this English translation, focusing on general approaches and specific studies on Lengshuigou.

2. By the 1970s, a new generation of scholars in Japan, as well as in the United States, became interested in using the materials for research on pre-Liberation China, and in 1980 the publisher put out a reprint edition.

3. Among these studies are Wang Yanyan's MA thesis examining urbanization and modernization in Lengshuigou, and Wei Ya'ni's MA thesis, which focused on changes as a result of the development of rural industrial parks.

4. Zhuang Kongshao's *The Silver Wing—Local Social Culture and Change*, and Zhou Daming's *Transitions in Fenghuang Village* are recent examples of follow-up studies.

Chapter One

Lengshuigou in Time and Space

Lengshuigou is situated in the piedmont region of north-central Shandong, fifteen kilometers east of the provincial capital of Jinan, in the rapidly industrializing and urbanizing suburbs of the city. In the second decade of the twenty-first century, the village is a complex mix of rural and urban features. Although it is now surrounded by highways and industrial parks, and soon to have more of its land taken for the construction of a new high-speed railway station, some of the village residents still farm small plots growing grain, and others work on the demonstration dairy farm, which is the largest provider of milk to the Jinan market. Although village families still have farmland allocated to them, most of them draw most of their income from non-farm activities, commuting to jobs in factories and businesses in the nearby town of Wangsheren or in Jinan. There are also many newcomer residents in the village, including people who work in the nearby town and industrial parks: some have bought flats in apartment buildings constructed by the village, while others rent rooms from village families.

The story of the transformation of Lengshuigou is the story of rural economic and social change in China's most rapidly developing coastal regions, and Lengshuigou—now on the verge of disappearing as a rural community—offers us an opportunity to explore how economic growth and transformation have impacted fundamental social structures, that is, ways of organizing and carrying out production and social affairs and individual lives. The materials for our exploration cover seven decades, beginning with the Japanese survey in 1940 that first drew attention to Lengshuigou and ending with our comprehensive survey conducted in 2010. Over those seven decades, the region has experienced tremendous change. When Japanese researchers first visited the village in 1940, the trip took considerable time: getting off the train at the Licheng station on the Jiaoji line that linked Jinan to Qingdao, researchers walked to and through the small market town of Wangsheren to reach the Licheng County seat,[1] which they described as isolated with few shops and only a few restaurants inside the city walls (KC VI, 515). It was a further long walk to Lengshuigou, and in an effort to save time, the researchers often summoned villagers to their office in the county seat rather than making the long walk to the village. Today the trip is much easier: paved highways link the city of Jinan to Wangsheren and Lengshuigou, and motorbikes, cars, and light vans are now parked along the side of many village lanes. Change in ease of access is only one aspect of the changes that have transformed the lives of Lengshuigou villagers.

This chapter introduces basic data about Lengshuigou that readers will need as they read the later chapters in our book. While our focus in the book is on the transformation of the village of Lengshuigou, developments in the village have been shaped by many factors including state policies, regional development plans and accomplishments, indigenous leadership decisions, and the strategies and life choices of families and individuals. In our brief introduction to the village, we will begin with the natural environment and then will move on to a quick survey of major changes in the state's governance policies that have directly impacted the village over the last seven decades. Readers can also refer to the chronology, which provides a timeline of important events in national and regional history and important developments in the village of Lengshuigou. Finally, we will provide a brief sketch of regional development, locating Lengshuigou in a comparative context.

NATURAL ENVIRONMENT

Lengshuigou lies on the North China plains, just south of the Yellow River and north of the Taishan Massif (map 1.1), which rises some 1,545 meters from the plains. The region shares many of the features of the North China plains: the soil is a mixture of river silt and loess blown in by wind from the northwest, and the climate is semi-arid, with annual rainfall of about 550 mm, most of which falls in the spring and summer seasons. Summers are hot, and winters are cold and windy. In the past, the region was subject to frequent flooding, and historical records show that the Yellow River burst its banks 1,593 times, with the river shifting its course to the sea from the southern part of Shandong province to its current course entering the sea on the northern side of the Shandong peninsula.

While much of the North China plains region struggles with lack of water resources for agriculture, the region around Lengshuigou benefits from a large karst aquifer that lies under the Jinan region and feeds the area's natural

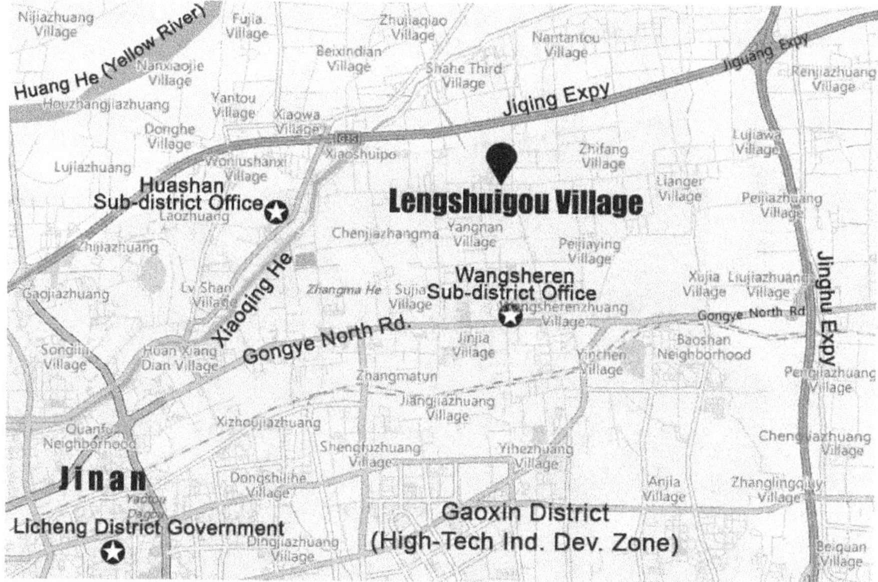

Map 1.1. Map showing Lengshuigou in the region
Based on Bing map

springs. The city of Jinan is known as "The City of Springs," thanks to the seventy-two famous artesian springs that provide water for the city and have made the spring-fed lakes in its parks a major tourist attraction. The springs are the result of the natural features of the landscape: lying in the intermediate zone between the Taishan Massif to the south and the Yellow River Valley to the north, a number of geological fault lines lie under the region, creating fissures in the limestone rock that bring water to the surface in natural springs.

Lengshuigou takes its name—which translates as "cold water ditch"—from these natural springs. A map of the village in the 1940s clearly shows the ditch cutting through the heart of the village that had been dug to drain off excessive water, as well as the pools in several parts of the village (map 1.2). At the time of the Japanese survey in the early 1940s, roughly one-third of the village's fields were planted in rice, with the rest planted in dry-field crops including wheat, corn, millet, sorghum, and soybeans. Lengshuigou villagers continued to cultivate rice paddies until the mid-1980s. However, the construction of three waterworks in Wangsheren, which draw water out of the aquifer to provide water to the city of Jinan, led to a decline in available spring water and brought an end to rice cultivation in the village. Today the village's remaining fields are planted in dry-field crops.

Map 1.2. Map of Lengshuigou in the 1940s showing water ponds
Designed by Li Xingwei

VILLAGE ORIGINS

Lengshuigou is located in the north-central part of Shandong province, an area on the North China plains where archaeologists have uncovered some of the earliest records of human civilization.[2] The North China plains region, however, was frequently affected by both natural and manmade disasters. One of the results was the frequent resettling of the region following such events. When the *Kankō Chōsa* investigators asked about the origins of the village, they were told that the current village traces its origins to resettlement after the wars at the end of the Yuan and beginning of the Ming dynasties. Early in the reign of the Hongwu emperor (1368–1398), the Chinese state organized a massive migration to resettle the war-ravaged North China plains. According to traditional Chinese accounts remembered by villagers in Hebei and Shandong, their ancestors gathered near a large ash tree in Hongdong County in Shanxi to begin the journey to the North China plains. Ancestors of the Wang and Du families seem to have been the first settlers, later joined by other families that moved to the region from Zaoqiang County in Hebei. In 1940, villagers gave the Japanese researchers the following account:

> During the Hongwu reign of the Ming dynasty, our ancestors moved here from Zaoqiang County in Hebei. They were following the Imperial court's order on migration, and this place was chosen because there was lots of land. According to the preface to the Li family genealogy edited in 1842 (Daoguang 22), the Li family's ancestors had moved from Zaoqiang in the early Ming. They first settled down in what is now the north part of the village. We have been told that the village name comes from the fact that there were very rich underground water resources, and that a long ditch traversed the village from southeast to the northwest. (KC IV, 55)

According to a stele inscription dated to 1622, Lengshuigou village took its current name when three small villages—Lengjigou, Lijiazhuang, and Renjiazhuang which later joined together. From these records we can see that the village has a history of at least 650 years (LCZ 2010, 3).

OVERVIEW OF HISTORICAL CHANGES

When the Japanese researchers visited in 1940, they found a large North China village in which most of the villagers farmed, growing rice and other grain crops in a largely self-sufficient economy. The village seemed to have been little touched by the turbulent political scene, which Prasenjit Duara noted was characterized by two broad historical processes. "The first was the series of economic changes stemming from the impact of the West. The second represented the efforts of the state to deepen and strengthen its command over rural society" (Duara 1988, 2). We see North China rural society before the founding of the PRC as fundamentally static, operating under the small peasant mode of production. To borrow the words of Fei Xiaotong, "China's basic economy structure was formed by the numerous independent small farmers coexisting in the village. Division of labor among small farmers was rare. Villagers grew the same kind of crops and got from the land enough for their subsistence" (Fei 2009 [1948], 29).

Lengshuigou before 1949

Before 1949, most villagers in Lengshuigou farmed their own land; only a handful of villagers rented the land from others, and only a small minority engaged in livestock breeding, including the breeding of domestic animals and poultry on a very small scale. Lengshuigou land was fertile, and water was abundant, and villagers grew rice, wheat, sorghum, soybeans, millet, and other grains. Rice accounted for an important part of rural income, and most of this crop was sold. Before the war, villagers took their rice to Jinan markets; under the Japanese occupation, peasants were ordered to sell their rice only to the Japanese puppet organization, the Xinminhui, at prices determined by that organization (KC IV, 2). There were several small handicraft workshops in the village, including several distilleries, one carpentry workshop, and three vinegar workshops. The village had three small restaurants offering noodles, steamed stuffed buns, and fried dishes, and several individuals produced steamed bread. Some villagers went into the city in the slack agricultural season to work as coolies. Overall, economic activity in the village followed time-honored patterns, with most village families farming their fields and gaining most of what they needed for consumption from their own work.

At the time the Japanese research team visited, there were some 370 households in the village, with a total population of about 1,800 (KC IV, 9). Although there were few dramatic changes in the economic life of Lengshuigou villagers in the period before 1949, there were significant changes in other fields. One of the changes that would have a long-term impact on the village was the development of modern education. Wealthier families in Lengshuigou were proud of their lineage's educational traditions; the genealogy of the Yang lineage, for example, listed two ancestors who had passed the provincial-level imperial examination, earning the second highest degrees. Yang Chunhua earned his degree during the Jiaqing reign (1796–1820) and Yang Enpei earned his during the Guangxu reign (1875–1908). The two members from the Yang family were famous in the eastern suburbs of Jinan, and Yang Enpei played a major role in developing modern education, establishing a village library, and educating village youth. The Yangs and other young boys in the village attended old-style private schools, where boys from wealthier families studied the Confucian classics, taught by private teachers who had also studied at such private schools.

While rural education in the late Qing followed patterns from the past, the Qing government, beginning with the 1898 reforms, began to reform the traditional examination system, finally abolishing it in September of 1905. Even after the end of the exams, some schools still operated on earlier principles. In the late Qing and early Republic, Lengshuigou had a number of private tutors who ran their own schools providing education for many village boys, and the village was always in the top ranks in the eastern suburbs. However, modern education was also beginning, and Lengshuigou became a regional pioneer in providing modern elementary education with the establishment of a lower primary school in 1913. By the 1930s, the school, located in buildings of the Guandi Temple, had developed into a senior primary school offering six years of education. Records from the period of Japanese occupation report that the school curriculum included classes in self-cultivation, Chinese, mathematics, science, history, geography, drawing, music, and physical education.

All of the students in the school were boys. At the time of the *Kankō Chōsa* survey, there were 150 boys in the school, 127 in the lower primary school and 23 in the higher primary school. Villagers told the Japanese researchers that girls did not attend the school because funds were insufficient to pay for female teachers. There were no tuition fees for attending the school, and lineages helped to pay the book fees of boys whose own families were too poor to pay (KC IV, 15, 16, 18).

Thanks to the development of the primary school, Lengshuigou men had a relatively high literacy rate and some of those who graduated from the primary school went on to get further education and take up positions in various fields outside the village. At the same time, the high levels of literacy meant that the village had a relatively large population of literate men who were better prepared to take on leadership roles during land reform and collectivization.

Collectivist Era: From 1949 to the Reforms

Following the end of the Anti-Japanese war in the summer of 1945, the Jinan area and Lengshuigou came under the control of the Guomindang (GMD). In September 1948, the Guomindang was driven out and Jinan was liberated by the Communist Party. At the beginning of 1949, a new administrative structure was established in the village, with Li Yuquan serving as village head and Li Xingfu as the vice-chairman of the newly established Peasant Association. This was the beginning of a long process of transformation that would eventually end the system of private land ownership and replace it with a system based on collective ownership and communal work.

The first step in the transformation came with land reform, which was completed in the fall of 1950. A land reform team dispatched by higher authorities led the village land reform process, determining class statuses (*chengfen*) for all village households; following the determination, the land reform team seized and redistributed land and property that had been taken from those who were classified as landlords and rich peasants. In Lengshuigou, thirty-two households were classified as landlords, eight households as rich peasants, and the rest as lower middle and poor peasants. While the land reform readjusted the distribution of land, the land system was still based on private ownership. All households now had land, but the plots were small, and farming was still relatively inefficient. In the spring of 1952, Lengshuigou village moved to the next step, the creation of mutual-aid teams. The mutual-aid teams were voluntary organizations set up by small groups of households who made arrangements to share equipment, plow animals, and labor, with each household keeping the harvest on its own fields.

At the same time that steps toward cooperation were being taken in the village, changes were made in the institutional framework for control of agriculture. In October 1953, the state established a monopoly over the purchase and sale of grain; households now had to sell their surplus output to the state. In 1954, Lengshuigou villagers sold a grain surplus of 1,500,000 *jin.*

The mutual-aid teams had made a start toward increasing efficiency in production, but the small size of plots blocked larger investment in agriculture. To deal with this problem, the state called on peasants to form producers' cooperatives. Participation was voluntary and involved the pooling of both land and labor, with calculation of returns based on a combination of each household's contributions in land and in labor. In 1954, Lengshuigou villagers set up eight lower level cooperatives. At this time there was great enthusiasm for rapid collectivization, a phenomenon that was referred to as a "socialist high tide." In the fall of 1955 orders were sent out to move from lower level cooperatives to higher level cooperatives. For the first time, membership was compulsory, and returns were calculated only on labor inputs. This step marked the end of private land ownership in rural China.

Lengshuigou established a higher level cooperative, taking the name "East Is Red" cooperative. Accompanying the push for reorganization of the rural economy was new investment in infrastructure, and Lengshuigou was one of the first beneficiaries of the push. In 1956, the village cooperated with several nearby villages to build a small hydroelectric power station, and Lengshuigou village became one of the first villages in Shandong province to have electricity.

In January 1958, the national government took another step that was to have momentous consequences for rural China, the establishment of a household registration system that registered all individuals in the place where they were living, assigning either a rural or urban residence status.[3] Those with rural resident status could no longer move freely into the cities, and their consumption needs, job assignments, and welfare were to be supplied by their rural collective. This created a dual social structure in which those with rural registration could only work in agriculture.

Inspired by the success of the cooperative movement, the Party's leaders decided to launch the "Great Leap Forward" in May 1958, with the aim of mobilizing manpower and resources to bring about a rapid transition to socialism. In the countryside, the Great Leap Forward brought another reorganization, this time creating people's communes. The commune joined together the lowest level of government administration with the basic unit of economic organization. The first people's commune in China was established in August 1958 following a visit by Mao Zedong to Shuitun village in Licheng County, where he put his seal of approval on the people's commune as an organizing principle. Within several months, Licheng County had combined more than five hundred higher level cooperatives into ten people's communes. Lengshuigou was assigned to the Eastern Suburb Commune, which had its headquarters in Wangsheren town. In the first years of the commune, the commune organization was modeled on the military, with villages combined to form battalions. Lengshuigou was joined with three other villages to form the Lengyang Battalion.

The large scale of the communes and the militarized organization led to multiple problems, and in 1959, the communes were reorganized on a smaller scale. Brigade units were established as sub-units of the commune. At first, Lengshuigou was divided into East and West brigades, but later the two were joined together so that the borders of the brigade matched the natural village. There were nineteen work teams below the brigade, with each work team serving as the unit for collective work and also for accounting.

Although the communes disbanded in 1984, and collective labor came to an end with the establishment of the household contracting system, elements of the commune system continue to influence rural China to the present day. In a preface to the second edition of his award-winning book on the commune system, *Gaobie Lixiang* (Farewell to Ideals), Zhang Letian argued that although the people's commune was born out of the Great Leap Forward and reflected conditions of the late 1950s, it has left a permanent mark on later developments.

> It was the people's commune that realized the collective ownership of land. It is precisely this system of land ownership that continues to be a symbol of development in rural areas. Under the people's communes, many small-scale industries developed (what are now called township and village industries), and they provided the economic and institutional base for the takeoff of the rural economy during the Reform era. This is certainly true for at least the coastal areas. Moreover, the commune created a complete and effective system that joined party and government power. Now it does not make any difference where you go in China—however remote a region—you can still see this system in operation. The people's commune is closely related to the present situation in China, and made major contributions to the formation of "socialism with Chinese characteristics." (Zhang 2005, 15)

When we look at Lengshuigou, we can see evidence of this kind of development. For example, in 1953 the village set up a branch of the supply and marketing cooperative, a kind of general store that sold various kinds of goods; 80 percent of the villagers became shareholders. The Lengshuigou brigade also started a number of small enterprises: in 1964, the village and the animal-products exporting company jointly set up a factory to process pig bristle, which was used to manufacture various kinds of brushes. In 1972, the factory expanded and came to employ two hundred villagers, producing an annual revenue of 200,000 RMB. Other factories were set up in the village, and when the reforms started, many of these factories were contracted out to their managers—which was an important part of the early reform policies.

During the collective years, life in the village improved in many ways. For example, the village was able to use its own funds in 1978 to build a water system that brought running water to village homes. No longer would people have to carry heavy containers of water from the wells. Another sign of improvement could be seen in the education and health systems.

Development of education: Educational reform was one of the pillars of the new socialist state, and education levels in Lengshuigou rose very rapidly in the early years after the founding of the PRC. The rise of educational levels was the result of two separate movements: first, the improvement of basic elementary education for all children and, second, remedial efforts to spread literacy, particularly among women who had been excluded from the village schools before 1949. Let us first look at the improvement in formal schooling.

In the second half of 1948, following the liberation of Jinan, two teachers came to teach in Lengshuigou. At the beginning, the school had only 80 or 90 students from grade one to grade four. The only textbooks they had were old; students were divided into two classes, with different grades sharing the same room. Soon the number of teachers and students increased: by 1949, there were 200 students and 5 teachers at the school, and in 1952, two additional grades were added, with 8 teachers. Between 1955 and 1957 the number of classes increased to 9, serving a total of 340 students, including some from nearby villages. The school followed a relatively simple curriculum, stressing Chinese language and mathematics. Morning classes began with assembly in the schoolyard where the national flag was raised, and students sang the national anthem, and ended with another assembly lowering the flag. Students were encouraged to link their educational goals with the establishment of a socialist China, mastering knowledge that would make contributions to the nation.

In the 1950s and early 1960s educational policies struggled with the question of how to provide education that would provide practical support for the building of socialism. One such effort was the Lengshuigou Agricultural Middle School, which ran from the autumn of 1958 to June 1961 and from the summer solstice in 1964 to July 1968. A total of 300 students studied there (LCZ 2010, 113). Growing out of the Great Leap Forward, this middle school combined education with productive labor; over 180 students from

Lengshuigou and neighboring villages studied in the middle school, attending classes on Mondays, Wednesdays, and Fridays, and engaging in farm work on Tuesdays, Thursdays, and Saturdays. Sometimes, the students studied in the morning and worked on farming in the afternoon, or vice versa. Following the end of the Great Leap, the school was suspended for several years. In 1964, a new Agricultural Middle School was established in Lengshuigou, following the directions of the Central Committee of the CPC (Chinese Communist Party) that institutions should strive to "walk on two legs" (*liang tiao tui zoulu*). Over 120 students were admitted to the school: the curriculum combined classes in agricultural knowledge with agricultural labor and middle school academic courses. The school also ran other practical classes, including training classes for barefoot doctors and classes to train accountants for production teams and brigades. The Lengshuigou school was regarded as a model and hosted visitors from the Soviet Union and Mexico.

Literacy education: Education policy in the 1950s not only developed formal schools but also stressed adult education in an effort to eliminate illiteracy. In 1950, Shandong province established a province-wide committee to organize the work, and a large-scale "literacy movement" was implemented from 1952 until the 1970s. The movement began with a "winter study movement" in 1952. The campaign used various methods, including quick literacy classes and night schools. Particular emphasis was given to eliminating illiteracy among women.

Literacy classes for women were held in Lengshuigou with 90 percent of the young women joining, including the "quick literacy class" (semiliterate young women were taught in the morning) and the "class for beginners" (married young women were taught during the rest time for over one hour at noon). While there were starts and stops in the campaigns, especially during the Great Leap Forward when many rural areas sought a "Great Leap Forward" in eliminating illiteracy, overall the movement gained success, and the literacy rate and cultural level among farmers showed great improvement.

Cultural Revolution and education in Lengshuigou: Education in Lengshuigou from 1966 until the conclusion of the Cultural Revolution in the 1970s was strongly impacted by leftist ideas that characterized education across rural China. Following the issuing of Mao Zedong's May Seventh (1968) directive on education, which stressed the studying of industrial, agricultural, and military skills, the school day was shortened, and a new curriculum stressing practical skills and work was instituted.

When the Cultural Revolution reached Lengshuigou, regular classes were suspended to allow students to take part in revolutionary activities. In

Lengshuigou, as was common throughout China, schools and schoolteachers were accused of promoting anti-party and anti-socialist forces: attacks claimed the schools had promoted feudalism, capitalism, and revisionism. Many teachers were subjected to strong criticism sessions, and many leaders were removed from their positions. Meanwhile, representatives of the poor and lower-middle peasants took responsibility for school affairs for the period of two years. During this period, class sessions, originally designed for reading books, studying, and disseminating knowledge, became a battlefield where students criticized the former school leaders, accusing them of being capitalist intellectuals. The group of representatives running the school during those two years advocated the ideas expressed by the slogans "study industrial skills, study farming skills" and "receive re-education from the poor and lower-middle peasants."

Although the curriculum was highly politicized during this period, the number of students attending school swelled. In 1969, Lengshuigou Primary School adopted the then-popular system of adding on two years of middle school, for a seven-year curriculum, a system referred to as a school with "two hats." The Lengshuigou village school had fourteen primary school

Photo 1.1. Lengshuigou Elementary School

classes and four middle school classes, serving somewhere between five hundred and six hundred students.

To meet the needs of the expanding student body, Lengshuigou schools introduced a new style of teachers, known as citizen-supported teachers (*minban jiaoshi*). While regular schoolteachers were certified and funded by the state, these new teachers were recruited by the village, which paid their salaries. At that time, about two-thirds of the teachers in the Lengshuigou school were in this category. *Minban* teachers came from rural areas and continued to engage in agricultural labor while also teaching in the school. Rural schools continued to employ *minban* teachers until 1998, when the system came to an end. These teachers played an important role in rural education and formed an important part of the teaching staff. When we conducted our survey, we interviewed a former *minban jiaoshi*, Liu Hua, who had continued to study on his own time and was eventually able to receive certification and continue teaching in the Lengshuigou Elementary School.

Development of health services: Development of rural medical and health services was one of the outstanding achievements of the period from 1949 to the launching of the reforms in 1978. In the early years, stress was put on disease prevention, with the state creating a system of prevention and health care in rural areas that stressed prevention of epidemics, control of endemic diseases, and improving the overall health environment. In the period before the establishment of the PRC, health care in rural areas had been spotty, with individuals turning to traditionally trained doctors and herbal medicine specialists: in general, rural China had high mortality rates and short life expectancy. Lengshuigou, like other villages in northern China, was no exception. Generally speaking, if a village had an herbalist and a midwife, it would already be regarded as having good medical services. At that time, villagers rarely sought medical treatment in a county town or city, and hardly anyone consulted Western medical doctors. Lengshuigou had no regular clinic, only a few medicinal herb stores and several folk practitioners. There were three traditional specialists, Li Yongfang, Li Defu, and Yang Jiechen, who treated diseases and prescribed traditional Chinese medicines; however, none of them had specialized training.

The rural health and medical systems developed rapidly in the early 1950s, beginning with a "patriotic health campaign" to eliminate the "four pests" (rats, bedbugs, flies, and mosquitoes) and improve basic hygiene. During this period, the village took steps to improve access to medical care, organizing a collective clinic in 1954 that employed the village's three traditional medical doctors along with one Western-trained doctor. In 1958, an obstetrics and gynecology clinic was established, and the new safer methods of childbirth led to a drop in infant mortality rates.

In 1965, China's rural primary medical and health-care network included county-level hospitals, commune-level public-health centers, and brigade-(village-)level clinics, which provided a comprehensive system stressing prevention and offering basic medical treatment. The village also strove to improve general sanitation, further contributing to the decline of disease.

Despite all of the improvements, there was a great shortage of trained doctors in the countryside. In June 1965, Mao Zedong put out a call to put greater efforts into rural medical care, creating a system of "barefoot doctors," who were local residents given basic medical education and charged with providing the first level of care in the villages. The goal of the rural cooperative medical services was to see that "small diseases should be cured in the village, while large diseases should be cured in the township." During this period, medical and health services in Lengshuigou developed rapidly. In Lengshuigou, at least nine people were trained as barefoot doctors, supplying low-cost medical care to villagers, who paid a small fee of five yuan to join the system.

From 1978 to the End of the Twentieth Century: The Village in the Context of the Reform and Opening Up Policies

After a decade of turmoil during the Cultural Revolution, the drawbacks of the planned-economy system became increasingly obvious: by the late 1970s, rural collectivization had reached an impasse. Slow economic development and low rates of productivity were characteristics of the rural economy all across the country. Living standards had shown little improvement: peasants made up more than 80 percent of the country's total population, and the rural labor productivity rate was one-tenth of that of urban workers. For instance, although the added value of agricultural production in Jinan had increased from 139 million to 394 million *yuan* between 1965 and 1978, the annual growth rate was significantly lower than in other periods. There had been a steady increase in the rural population, and thus when we look at per capita income and expenditures, we can see that they showed little improvement, and in some cases actually declined. This was because production rose at a slower rate than population growth (table 1.1).

Under the planned-economy and dual urban-rural structure, China's development policies embodied an urban bias, meaning that urban development happened at the expense of rural development. As a result, the countryside and the peasants became the biggest victims of China's development policies. There were major imbalances between industry and agriculture and between urban and rural areas. Although there was major industrial development during this period, the benefits were not shared by the rural population, with the

Table 1.1. Living conditions of Jinan's rural residents, 1965–1978

Year	*Per capita net income (yuan)*	*Per capita living expenditure (yuan)*	*Per capita residential area (m2)*	*Rural population proportion (%)*
1965	92.6	69.7	8.2	47.3
1970	82.7	67.2	8.5	51.6
1975	79.1	59.5	9.0	51.9
1978	110.5	83.2	9.6	50.0

Source: BSJ/NBS 2011, 142 and 211.

gap between urban and rural residents showing steady growth. In 1965, the urban population's income was 2.37 times higher than the rural population's, and by 1978, the urban-rural income ratio had grown to 3.06.

Something had to be done to resolve these growing gaps. Change began with experiments in Anhui, Sichuan, and other places that experimented with rural reforms in which farming was contracted to individual households (*dabaogan*). After some exploration and experiments, the household contract responsibility system obtained government approval and quickly spread across rural China. The household contract responsibility system (*jiating lianchan chengbao zerenzhi*), which formed the core of the rural reform policies, was a grassroots initiative that was based on a series of major institutional changes.

First, the responsibility for management of agriculture shifted from the collective unit to the household. Following the implementation of this system, rural labor productivity rose. The first experiments with household contracts in pioneering villages like Xiaogang village in Fengyang county, Anhui, in 1978, involved the setting of grain output quotas for each individual household. By the end of 1983 more than 90 percent of China's villages had implemented the system. Lengshuigou shifted to this system in August 1983, and the results were dramatic: grain output in 1989 stood at 2,481,180 kilograms, 2.2 times the level of 1974. As Du Runsheng, a Chinese social scientist, noted, the "household contract responsibility system led us to rediscover the significance and function of family farming" (Du 2003, 189).

Second, the commune system was abolished, and a new form of rural governance was established. With the implementation of the household contract responsibility system, the management system that blended government administration with the management of the communes lost its function as a promoter of development. On October 12, 1983, the State Council issued a guideline called "Notice on the Separation of Government Administration from Commune Management and Establishment of Township Government." By the end of 1984, almost all rural areas in China had abolished the commune system, transforming the brigades and production teams into a "dual organization" formed by the "village committee" (*cunmin weiyuan hui*, the former brigade) and the "village group" (*cunmin xiaozu*, former work team) referred to as "village Party branch and village committee." Thus, rural villages set up a new grassroots democratic management system, with the village committee as a self-government organization democratically elected by the villagers. Such a dual organization had a mandate to manage the village's affairs, bringing to an end the twenty-six-year history of the commune system. The village Party branch and the village committee were set up in Lengshuigou in 1984, with Cheng Kexing serving as the village head and Ren Yanting as the village Party branch secretary.

Third, the transition from a planned economy to a market-oriented economy changed the factors controlling production allocation. The introduction of market-economy mechanisms has become a powerful driving force for rural development. Under the system of state planning, the state held the monopoly over the purchasing and marketing of grains, that is, the market was entirely absorbed into the state's structure; grain purchasing and marketing happened between and within government departments, and products could not be traded freely.

Following the famine of the late 1950s and early 1960s, the state had instituted an agriculture policy known as "taking grain as the key link" that forced all rural areas to concentrate their production efforts on grain. This policy had given rise to a number of undesirable side effects and was one of the factors that had contributed to low productivity and low labor performance. This highly centralized and unified production and management system seriously restricted the development of rural production and the increase of income among villagers. One of the most effective measures under the reform policies was the introduction of market mechanisms, which granted producers some freedom in choice of crops and also allowed them to dispose of their output once they had turned the contracted amount over to the state. The incentives introduced by this reform led villagers to get involved in many new kinds of business.

Another major feature of the early reform era was the rise in the 1980s of township and village enterprises (TVEs). For example, Shandong province had only 100 registered township and village enterprises in 1963, but the number had jumped to 122,000 units in 1977. Township and village enterprises developed rapidly in Shandong in the 1980s; in 1987, the revenue generated by Shandong's township and village enterprises accounted for 53.4 percent of the province's total agricultural output value or 40 percent of the total industrial and agricultural output. These TVE companies employed about 27 percent of the rural labor force. By the end of 1990, there were 1,440,000 township and village enterprises in Shandong, with a total output value that exceed 100 billion *yuan* (Gao, Li, and Qin 2009, 4). The development of TVEs not only changed the industrial and employment structure of rural areas, it also increased income in rural areas.

Lengshuigou developed many township and village enterprises. With the Reform and Opening Up Policies, more than 40 enterprises of all types opened in the village in the 1990s. However, as the reforms progressed, many of the village factories were closed. The largest of these enterprises was the bristle factory, which was jointly run by the village and Jinan's livestock export company. The bristle factory was contracted out to its managers in the early 1990s. In 1978, the village jointly ran a leather-shoe factory with Jinan Number Two Leather Shoe Factory, but this enterprise also was closed in 1984. In 1984, the village invested in a fertilizer factory, which was shut down in 1998, and in 1990, the village invested in a chemical plant, which closed down in 1993.

Not all of the village's enterprises ended in failure. Lengshuigou's most successful venture has been dairy farming. The first dairy farm was launched in 1986. In 1999, a cow breeding demonstration base was built on an area of 80 *mu*, employing 17 families. The second phase of the breeding demonstration base was concluded in 2001 on a area that reached 300 *mu*. The total dairy cattle population reached 5,000 heads, producing about 30 tons of milk on a daily basis. This dairy farm became one of the major industries in Lengshuigou. In sum, this series of initiatives during the 1980s promoted rapid development in the village, thereby improving the villagers' living standard. The urban-rural income ratio in Jinan declined from 3.06 in 1978 to 1.78 in 1985; but in the 1990s, it began to increase again, reaching 2.22 in 1990 and rising to 2.60 in 1995 and 2.78 in 2000 (BSJ/NBS 2011, 211 and 189).

With the Reform and Opening Up Policies, which put the focus of development policies in urban areas, the urban-rural gap gradually increased. In 2000, urban residents were making 2.78 times more than rural residents. It was at this time that national concern about the "three rural concerns" (*sannong*) became a major policy concern, and former premier Wen Jiabao announced new policy initiatives to try to improve rural life. These efforts kicked off a new stage of social transformation in the early twentieth-first century.

Before moving on to the most recent stage of reforms, we need to briefly sketch in one of the most important policy shifts of the early stages of the reform movement, the initiative to limit population growth known as the "one child policy."

Population Growth and Family Planning

Thanks to the end of armed conflict and improvements in health care, Lengshuigou's population grew rapidly during the collective period, rising from 1,800 in the early 1940s to 3,317 in 1974; by the late 1970s, the village population had reached 3,500, or almost double the 1940 population. In 2010, the village population included 1,450 households, and 4,271 people.[4] Between 1948 and the implementation of the Family Planning Policy, the transformation of the village's population can be divided into three phases.

Phase one, from 1949 to 1956, was a period of fast population growth; the fertility rate rose, the mortality rate declined, and the population's natural growth rate rose significantly, as we can see in figure 1.1.

In phase two, from 1957 to 1965, population fluctuated. This was an era of radical social movements, including the Great Leap Forward and the establishment of the people's commune system. From 1959 to 1961, rural China experienced a serious famine, during which a great number of people died from natural disasters and manmade calamities. This resulted in significant negative population growth, especially in 1960. Production and life recovered only after 1962, when the fertility rate rose again, reaching a new peak.

Population change in Lengshuigou reflected these more general trends. The village's fertility rate and population growth in 1960 reached a low point; in 1962 and 1964, however, it registered new peaks. Moreover, population mobility was restricted following the implementation of the household registration system in 1958.

Phase three, from 1966 to 1976, was a period of stable population growth. The Cultural Revolution broke out in China in 1966, and the whole society

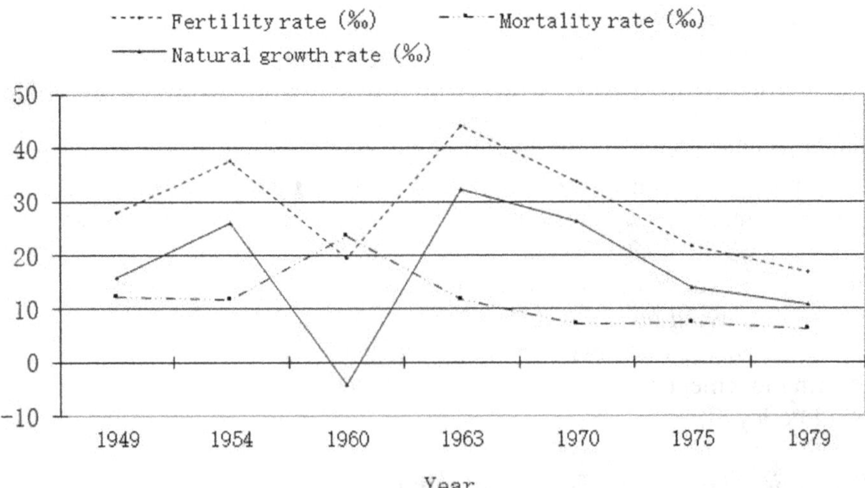

Figure 1.1. Fertility and mortality rates and natural population growth in Shandong Province, 1949–1979
SSY 2011, 58

entered a ten-year period of political and economic turmoil, which strongly affected daily life. During this period, educated youth were sent to the country as part of the campaign to "go and work in the countryside and mountainous areas" (*shangshan xiaxiang*). Lengshuigou received about one hundred educated youth, who arrived in three groups. While they brought a temporary increase to the village's population, all returned to the city at the end of the campaign.

Family Planning and the One Child Policy: Family Planning was incorporated as a state policy in the new constitution, approved by the Fifth National People's Congress in 1978, which clearly stated the state's interest in controlling population and presented for the first time the outlines of the one child policy. The stated aim was to restrict population growth and improve the quality of the population (*renkou suzhi*) by promoting late marriage, delayed childbirth, and fewer, healthier, children. The campaigns began immediately, and couples who already had several children were mobilized to have contraceptive operations.

Shandong province was an early player in family planning, drafting its own policies beginning in 1973 that encouraged families to have only two children. In March 1980, the province launched the one child campaign and began to issue certificates to couples promising not to have a second child. The certificate entitled the first child to priorities in school acceptance and job placement. Following the implementation of these policies, Shandong's fertility rate declined sharply from 21.6 per thousand in 1975 to 13.9 in 1980 and 11.8 in 1985 (SSY 2011, 58).

Influenced by traditional ideas about childbearing, the peasantry initially resisted the one child policy. Zhao Fuzhen, former director of the Women's Association in Lengshuigou, recalled that it was hard to control family planning; although more than 650 childbearing couples voluntarily had contraceptive operations, there were still births that violated the guidelines. Villagers had to pay fines that varied from 2,000 to 3,000 RMB for each extra birth. The policy was particularly strict in 1984. At that time, Lengshuigou's village committee arranged contraceptive operations twice a year for women of childbearing age who had given birth in the previous year and were not using an intrauterine device. The committee also provided contraceptive pills to women who did not want to use an intrauterine device. Individuals who worked outside the village needed to present certifications proving that they had submitted to a contraceptive operation elsewhere. To encourage families to comply with the regulations, fees for contraceptive operations were borne by the village committee.

There have been a number of adjustments to China's birth control policy, including changes that allowed families whose first child was a daughter to have a second child, and that allowed those who were single children to have a second child.

The family planning policies have been very successful in limiting population growth, but have contributed to a new problem—a rapidly aging society. We can see this clearly in a comparison of population pyramids of the population in 1985 and 2008. The first of these population pyramids, produced by the Japanese scholar Nakao Katsumi, shows the beginning of the decline in population growth among the youngest cohort, and the second, based on 2008 census figures, shows even more clearly the impact of family planning policies (figures 1.2 and 1.3).

Skewed gender balance: one of the unintended consequences of the family planning policies has been a change in the gender ratio of the population. As we can see from the pyramids, there are consistently more males than females

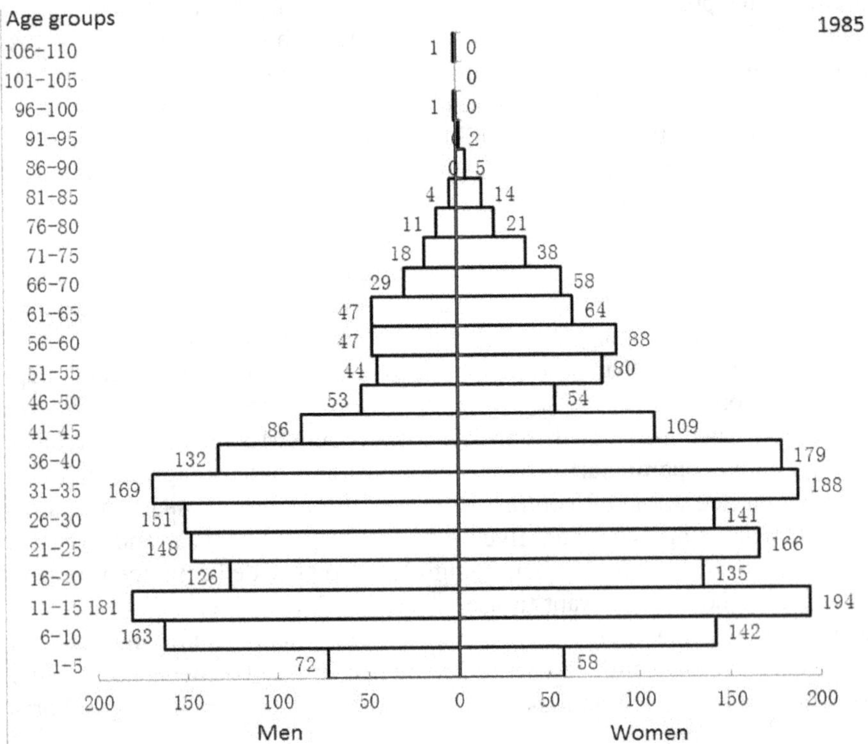

Figure 1.2. Population Pyramid, Lengshuigou, 1985
Nakao 1990, 15.

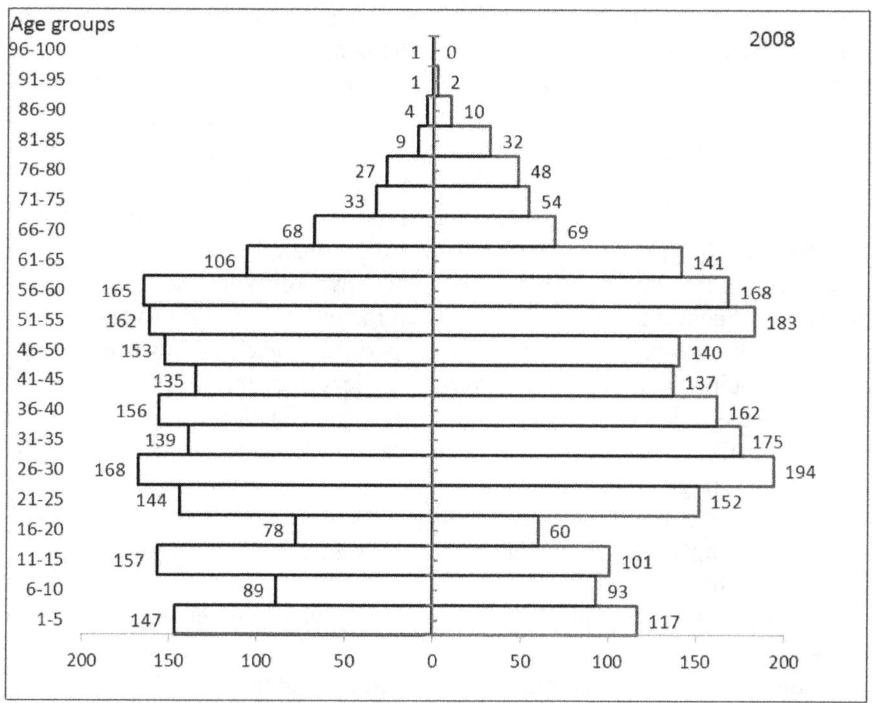

Figure 1.3. Population Pyramid, Lengshuigou, 2008
Based on the statistics from the Village Committee of Lengshuigou

in the younger age cohorts. This is a reflection of the policy that allows a family whose first child is a girl to try for a second child.

Summary of population changes: The family planning policies have produced a dramatic impact on population change in Lengshuigou. Population expansion has slowed, and the ratio of elderly has risen sharply. In recent years, the opening of job opportunities outside has also contributed to population change, as members of younger generations have left the village for school, to join the army, and for employment. The minority in the village who are still actively engaged in agriculture are mostly women and older men.

Changes in Health Care

Lengshuigou, like most other rural areas in China, struggled with providing health care during the early reform period. Under the commune, health care had been provided collectively, but the dissolution of the commune also brought the end of fiscal support for such a system. Where under the commune the principle had been "service to the people," during the early reform period stress was placed on financial sustainability. Some of those who had worked in the Lengshuigou clinic were not able to make a living under this new system and abandoned medical service for other occupations; some with better medical skills opened their own small private clinics.

In 1983, Lengshuigou village, worried about the lack of adequate medical care, decided to invest 50,000 RMB to reconstruct a village clinic and purchase medical equipment. In 1999, the town of Wangsheren reclaimed the right to operate the clinic and then contracted out the right to operate the clinic to individuals. Wangsheren town supervised the clinic, insuring that all of the medicines came from approved suppliers and checking to be certain that all of the medical personnel had proper qualifications. However, while the clinic could handle fairly simple medical problems, villagers with serious illnesses had to go to the county hospital or to specialized hospitals in Jinan city. At the time, good medical care was expensive and difficult to get, and according to our survey, villagers were not satisfied with either the care they got or the costs.

This crisis in rural medical care was a nationwide problem coming just at the time that increasing prosperity led to a greater demand for better services. After much debate, the national government instituted a new rural cooperative medical-care system in 2003. Rural residents were urged to join the new cooperative medical system, paying an annual insurance fee that covered basic medical care. Our survey of attitudes showed that there were still many problems with the system—for example, there were restrictions on the hospitals that would accept the villagers' medical insurance, and the procedures for using medical insurance required a great deal of paperwork, which was difficult for some older members of the population with relatively low levels of literacy. Nevertheless, the system provided at least minimal guarantees in case of illness.

The New Century: Urbanization-Driven Transformation

New rural development opportunities appeared as China entered the twenty-first century. Rural transformation has entered a new phase in response to a number of new conditions, including changes in the tax system, campaigns to improve rural life, and a stepped-up pace of urbanization. Let us look at each in turn and its impact on Lengshuigou.

For more than 2,000 years, agricultural taxes were crucial to the Chinese fiscal state. The decision in 2004 to eliminate the land tax, fully implemented in 2006, thus represented a major change for Chinese rural dwellers. Elimination of the tax was one of the pillars of the state's efforts, under Premier Wen Jiabao, to try to shrink the gap in living standards between rural and urban dwellers.

A second building block of the new policies was efforts to "build a new socialist countryside." This policy, which also targeted the "three rural" problems, had five major aspects: developing production. improving living conditions, civilizing customs, cleaning the environment, and improving management through democracy. These five aspects were designed to promote economy, politics, culture, and broader social development in rural areas. They also contributed to raising the income level of rural residents and narrowing the gap between urbanites and rural residents.

The third major condition that affected rural development was the speeding up of urbanization. By 2010, Shandong's urban population had reached 47.621 million people, or 49.7 percent of the total population. This was 3.68 times higher than the urban population in 1978, which was 13.5 percent of the total population. Urban areas were expanding at a fast pace, especially those administratively classified as "towns."[5] It will not be long before urban society—including both large cities and somewhat smaller towns—replace agricultural communities. One of the key features of this planned transition has been a government effort to create new intermediate-size urban settlements—what we might call "townization" of the countryside. Under this plan, the government is promoting the construction of new communities in the countryside, moving from villages to residential areas (*cun gai ju*), a process that involves the transformation of villages into urban-style residential areas.

We can clearly see these processes at work in Lengshuigou. The village has developed a number of new-style enterprises, including the dairy business. In 2002, with the help of the local government, Lengshuigou village cofounded an industrial park "Xingfuliu Industrial Development Zone," leasing 1,000 *mu* of its land and recruiting dozens of enterprises that employ more than five hundred people in the village. Thus, Lengshuigou has followed the path of agricultural industrialization and diversification.

Along with industrialization and urbanization, Lengshuigou has invested in infrastructure to improve the living conditions of its residents. Between 2002 and 2007, the village invested more than 800,000 *yuan* to build a three-story office building for the village committee, and in 2007, the village invested 550,000 *yuan* to purchase an excavator and a forklift, which have been used to improve and repair village streets. In total, the village spent about 5 million *yuan* to pave its roads. The village has also invested in apartment buildings and undertaken various other activities to support cultural life.

As Wangsheren town was reclassified as a sub-district (*jiedao*) in May 2010, Lengshuigou village had its administrative classification changed to "town" (*chengzhen*). This change recognizes the rapid transformation of Lengshuigou from a rural to an urban area.

NOTES

1. Licheng is now a district of Jinan, and its government headquarters are in Jinan city. However, at the time of the Japanese survey, the county government was in the countryside, having moved out of the city shortly before the start of the war in 1937.

2. The well-known Neolithic archaeological sites of Longshan and Dawenkou are not far away.

3. Under the household registration system, people were, in theory, registered where they lived. However, in subsequent movements in the late 1950s and early 1960s some recent migrants to the city were forced to return to rural areas.

4. The population figures given here include all of those who have their household registration (*hukou*) in Lengshuigou. Thus, the number includes individuals with *hukou* in Lengshuigou, who may be working and living elsewhere; on the other hand, it does not include some who actually physically live in Lengshuigou—for example, those who work in local enterprises and rent rooms or have bought apartments—but whose household registration is elsewhere.

5. China is seeking to develop a new paradigm regarding urbanization and city building. China's urbanization model focuses on transforming rural villages into small towns (*chengzhen*). These newly built or retrofitted former rural villages are administratively treated as urban communities under the jurisdiction of the next larger town. However, larger towns preexisting the current urbanization model are being upgraded to *jiedao* or sub-districts of a given city.

Chapter Two

Changes in Village Politics and Village Elites

One of the central stories of rural change in twentieth-century China has been the effort of the state to gain control over rural society. We commonly assume that under the last imperial dynasty, village governance was relatively autonomous, with members of the local elite, often referred to as "local gentry" (*xiangshen*), managing village affairs. Beginning in the last decade of the Qing dynasty, the state initiated efforts to formalize the practices of local governance, efforts that were strengthened during the Republican era. As these efforts impacted the village, the traditional forms of elite management of local affairs were weakened, but the new institutions were not able to create an alternative governance regime. The CPC-led regime after 1949 was the first national government able to successfully penetrate to the grassroots level, creating a system of rural control that reached down to the most basic level of society. The changes in administration brought about changes in the local elite. In this chapter, we first look at the changes in institutions and then at the changes in the village elite and their participation in politics.

CHANGES IN VILLAGE POLITICS

Under the imperial system, it was commonly said that the power of the state stopped at the walls of the county seat. Beyond the county seat lay the vast world of rural China, where peasants whose families had lived in the same communities for generations worked through the lineage and other village organizations to manage their own affairs. Although villages were relatively autonomous, communicating with the county government primarily with regard to basic issues like tax collection and local security, it is important to remember that this was not the way the state envisioned the ideal relationship.

Beginning from the time of the first unified state some two thousand years ago, Chinese imperial authorities had attempted to incorporate the countryside more tightly into the formal administrative system. However, state efforts to push control into the vast rural areas continually failed, leaving a situation in which actual power in the village formally followed state forms, but with an internal system of control based on indigenous elite politics. As the well-known political scientist Yu Jianrong has noted, "Below the county there was a kind of rural political autonomy which took the *baojia*[1] system which represented imperial authority as its frame, but took lineage power as its base, and which was all managed by the local elite who acted as the connecting agents operating on the basis of an understanding of gentry responsibilities" (Yu 2001, 52). In this way, a dual-authority structure of state and lineage was formed, represented in the two forms of the lineage and the *baojia*. The former was based on the indigenous authority of the traditional kinship system, while the latter represented the external authority of the state.

For peasants, the emperor, who was far away, was not an abstraction but an actual authority whose will had to be respected. Peasants understood the responsibility to pay the land tax and to participate in labor service (*corvée*), but beyond those obligations, the state had little impact on their daily lives. The well-known anthropologist Fei Xiaotong described the role of the state as follows: "Judging from the reality of people's lives in agrarian societies, then, we can see that the power structure, although it may be labeled a 'dictatorship' is actually loose, weak, and nominal. It is a government that does not actively govern at all" (Fei 1992 [1948], 113).

In order to create the population registers, which were the basis for levying taxes and *corvée* labor responsibilities, the state imposed organizations like the *lishe* and *baojia* on rural society. Although these organizations, which divided the village community into sub-units of families responsible for assuring compliance with tax payment and other affairs, were imposed by the state, they were not part of the formal government institutional apparatus. Village officials, including the heads of *lijia* and *baojia* units, usually received no salaries and were elected by the people. Village communities usually chose people with good reputations, social status, money, and power to head such units, and thus we can see that there was a relatively high degree of autonomy in village management. The system that emerged can be described as one of "gentry governance under state supervision," that is, the government controlling rural society through the village elite.

According to the 1940s *Kankō Chōsa* study of Lengshuigou, lineage involvement in local management was not very strong. The Japanese researchers speculated that because of its proximity to the provincial capital of Jinan, there had been significant sales of land to outside landlords, including those from Jinan. As a result, the original spatial arrangement of village housing in which members of the same lineage lived close to each other had been replaced by a more dispersed arrangement of households, weakening the power of the lineage. While the power of the lineage had been weakened, this did not mean that it was nonexistent. We know, for example, that the village's largest Li lineage had a genealogy recording all members as well as an ancestral temple. Lineage groups still played some role in village management.

Religious institutions—including temples and shrines—also played a role in managing village affairs. Among the six villages studied in the *Kankō Chōsa,* Lengshuigou was remarkable for the strong role religious institutions played in village management. During the Qing dynasty, members of the village elite played very active roles in religious activities, as we can see from the records on twenty-five temple and shrine stelae. A number of temples—including the temples to Yuhuang (Jade Emperor) and Guandi (Daoist God of War)—served as foci for religious activities into the Republican period. The most important religious activity was the ceremony to pray for rain that was held when there were droughts. These were elaborate ceremonies that mobilized well over fifty villagers divided into different sub-groups to handle different parts of the ceremony. The ceremony was regarded as an act of the whole village, and the organization to carry it out was closely related to other village management organizations. When the temples needed to be repaired, the village leaders took the lead in collecting money, and the committee conducting the prayers for rain was made up of the wealthiest leaders of the village community (KC 1955, 31, 43, and 56). The ceremonies were an important stage for village leaders to display their leadership qualities and to exercise influence over village society. Through such acts, they played a leading role in maintaining the natural order of rural society.

The *Baojia* System in the Republican Period

In the late nineteenth and early twentieth centuries, the Qing state was challenged on all sides, facing foreign aggression along its coast and internal rebellion in the heartland. Following the Boxer Rebellion and temporary occupation of the national capital by foreign powers, the Qing court turned to reform. The "New Government" policies, modeled on Meiji Japan, abolished the imperial examination system and took steps to create new institutions—including the first steps toward representative institutions. Local self-government was an essential part of the New Government initiatives. Regulations for local self-government issued in 1908 officially established sub-county units—towns and rural townships (*xiang*)—as part of the administrative hierarchy. However, the regulations were issued only three years before the fall of the Qing dynasty and were not effectively implemented. The new Republican government continued the efforts for local self-government begun under the Qing, appointing officials to sub-county administrative offices. The *baojia* system for collective security continued. While the late Qing reforms had envisioned these new institutions as part of a system of self-government in the early Republican period, they came to reflect the views of the state.

In the 1930s, following the establishment of the Guomindang government in Nanjing, the state launched a new effort to extend its authority over rural areas, striving to replace the lineage-based system of village control with one more subordinate to the state. During the teens, China had been split up among a number of different regional authorities, each with its own approaches to local government. In 1928, after the Northern Expedition succeeded in bringing about a nominal unification of the country, the Republican government set out to standardize rural organization. The new system set up administrative districts (*qu*) under the county.[2] Each district was then divided into sub-units (towns or rural townships), with the village now recognized as the lowest unit in the new administrative structure. Under this new organization system, the state officially recognized village heads as representatives of a legitimate village authority. In 1929, the Nanjing government issued regulations officially establishing the new administrative hierarchy for local government as county, district (*qu*), town (*zhen*) or rural township (*xiang*), and village. According to the regulations, the villages and towns were to have representative assemblies to implement self-government, but in fact this was not realized in most places. Counties were ordered to organize a new system of collective responsibility in the villages known as *lülin*, in which five households were joined together as a *lin*, with five groups of five, or twenty-five households, as a *lü*.[3]

Let us now turn to see how these general principles were implemented in Lengshuigou. Lengshuigou was one of many villages in Licheng County. The county was divided into districts, and our village was part of the Northeastern District's Minxiaosanli sub-district. The village head was a man named Xie Chaoli. Villages in this part of Shandong commonly established sub-village sections (*duan*), with the village head deciding the number of sections. Each section was represented by a councilor (*shoushi*). Sizes of the sections varied, depending on the reputation of the councilor. The councilors were expected to manage village affairs, including mediating disputes, managing temple properties, carrying out sacrificial rituals, and organizing crop watching. This position, which was often passed from father to son, usually went to someone who was relatively wealthy and had earned the respect of other villagers. The councilors in turn nominated a candidate to be the village head (KC 1955, 7–8).

In 1928, Xie Chaoli resigned his position as village head, and the councilors reorganized the village, going from thirteen sections to eight. The councilors nominated Du Fengshan as village head. Du Fengshan said he was unwilling to assume the positions and offered to resign many times, but the councilors insisted that he should continue. One of the reasons men were reluctant to assume the position was that it brought an immense amount of work but no pay. To induce Du to take the job, the village decided to raise one hundred *yuan* a year out of donations to provide an allowance in thanks for his work.

The 1926 regulations on village and town self-governance stipulated that the population should be organized under the *lülin* (collective responsibility system) and, given its population, Lengshuigou should have established fourteen *lü*, each with its own head (*lüzhang*), but the village only nominally followed the rules. The population was registered into the *lü* units, but no heads were appointed. As for the village head, Lengshuigou did go through a formal election process in which each household got one vote. The election was held at the village's primary school, and women were allowed to represent their families. On the day of the election, officials from the sub-county administration supervised the proceedings, reporting back to the county government when the election was over. The *Kankō Chōsa* records have a detailed account of the procedures for electing village heads:

> There are no restrictions on the village head's tenure, and the village head can resign. . . . Township (*xiang*) and district heads should be well educated, while the village head should be popular among villagers, should have a good reputation, should be enthusiastic in managing village affairs, and be regarded as fair. There are no restrictions on the basis of age, property and education. . . . The village head receives no official salary, only 120 yuan collected by villagers at the end of year. The amount of money given by each household is based on the amount of land they own. . . . The village head is responsible for delivering tax payments to the county, assisting the police in household investigation, keeping registers, mediating conflicts, greeting inspectors, and organizing villagers to repair temples, schools and roads. . . . Usually villagers obey the village head absolutely. But if someone refuses to follow, the village head has no authority to order punishment. Such cases, however, are quite rare. . . . The village head has no priority in access to public facilities (such as temples and schools) and pays the same tax as other villagers. Overall the village head enjoys no special privileges. (KC 1955, 6–8)

Under the Japanese occupation from 1938 to 1945, Lengshuigou was subordinate to Zhangma District, Licheng, and the system of collective responsibility changed from the *lülin* to the *baojia*. As a result of this shift in organization, the village head was referred to as the *baozhang*, rather than village head. Du Fengshan continued in the position until he retired in 1943. There were four *bao* in the village, each with ten subordinate *jia* (ten family groups). The heads of the *jia* were elected by a vote of the constituent households, with the ten *jia* heads then voting to decide the head of the *bao*. In choosing the *bao* heads, attention was given to the personal skills of the individual, his level of literacy, and his financial standing. Most of the *bao* heads were relatively well off. There was no fixed tenure for the positions, nor did they receive salary. The only reward was recognition of a somewhat higher status than ordinary peasants. Their jobs involved registering the population of their unit, tracking and recording those who migrated in and out, and assisting with the work of the self-defense militia—much of which had to do with paying the grain tax collected by the Japanese occupation authorities (KC 1955, 336).[4]

When villagers were asked about the *baojia* system instituted under the Japanese occupation, they had this to say (Duara 1988, 171):

> Q: What is the difference between the neighborhood (*duan*) and the *baojia* systems [introduced in 1940 and not very different from the *lülin* systems]?
>
> A: The *baojia* was imposed from above. The neighborhood emerged spontaneously.
>
> Q: Were the households in the neighborhood closer to each other than to outsiders?
>
> A: A little more. Certainly, they were closer than the present *jia*.
>
> Q: Did the councilors [*shoushiren*] of the neighborhood mediate quarrels between two fellow members of the neighborhood?
>
> A: Certainly, they did.
>
> Q: What about the present head of the *jia*?
>
> A: Not necessarily. It depends on his ability.

We can see that under the Japanese occupation, the relationship between the leaders and the people changed. The traditional village councilor had authority within his own *duan* on the basis of his own personal reputation, while the *jiazhang* under the Japanese did not necessarily have such personal authority. The relationship between the village head and the sub-unit heads also changed. Under the traditional system, the councilors had selected the village head; under the system in place under the Japanese, the lines were reversed, and the village head appointed the heads of the sub-units.

Under the Nationalist government, the state not only tried to gain tighter control over rural areas, it also tried to curb lineage influence. At the time, the number of lineages that maintained genealogies and ancestral halls was declining, and group rituals in memory of ancestors were also increasingly rare. Anti-superstition movements in the late 1920s and early 1930s, which were part of the modernizing and secularizing agenda of the Nationalist Party, also impacted rural areas. Rural communities were urged to take over religious property, including temple land, and convert it to public use. In the past, Lengshuigou reportedly had a great deal of land that had been set aside to support village religious institutions; by the late 1930s, there was only two *mu* left. In this period, the rural elite also experienced dramatic change: some members of the traditional gentry elite lost their property or moved to urban centers. With the end of the imperial examination system, rural men no longer had an easy route to elite status. As warlords moved back and forth across the North China plains, the elite were increasingly militarized, just at the time that the old-elite of gentry with examination credentials were retiring. This left a situation in which there was little strong leadership at the grassroots level. Lengshuigou was relatively lucky, but even in this relatively stable village, residents felt it was necessary to set up a voluntary self-defense force.

In 1945, the Japanese army surrendered, and the Guomindang returned to control in the region. For the first half year, they continued the wartime system and then later reorganized the system following *baojia* regulations. It was not long before civil war broke out between the Guomindang and the Communist forces, and the Guomindang government used the *baojia* system to mobilize labor and financial resources for their war effort. The major duties of the *baojia* units were collecting grain and taxes, recruiting soldiers, and training militia. There were numerous changes in the organization during this period, but little change in functions.

Throughout the turbulent first half of the twentieth century, the Chinese state—first under the late Qing, then under successive Republican governments, as well as under the Japanese occupation—made efforts to gain greater control over the countryside, partly in an effort to mobilize financial and human resources to support different factions, partly to push modernizing agendas that were a central part of the efforts of those regimes to build a new Chinese society. None of those efforts were completely successful, in large measure due to resistance on the part of villagers who continued to rely on the traditional mechanisms of organization and power internal to the village.

Village Administrative System after 1949

During the first half of the twentieth century, the state tried to work through indigenous village structures to extend its control into the countryside, in efforts that were only partially successful. After 1949, the newly established

PRC state—which was much stronger than its predecessors—used its absolute power and control over propaganda to extend its control to the grassroots level. In the early years after the establishment of the PRC, the state began, through a staged process, to create new institutions including the administrative village. Work teams, sent in by the new national government, established peasant associations led by poor peasants that came to play a crucial role in the land-reform campaign and the movement to introduce cooperation in agricultural activities. The peasant association replaced the earlier *baojia* system as the fundamental unit of village self-government. New mass organizations, created at the village level, mediated the push by the Communist Party and state to extend control over the grassroots level.

The new arrangements for village control brought a major revolution: for centuries village affairs had been in the hands of those who were literate and relatively prosperous. Under the post-1949 system, the president and members of the peasant association were selected from among the poor peasants. The work teams sent in by higher authorities identified poor peasants who they believed had leadership potential, and those individuals took on village leadership roles, including head and deputy head of the peasant association, accountants, militiamen, and members of the security and defense units. The peasant association played a central role in village affairs until the establishment of the People's Commune in 1958 when it was replaced by new organizations. In contrast to the pre-1949 village self-government organizations, the Peasant Association was a much more powerful and comprehensive organization, handling administrative, military and security functions. It also played a central role in the efforts to transform village society and economy.

Land Reform

Land reform was the first large-scale effort to transform the fundamental conditions of Chinese rural society after 1949 and was also the village community's first encounter with the Chinese Communist Party's use of "campaign tactics" to transform society. Under the direction of land-reform work teams sent in by higher authorities, the Lengshuigou Peasant Association began to mobilize the population, beginning with propaganda meetings to explain the principles of land reform (Land Reform Act). Mass meetings were held to explain ideas about political classes—meetings in which poor peasants were encouraged to talk about past misery and compare it with present happiness. For peasants who had long believed in the power of fate, the new political education introduced ideas about class exploitation as the cause of poverty and suffering and encouraged the peasants to think about new ways of dealing with social injustice. The poor were encouraged to rely on each other and to challenge the dominance of the rich peasants and the landlords. Following the political education campaign, land reform moved on to assigning class statuses to individuals and households: in Lengshuigou thirty-two households were identified as landlords, and eight households were assigned the status of rich peasants.

Following the outlines of the Land Reform Act, extra land, buildings, and farming tools were taken from the landlords and rich peasants and distributed among poor peasants and hired laborers who had a little or no land. At the end of the movement, land ownership certificates were given to the formerly poor, realizing one of the goals of the revolution, "land to the tiller." Li Wencai, an activist in the land reform movement who came from a poor peasant family, was appointed as head of the Peasant Association and was approved for membership in the Communist Party. As a result of the land reform movement, the structure of village power was radically changed: poor and lower-middle peasants not only gained economically but also became the holders of political power. This group—which to use the language of the time had "turned over" (*fanshen*) their lives,[5] had much higher levels of political consciousness, were loyal and obedient to the state, and became powerful supporters of the state in its efforts to control rural society. Through land reform and the movements that followed, state power successfully penetrated rural society, and the poor-peasant cadre became the heads of village organizations replacing traditional gentry or old rural elite as the leaders in rural society.

Following the conclusion of the land reform movement, the administrative village (or *xiang*) was established as the lowest level of administration in the countryside.[6] Under the new system, a People's Representative Assembly was established at the village level, with representatives chosen for one-year terms; members could be reelected. During periods when the People's Representative Assembly was not in session, the administrative village was responsible for running affairs, under the supervision of higher-level units of the people's government. The administrative village was responsible for maintaining public security, mediating conflicts, supporting the army and giving preferential treatment to families of army men and martyrs,[7] issuing social pensions, offering relief aid, and organizing agricultural and sideline production of the village.

During the early years of the PRC, Lengshuigou was subordinate to Zhangma District, Lengshuigou Xiang, whose jurisdiction also covered the natural villages of Shahe, Yangjiatun, and Shuipo. One of our elderly informants (seventy-one years old) was asked why Li Yuquan was selected as village head. She replied, "He was a good man coming from a poor peasant family, with a high political awareness." From this we can see that class status was an important criterion for office, as was personal performance as a political activist in earlier movements. Others who later served as village head were Li Changxin, Li Changan, Liu Rusheng, Wang Jinting, Xie Changji, Li Zhanqi, and Xie Jinghe (LCZ 2010, 51).

Organizations during the Cooperative Movement

The Land Reform movement had rectified some of the greatest inequalities in land distribution, but it had not resolved many of the fundamental problems of agricultural production. Land holdings were still small and scattered, and many households lacked farm animals, agricultural implements, and labor. The new regime soon launched a movement to create agricultural cooperatives, which were designed to improve production and prevent change that might lead to a return to an economically polarized rural society.

In 1951, the Chinese Communist Party (CPC) central committee issued *The Resolution on Mutual Cooperation in Agricultural Production.* Following the guidelines in this national policy, villagers in Lengshuigou set up several voluntary mutual-aid groups. One of our informants recalled: "Usually four or five households voluntarily formed a mutual-aid group. Each group elected a member who had progressive ideas and was willing to be of service to others as its head. In the busy season, members of the group helped each other. When work in one household was done, they moved on to the next. But farmland was still privately owned."

In 1954, on the basis of the mutual-aid groups, Lengshuigou set up eight lower level agricultural cooperatives. In the same year, the Party directed party members in Lengshuigou and Shuipo to form a Party branch, with Xie Changjiu as party secretary. While joining the lower level cooperatives was voluntary, these new cooperatives were different from the loose form of cooperation of the mutual-aid teams. The lower level cooperatives separated land ownership rights and rights of use, pooling land as shares in the cooperative. Villagers who wanted to join a cooperative had to make a formal application and gain approval; withdrawal was also permitted. Each cooperative had a head, with the members divided into a number of smaller working groups, each with its own head. In addition to the heads, each group had an accountant and one or more members who recorded the work contributions of each member. The lower level cooperative was responsible for arranging production and distribution, assuming many functions of local political organizations, and became the basic social unit through which the state controlled rural areas.

At this time, there was a nationwide rising tide of enthusiasm for a more egalitarian economic system. While the lower level cooperatives had made major gains in improving cooperation in agricultural activities, there were still problems. Under the lower level cooperatives, cooperative members received returns in kind and cash based on a two-part calculation: part of the distribution was based on work contributions, part was calculated as a return for the contribution of land and means of production. While land reform had removed the extremes of inequality in distribution of land and other means of production, it had not made households equal. Debates at the time argued that the lower level cooperatives still embodied some elements of exploitation—since better-off households contributed more land and other items and received more than poorer households because of these contributions. This inequality in returns was seen as a remnant of inequalities from the pre–land reform system of unequal distribution of land.

The national government decided to move to higher level cooperatives, compelling all members of rural society to join the new organizations. All land and means of production became the property of the collective, and returns were based only on labor contributions. In the autumn of 1955, Lengshuigou and Shuipo together set up the East Is Red higher level agricultural producers' cooperative. The cooperative adopted a uniform accounting system, and introduced collective production. Wang Yonggui was appointed as head of the cooperative by the *xiang* government. According to one of our informants, the movement to create higher level cooperatives began with a propaganda campaign encouraging people to join, but in the end membership became mandatory.

As we can see from this brief description of changes, the state moved very quickly in the early 1950s to transform rural society, successfully creating mass organizations at the village level (Peasant Association, lower level and higher level cooperatives). A range of other mass organizations were created at the grassroots level, including a branch of the Youth League, a Women's Representative Congress, and a militia responsible for self-defense. At the same time, the Communist Party set up organizations at the grassroots level, which successfully brought the power of the state and Party into the village.

As for traditional village organizations that had been based on lineage and neighbor relations in the village, through a series of educational and struggle campaigns, the state pursued efforts to eliminate what it regarded as "feudal" and "superstitious" activities. Overall, all these new organizations and campaigns broke the hold of former institutions and ideas that had together played a role in isolating and protecting the village from external forces. The village was now integrated into a single structure of leadership and was controlled directly under the authority of the unified national state (Mao 2000, 40).

Village Administration under the People's Commune

In August 1958, Mao Zedong visited Licheng County, inspecting the nearby village of Shuitun in Beiyuan xiang. During that visit, Mao was asked about rural organization and remarked, "The People's Commune is good. Its advantage is to combine workers, peasants, merchants, students, soldiers and intellectuals together, easy to lead" (SHZ 1989, 118–19). Publication of Mao's words in the *People's Daily* on August 13 touched off a movement to form communes all over the country. Within months the more than 740,000 higher level cooperatives in China were reorganized into 23,284 people's communes, with an average of 4,767 households in each. The people's communes integrated government administration, economic production, and social welfare in one unit.

The people's commune followed a military-style organization. Under the aegis of the commune headquarters, groups of villages were organized into battalions, and smaller groups of four to five villages were formed into companies. Lengshuigou, together with Shuipo, Yangjiatun, and Lijiacun, were combined into the Lengyang battalion, under the Dongjiao (East Gate) People's Commune; Ren Zongxiang was appointed as battalion commander. Under the battalion, there were four companies, and the four villages that were joined together as a battalion shared a common Party branch, with Yang Hongbao as the Party branch secretary. During the early, heady days of the People's Commune, national policies called for "huge in scale and collective

Photo 2.1. Chairman Mao visits the Dongjiao Commune. Photo provided by the district government.

in nature," arguing that "equalitarianism and equal distribution of resources" would soon produce a communist paradise. People in the commune were urged to overcome physical challenges, treating production as a form of battle. This was the era when all of life was collectivized—people worked in teams, often working for long hours away from home, eating together in collective dining halls.

Agricultural cooperatives were changed to production brigades that were divided into several small production teams. The commune adopted a system of unified management and allocation, which meant that everyone worked together and received in kind the food and other goods they needed to sustain life. The commune set up collective dining halls for meals, nurseries to provide child care so that women could join in agricultural labor, and homes to care for the elderly. The new organizations went beyond the limits of kinship and collectivized all labor and consumption. The commune was both a collective economic organization and a basic-level political organization. Economic rights, including the right to make decisions with regard to production and consumption, which had for several millennia belonged to households in the village, were now put in the hands of the state.

The sudden rush to communism soon produced disaster resulting in famine conditions in many parts of China. In response to the crisis, in 1959 the CCP central committee issued *Eighteen Questions about People's Communes*, placing restrictions on ownership and functions and powers of communes and production brigades, demanding protection of commune members' rights, giving permission for household sidelines, recovering private land, ending the commune dining halls, and making the production team the basic accounting unit. In the following months, military-style organization was reversed, and battalions were renamed as brigades. Lengshuigou village was divided into two brigades, the Lengshuigou East Brigade and the Lengshuigou West Brigade, with Li Fengke as East Brigade leader and Ren Zongxiang as West Brigade leader. In 1963, the East and West Brigades were rejoined into one unit, the Lengshuigou Brigade, with Li Fengke as the brigade leader (LCZ 2010, 51).

Former village director Cheng Kexing had this to say about those times:

> During the People's Commune period, I was the leader of the tenth production team. I joined the Party in 1971 and was appointed team leader in 1975, responsible for distributing assignments and arranging and inspecting production. At that time, our brigade was doing very well. The Lengshuigou Brigade had organizations such as the Party branch, a management committee, a militia unit, a Youth League branch, an association for the poor, an association for women and a public security committee, among which the Party branch was the core with supreme authority. On the next level, there were 19 production teams,

> each with its respective team leader and vice–team leader. The brigade leader was responsible for organizing agriculture production, ensuring implementation of missions from superiors, turning in grain tax and agriculture taxes, final accounting of revenue and expenditure, managing village collective property and maintaining social security. The team leader should be a peasant who came from a good class background, worked hard, had rich experience in agriculture, knew how to negotiate with people, and was fair in judgments. There were also men responsible for the warehouses, work point recorders, accountants, cashiers and a leader of a women's team.

About villagers' life in the period of the People's Commune, a villager (fifty-three years old) who had served as a work point recorder, recalled:

> I was in the nineteenth production team and worked with everybody. At 6 in the morning we went out together and returned home at 7:30 to have breakfast. Afterward the dining hall was built and we were required to eat there, but I could not get used to it. One was not free and had to ask for leave for visiting relatives and going to the periodic market. Meetings were often held. Twenty days out of a month there were meetings for villagers, most of which were about production, how to arrange production, and there were political meetings for political education, such as reading quotations from Chairman Mao Zedong, criticizing Lin and Kong,[8] contrasting past misery with present happiness and learning from Dazhai.[9] There were posters and slogans everywhere in the village. Villagers were required to attend meetings. Work points were added for attendance and deducted for absence.

During the People's Commune era, new collective-living styles replaced the traditional rural lifestyles. The family, which for millennia had been the center of village economic and social life, came to play a minor role, supplanted by collective production. Individual peasants and their families were subordinated to collective institutions, and ultimately to the state. The movement for collectivization, which had begun with very high hopes, was transformed into a system that took away peasants' freedom to speak and left them with little enthusiasm or incentive for collective work. Moreover, repeated political campaigns interrupted the normal work of agricultural production. The mistaken political lines adopted after 1958 sent the Lengshuigou economy into a tailspin, and agricultural output fell. In the two years following the launch of the Great Leap Forward, the lives of ordinary people were pushed into extreme difficulties, and the result of mistaken policies and three years of natural disasters was a large-scale famine.

Beginning in 1966, the village was influenced by the waves of the Cultural Revolution, and some villagers spontaneously formed Red Guard units. The village Red Guards began to attack village cadres, holding struggle meetings against those in power, parading them through the streets, and denouncing them in big-character posters. Some village cadres were beaten and forced to kneel down as punishment. The Cultural Revolution presented some villagers who had been unhappy—but passive and obedient—with an opportunity to express their resentment toward the village leaders. In Lengshuigou, as in villages across China, a new organization known as a "revolutionary committee" replaced existing power structures. Gao Fuxing and Li Yanwu successively held the position of chair of the village revolutionary committee. In 1975 the revolutionary committee was abolished, and the production brigade was restored as the center of village governance, with Ren Yanting as Party branch secretary and Cheng Kexing as the brigade leader.

Township Government and Village Self-Governance Since 1978

In December 1978, the Central Committee of the Chinese Communist Party announced the first steps in the "reform and opening up" policies that over the last decades have transformed Chinese economy and society. The reforms began in agriculture introducing the "household responsibility system" which brought an end to collective cultivation and revived household-based production. This shift in the fundamental system of rural economic organization radically changed the responsibilities of local government and demanded changes in the commune system, which had unified economic and political control in a single institutional framework.

Four years later, in December 1982, the new Constitution of the People's Republic of China officially abolished the people's communes and created new grassroots political institutions including the township (*xiang*), ethnic township (*minzu xiang*),[10] and town (*zhen*) as sub-county administrative units (1982 Article 30). At the village level, village committees elected by the residents were established as self-government institutions. The village committee, with a head and deputy head, was given responsibility for mediation of disputes, security, and public welfare; assisting in the maintenance of social security; dealing with people's complaints and demands; and offering suggestions to the government (1982 Article 111). These stipulations in the Constitution provided legal grounds for village self-governance.

In August of 1984, Lengshuigou Brigade officially disbanded as a "brigade" and established a village committee, and the former production teams were transformed into small groups (*cunmin xiaozu*). Cheng Kexing, who had been the brigade leader, was elected as the first director of the village committee; he was subsequently reelected several times, serving until 1999.

The new institutional framework represented a major change from the commune system. As we have seen earlier, although the commune and brigade headquarters were located in the rural countryside, institutionally they were official government institutions rather than village self-government organizations. The commune, which was responsible for management of economic, political, and social affairs, had been the lowest level of the national government; the brigade office had been subordinate to and under the leadership of the commune. Under the new system, the township was the lowest official level of government, and the institutions at the village level were designated as self-governing organizations that elected their own leaders. Although the village-level organizations were officially and legally designed as self-governing mass organizations, there is no question that they operated under the guidance of the township, which served as the lowest level official government institution.

Organization on the Village Level

In contemporary Lengshuigou, there is a variety of party, government, and mass organizations that together work to manage village affairs. Let us look now at some of those organizations and see what they do.

Village Party branch: According to the Constitution, the village committee replaced the production brigade as the institution with primary responsibility for village governance. However, there is no question that it is actually the village Party branch that plays the central role in managing village affairs. Under the present Chinese political structure, the village Party branch plays the leading role in implementing political directives, doing propaganda and political education work, and providing leadership for other village organizations. It plays the decisive role in making and implementing policy. The village Party branch leads the village committee, village collective economic organizations, the Communist Youth League, the Women's Congress at the village level, the village militia, and other mass organizations.

Party membership in Lengshuigou has increased since 1980, and in 1994 it was designated as a general party branch (*zongdangbu*), a status given to local party organizations with more than 50 members. At the end of 2007, there were 77 Party members in the village, including 68 men and 9 women. An examination of the educational background of party members showed that 9 (11.68 percent) held college degrees, 16 (20.78 percent) were graduates of high school or technical secondary school, 34 (44.15 percent) were graduates of middle school, and 18 (23.38 percent) had only a primary school education. In terms of age distribution, there was only 1 (1.3 percent) Party member in the age range of 18 to 25, 10 (13 percent) Party members were in the age range of 26 to 35, 4 (5.19 percent) Party members were in the age range of 36 to 45, 21 (27.27 percent) Party members in the age range of 46 to 55, and

41 (53.24 percent) Party members were over the age of 56 (LCZ 2010, 45). The party membership in Lengshuigou reflects patterns in other rural areas of China with a predominance of older members, many of whom have lower levels of education. Thus, the village party faces the problems of aging and a shortage of young candidates.

According to regulations, branch committee members served for three years. Candidates for committee membership could be nominated either by villagers or by party members. Once a Party working committee had considered and approved the eligibility of candidates, all party members had the right to vote. To see what actually happens in such a vote, we will turn to an account of the election for the branch committee members held on February 25, 2011. Zhang Yuanxiu (female, sixty-two years old, former Lengshuigou Party branch secretary) gave us a brief description. According to her description, there was a three-stage electoral process:

> In this election candidates were first recommended by villagers, then by Party members, and finally selected by a vote of all Party members in the village. Villagers' recommendations were based on villagers' small groups. The day before the election villager representatives distributed a formal notice and a formal table of basic information about a Party member to every household. In every villagers' small group there were three people in charge of the election. To avoid conflicting with work, the election started early at 7 o'clock in the morning and the staff delivered ballots to every village house, with every household receiving one ballot. Villagers had to choose 5 Party members from 98 formal Party members, usually choosing someone who they thought was capable, responsible and had a high level of political awareness. There was a polling place for every villagers' small group, and villagers had to vote at the scheduled time. When voting was over, every group delivered the ballot box to the yard of the village committee and votes were recorded publicly. The ten persons who received the most votes were qualified to be candidates, and results were posted on the billboard of village affairs. Then a conference of all Party members was called under the direction and supervision of the Party secretary of the sub-district office. In this election 6 candidates should be elected out of 10 candidates selected by the villagers; finally 5 should be elected as Party branch committee members out of 6 candidates. Then the new branch members meeting would be held to confirm the list for secretary, assistant secretary and committee members, which should be reported to the Street Party Working Committee. The final result was announced after being finally approved by the Town Party committee.

In this election, Liu Chuncai was elected Party branch secretary, Li Lide was assistant secretary, and Xie Zhaoyi, Li Zhongcheng, and Zhang Yuancheng were elected as committee members. Of the five successful candidates, three had college degrees, and the youngest, Li Lide, was only thirty-three. Within the Party branch, the village Party secretary had absolute authority. In Lengshuigou members of the Party branch committee were also members of the village committee, and there was no clear separation of responsibilities. The Party branch committee provided leadership for the village committee, and the Party secretary had supreme authority in the village and could inquire into all village affairs. When there were important issues to decide, the Party branch secretary would call a meeting with members of the branch committee and the village committee, and after discussion, the Party branch secretary would make the final decision.

Contemporary village leaders are quite different from those of the pre-reform era. At that time, leaders were selected on the basis of their class origin, political awareness, and loyalty. Leaders of the new generation are selected on the basis of their capacity and experience, economic strength, and wide range of social connections. The present Party branch secretary Liu Chuncai and committee member Xie Zhaoyi are examples of this new spirit. Liu Chuncai is an army veteran who took the leading role in developing the village's dairy business, thus demonstrating his entrepreneurial capabilities. Xie Zhaoyi, director of the mediation committee, was head of the people's militia under the commune, and later served as director of one of the village-owned factories. He has a good knowledge of the law, so villagers go to him for mediation when there are disputes.

Village committee: The village committee has between three and seven members, including a head, a deputy head, and general members. Under the committee, there are various committees to handle village affairs including management of economic affairs, maintenance of public security, public health, management of housing areas, and birth control. Villagers elect the members of the village committee.

At present, the village has four subdivisions known as *pian*, and each *pian* has a head responsible for conveying information between the people and the party. Land is now contracted to individual households, and following the reform in rural land taxes, the village committee's responsibilities for managing production and tax payment have disappeared. In contemporary Lengshuigou, the main tasks of the village committee are supervising enforcement of the birth control regulations, mediation of civil disputes, and management tasks related to village housing areas. Where the brigade cadre under the commune had played a major role in organizing production and distribution, activities that affected the daily lives of all village households, the contemporary village committee's tasks are much more limited, and most villagers are hardly aware of its presence in their everyday lives.

Women's Representative Association: The Women's Representative Association is the lowest level branch of the All China Women's Federation. According to formal regulations, its major duties include protecting and safeguarding women's rights, solving problems for women, maintaining harmony within families, and encouraging women of childbearing age to follow birth control measures. In practice, the main task of the village women's association is promotion and supervision of birth control. The present director, Zhang Yuanxiu, has been very successful in these efforts, and she and the village have won awards for their compliance with birth control regulations.

Association for the Elderly: The Association for the Elderly, founded in 1989, is Lengshuigou's only official NGO. When the association was first created, it had only five members, most of whom were retired cadres or retired teachers. Ren Yanting and Cheng Kexing, who had been important village leaders, have both served terms as chairman. The village has set up a social space for older villagers with rooms where they can play chess, cards, and *majiang*. Every year at the Spring Festival, the association sponsors competitions in chess and *majiang*, and it also holds contests testing people's knowledge of current affairs and health-care knowledge. In 1998, Li Xingshi, a native of Lengshuigou who now lives in Taiwan, donated US $1200 to the center, which the association used to repair the roof and buy office supplies; they also set up a "Xingshi" Cup Chess Competition. In 2001, two committees in the village invested over 30,000 *yuan* to build a gate ball court, added a room for Ping-Pong and a practice room for calligraphy, and bought sports equipment and sportswear. Gate ball has become one of the prime forms of recreation among village seniors, and Lengshuigou has twice won the annual competition run by the Licheng district (LCZ 2010, 103).

In February 2007, a group of retired schoolteachers who were alumni of Jinan Normal School founded a social club, known as the Lengshuigou Huanian Association. This group, with about twenty-five members, focuses on cultural activities, including compiling materials on village history, and played a central role in editing the village gazetteer (LCZ 2010, 55–56). The activities of these organizations, in collaboration with the party branch and village committees, have won the village many awards.

Contemporary Electoral Participation

Not long after the Party branch election, a second election was held to select members of the village committee. The Licheng District People's Government Office posted detailed guidelines for elections for the "two committees" (Party and village). Elections for the village committee also followed a two-stage process that began with public education and propaganda, a nominating process that led to selection of a slate of candidates, and the vote to determine winners. Regulations stipulated that the slate of candidates should include more names than the number of positions on the committee. An election committee made up of villagers was selected to supervise the election and see that voters' rights were protected. Once the slate of candidates had been approved, candidates were invited to give speeches about what they wanted to do as members of the village committee. The election was held on April 25, 2011, with voters gathering in the courtyard of the village committee to cast their ballots. Votes were publicly counted and the results announced and posted on the village billboards. Liu Chuncai, who had several weeks earlier been elected as Party secretary was chosen to concurrently serve as village head.

Following the elections, our research team conducted a survey of voters about political participation. Our survey results show that villagers had many questions about the electoral process. In answer to a question about whether they thought village elections were fair, only 2 percent of those surveyed answered yes; 24.1 percent thought it was just so-so, 28.1 percent thought the election was useless, 29.3 percent thought the effect of the election was not so good, and 16.5 percent thought it was very bad. As for what should be prohibited in an election, 38.5 percent replied that bribery and vote buying were out of control, and 36.9 percent thought some individuals had manipulated the election by illegal means. In addition, 4.6 percent thought the election was influenced by lineage and family powers, and 4.4 percent thought that the town government and villagers did not see eye to eye on the election. It was obvious that in the village committee election, lineage power and government interference did not have much influence, and people were concerned about bribery, vote buying, and illegal manipulation of the election.

In fact, villagers want to participate in elections and expect greater supervision and a more democratic process. For example, when asked "will you vote if the village organized an election for village committee," 65.9 percent answered "yes," 21.9 percent answered "no," and 12.2 percent answered "not sure." As for selection of candidates, most people supported election "through villagers' meetings" and other democratic measures. Despite their doubts about the election process, most of the respondents recognized the important role that the village committee and other village organizations play in village development and management of village affairs. For example, from the survey, we know that 88.7 percent recognized the committee's influence in making decisions about important affairs. In answer to the question, "Who is often consulted when there are problems or disputes," over half replied "village cadres and the mediation committee" (46.2 percent), while 30.5 percent chose relatives.

However, when we probed further, we learned that most villagers were not very interested in village affairs. In answer to a question about this, only 39.8 percent of our respondents said they were interested in village affairs, while 60.2 percent said they were not interested at all. From these responses, we can see that the impact of economic development has created a situation where many villagers work outside the village and have many more choices. Mobility of the population, together with involvement in occupations unconnected to village affairs, has led to a situation where villagers care less about collective affairs. The survey confirmed what we learned from interviews: because of the village's proximity to Jinan, many people work outside the village during the day and spend only a little time at home. Tired from work, they have little energy for village affairs and don't really care who becomes a village cadre since makeup of village leadership has little influence on their lives.

Experts disagree about the meaning of "self-government" in contemporary rural society. Some argue that contemporary post-commune "self-government" institutions represent a withdrawal of the state from efforts to control grassroots rural society, while others believe that what we see is simply reconstruction of a system of state control over rural society in a different form. Those who hold to the latter view believe that the state has consciously used the resources of traditional society to realize modernist agendas during a period of "planned social transition," creating a new institutional framework that blends state power with traditional rural methods of mutual assistance. Lu Xueyi has argued that control by the village committee does represent a form of self-government. Only by combining state institutional power with indigenous systems of power of the village can a new form of local organization emerge that can effectively govern the vast area of rural villages and peasants. Many problems remain: how to cultivate and nurture villagers' understanding of democracy and political participation, how to standardize village elections, and how to make use of peasants' talents and strengths are all problems that will require significant time to resolve.

VILLAGE ELITE

In the first part of this chapter, we have described the institutional structure of village politics. This latter section turns to the village elite who played central roles in the development of village politics. These are the men—for all the people we will consider are men—who were able, on the basis of the resources they controlled—including economic as well as cultural and social resources—to make successful lives and to play leading roles in shaping village affairs.

Classical elite theory holds that in any society, the elite does not stay the same but circulates and flows. Vilfredo Pareto, the social scientist who first developed theories about the elite, held that human history is a process of constant circulation of elites in which one elite rises and the former declines. There are two circulation modes for elites, one of which is internal circulation within the elite group, the replacement of one member of the elite by another; the other is mobility between elite and non-elite groups, a circulation that involves changes in the relative positions of the social strata. Twentieth-century rural China went through dramatic social change, from the fall of the last imperial dynasty to internal disruptions of the warlord era, invasion and war, civil war, and the socialist revolution. Each era gave birth to new social institutions and economic systems, and village elites were generated following both of the circulation modes. Let us now look at changes in elite composition in Lengshuigou through the three historical periods.

From the End of the Nineteenth Century to the Republican Period—Village Elite Composition

In the first half of the twentieth century, Chinese rural society went through constant change as the old social order created under the imperial system was slowly dismantled and new institutions were created. If we could visit late imperial society, we would see a village community in which gentry with educational and economic qualifications managed village affairs. These were men who had studied for the imperial exams, sometimes earning the lowest level degrees and who held respected positions within their own lineages. In traditional society, these gentry members performed their duties of "managing the village under government supervision," passing on ancient culture and customs, and maintaining social stability.

Following the overthrow of the Qing dynasty, new institutions were born, a process that has been explained in the first part of this chapter. Responding to government directives, villages were reorganized under the *lülin* and *baojia*, and villagers were selected to take on responsibilities as village head and heads of the subordinate units. The men who assumed these positions formed a new village elite. We can identify four general types of the Republican village elite.

New Middle-Peasant "Gentry"

Originally, only the wealthy could assume the position of village head. Under the Republic, however, the abolition of the imperial examinations broke the link between the village educated and state power. At the same time, there were increasing demands for extralegal tax assessments (*tankuan*) to carry out various modernizing agendas, and the traditional gentry—seeing no economic or prestige benefits—began to avoid holding office. This situation reached an acute stage during the time that the warlord Zhang Zongchang occupied Shandong, demanding both cash and provisions for his army.[11] The traditional elite was unwilling to become the agents of the state in exploiting the rural population; many powerful village leaders left the village, and others refused to serve in public offices. Middle peasants or poor peasants assumed the positions once held by rich landlords, as the old elite came to believe that a "good person" was not willing to serve (Duara 1988, 172).

In Lengshuigou, the former village head Xie Chaoli resigned in 1928, and the village councilors recommended Du Fengshan to be village head. Du Fengshan repeatedly declined the nomination, but the village councilors were unwilling to accept his refusal. In 1929, two-thirds of the village households voted for him to be reelected as village head. Du Fengshan is a good example of this shift in the elite. He was an ordinary peasant, illiterate, neither a local tyrant nor a rogue. His family was not financially well-off. They had only several *mu* of land and earned extra income from raising chickens and ducks. However, he was very capable and had a good reputation in the village. He tried to do all kinds of good things, winning villagers' trust and respect. He was so trusted that he was often invited to mediate disputes between landlords and tenants. It was said that when he acted as a middleman facilitating land purchases, or agreeing on loans, or negotiating prices in the market, business was handled smoothly. In the 1930s and 1940s, there were very few men like Du who could serve as village head for such a long period of time and still enjoy a good reputation.

However, during this period, most of the village councilors as well as the *lü* and *baojia* heads were relatively wealthy, owning more land than ordinary villagers. After 1928, the average amount of land owned by this group of people declined. According to the *Kankō Chōsa* survey, among the councilors who held office before 1928, the wealthiest individual had 80 *mu* of land and the least wealthy had 20 *mu*, with an average holding of 52.5 *mu*. But after 1928, the largest landowner among the fourteen *lü* heads owned 60 *mu* and the smallest 6 *mu*, with an average of 26 *mu* (KC 1955, 25).

Lineage Elite

Although the state was slowly encroaching on the structure of power in the village as the local government tried to bring the village leaders under their control, within the village, the lineage elite continued to protect the interests of their own lineages and continued to play important roles in village affairs. On the one hand, although the elite chose to "withdraw" politically they still had social prestige; on the other hand, members of the elite had long years of experience in carrying out village affairs, including collective prayers for rain and other ceremonies, and their participation guaranteed success in carrying out such public activities. The *Kankō Chōsa* materials include numerous records of such activities and record the names of members of the lineage elite who participated. These lineage leaders continued to play a central role in preserving village traditional culture.

Commoner Landlords

Land was the material basis for peasants' production and life. Farmland was quite abundant in Lengshuigou and commoner landlords owned a large amount of land, and the economic power of this relatively well-off group gave them a position in village affairs. We should note, however, that there were different types of landlords. Although most landlords had gotten rich by working hard and saving money, there were a few who got rich overnight by manipulating connections to political power holders outside the village. Ren Yanming, a large Lengshuigou landlord, is a good example of this second type: he became wealthy by manipulating connections with the Japanese. These commoner landlords participated enthusiastically in all kinds of public activities and village affairs as a way to protect their own land and property; and through those activities, they gained a certain degree of social prestige and played roles within the village in mediating disputes.

For example, Yang Changlu, who served as Zhangma district head (*qu-zhang*) in the 1930s and 1940s was the wealthiest man in Lengshuigou. At that time, his family owned over 100 *mu* and had two houses and a brewery, which hired two or three workers. He owned two horse-drawn carts (*mache*), and hired three or four long-term agricultural workers as well as short-term workers during busy agricultural seasons. Agricultural production was the key to his family's income; they produced 30,000 to 40,000 *jin* of grain a year, which was sufficient to support more than 1,000 people. His second son, Yang Mutao, joined the Eighth Route Army in 1939 becoming a professional revolutionary and retiring with the pension and privileges of a military officer (Li 2011, 25).

Xiang Head

As we have seen earlier, Du Fengshan, who served as village head in the 1930s and 1940s, repeatedly tried to resign, but was persuaded by fellow villagers to continue in the office. He had an assistant who served as *dibao* and worked as a liaison between the village head and the county government. The Japanese invasion made already-complicated politics more difficult, and the village set up a self-defense organization responsible for patrolling the village and maintaining public order. At the same time, the semi-militarized organization of the *baojia* was imposed by the Japanese occupation, and villagers participated in order to preserve their own interests. Under this system, the district head (*xiangbao*) also played a role in defending the interests of villagers, protecting their property and assets, and he came to benefit from a certain degree of respect and reputation among the villagers.

While the general political situation surrounding Lengshuigou during the Republican period was very complicated, there were no big conflicts in the village. This was true even during the period of Japanese occupation, when Lengshuigou was relatively stable. Various members of the village elite worked together, balancing their skills and interests, to keep the village in a relatively stable state.

From 1949 to the Eve of Reforms

Jinan was liberated in 1948, and it was not long before land reform and the movement for collectivization radically altered the social scene, turning the class structure upside down. Those who had been members of the elite before were the targets of the land reform, losing much of their land and other property and being assigned the bad "class labels" of "landlord" and "rich peasant." They and their descendants would be excluded from participation in village management. In their place, a new elite was created drawn from those who had been poor peasants in the old society. Our older informants remember those days when village standards with regard to personal prestige were turned upside down and when those who had been members of the elite came to be seen as "backward." The old elite would remain in that disadvantaged state, becoming targets of criticism during political movements culminating in the Cultural Revolution. Their children, who inherited their political status, were also kept out of leadership positions and were not able to play a role in village governance.

Once the old village elite had been displaced, Party leaders began to recruit a new group of individuals to assume leadership roles. The new leaders were all people of "good" class status, that is, those who, because of their family's poverty, were classified as "poor peasants." Party leaders recruited members of this poor peasant class who had demonstrated leadership qualities in the various political movements to serve as a new village managerial elite. There was some mobility within this new leadership group, as some individuals responded more quickly to changes in political lines, but all of those changes represented flows within the same elite stratum, not recruitment from other strata.

Rise of the Poor and Middle Peasant

Xie Changqi, leader of the early Peasant Association, and Wang Yonggui, who assumed important positions in the village after land reform, were both from the poor or middle peasant class. They came forward as leaders in large part due to their enthusiastic participation in political movements and their diligence in studying Party policies.

Literate and Educated

Lengshuigou had its own elementary school from early in the Republican period, and as a result, many male villagers were literate and able to quickly understand Party policies, which gave them an edge as administrative leaders. It is important to note that this was not true of all rural villages in China at the time, and many villages struggled with administration under leaders who were not literate.

Party Membership

The Party branch was the core institution of village management. Anyone who wanted to participate in development and decision making in the village needed to join the Party. All of the members of the village political elite were Party members, and they built their careers as leaders with the help of the Youth League and Party organizations.

Fair and Having a Sense of Public Service

We might think of the three criteria cited above—class status, some degree of education, and Party membership—as the hard qualifications for becoming a member of the elite. There were other qualifications that we might call "soft qualifications," which referred to personal attitudes. The village was a small social world in which everyone was acquainted—and villagers were always aware of the personal attributes of the leaders. If a leader wanted to gain the trust of his fellow villagers and persuade them to work together, then he needed a certain reputation for being fair and having a sense of public service.

After the Reforms—Coexistence of Elites of Different Types

The initiation of reforms in December 1978 touched off changes that would radically change the structure of village power. The adoption of the household responsibility system and the subsequent dissolution of the commune were signs of the weakening of state power in the village. As the reforms developed, the state abandoned its monopoly on the distribution of rights to public resources, giving individuals and villages greater freedom in pursuit of economic activities. Introduction of the market economy offered incentives to those who had managerial and entrepreneurial skills, and a new diversified elite was slowly formed. Class status disappeared as a condition for holding office, and Lengshuigou, like other rural communities, came to have a new more diversified elite based on political, economic, cultural, and social qualifications.

Although villagers eventually accepted the changes, former Party branch secretary Ren Yanting recalled that Lengshuigou villagers had at first resisted the household responsibility system. Backed by the support of the town government, Ren Yanting undertook the difficult mission of convincing villagers to accept the new system. For his hard work, he received honors from the town government.

The village entered a new stage of rapid growth after the implementation of the household responsibility system: grain output soared, and the village established several village-owned enterprises. When Secretary Ren Yanting retired, he was replaced by Secretary Liu Chuncai, who had gained respect in the village as a result of his efforts to build a large-scale dairy enterprise, which had significantly increased income for many village families. Building on his contacts with the town government, Liu successfully convinced the town to set up an industrial park on Lengshuigou land, bringing in many enterprises that offered jobs to unemployed or partially employed labor. This also contributed to a general rise in living standards.

These were times of great changes, and the transition was not always easy. As Lengshuigou was plunged into the rapid changes that accompanied the introduction of the market, a new type of elite began to emerge, no longer determined by class status but rather by its ability to succeed in the new market economy. The commune was replaced by a new social and political order with a much more diverse village elite. We can see this clearly in the replacement of the top-down system of political control, with new village institutions with a greater degree of self-government, as seen in the elections for Party and village committees. With the end of collective labor, villagers were now free to pursue economic activities. Many found jobs outside the village, and within the village they began to seek leaders who had demonstrated an ability to deal with the rapidly changing social and economic situations.

New-Style Political Elite

The reform policies gave rise to a new style of village political leaders. Ren Yanting, who was Party secretary during the transition, represented the first generation of new leadership, and the current Party secretary, Liu Chuncai, represents the second generation of this more entrepreneurial-oriented elite.

Photo 2.2. Contemporary village Leaders

Ren Yanting: Ren Yanting was born in 1938. After graduating from middle school, he served as an elementary school teacher from 1956 to 1962, earning an award from the city of Jinan as a "Distinguished Teacher." Later he returned to the village and worked as a village accountant and vice-secretary of the League branch. In 1972, he joined the Communist Party and successively held positions as vice–Party branch secretary, head of the village militia, and from 1975 as Party branch secretary; he retired in 1993. Ren was Party secretary during the transition to the household responsibility system, and he developed village enterprises, winning a number of awards for his efforts.

Ren Yanting was both a leader and participant in Lengshuigou's reforms; the household contract responsibility system was carried out under his leadership. Ren recalled that villagers were reluctant and resisted the policy. Entrusted with this mission at a critical and difficult time, he negotiated with the town leadership in an effort to assure speedy accomplishment of the task. With the assistance of other village cadres, he was able to overcome the crisis and to implement the new system without any major conflicts—earning a designation as a "model Party member."

Ren Yanting had the characteristics of the pre-reform village political elite, but also had a strong commercial consciousness. He not only pushed for the implementation of the household contract responsibility system but also developed many village enterprises, and as a result of his efforts, many villagers were able to find employment in non-agricultural activities. Under his leadership, the village invested 30,000 to build the first village collective enterprise—a bristle processing factory. He introduced new methods of choosing leaders: for example, the factory manager was chosen on the basis of recommendations from the masses and approved by the Party and village committees. Most of those chosen to manage the village enterprises were Party members. The bristle factory developed very quickly, and at its peak, produced an annual income of 400,000 *yuan*. Ren also initiated other enterprises, including a shoe factory, a fertilizer factory, a dairy farm, a mineral-processing plant, and orchards. The workers in these enterprises were all Lengshuigou villagers. By providing employment opportunities, the enterprises not only increased the income of village families, but also introduced village labor to technology and allowed some to develop managerial skills that would be very useful as the reforms moved ahead and an increasing percentage of the village population gave up agriculture. While a number of these enterprises were later forced out of business as a result of changes in the market and regulatory regimes, they provided an important bridge during the transition out of the collective economy and played an important role in developing popular consciousness of the opportunities in the new market economy. Experiences gained during this stage of development laid the foundation for further village development.

At the same time, the profits from the village's collective enterprises supported the development of important village infrastructure. In 1979, the village invested 100,000 *yuan* to construct pipelines to bring water to village homes, and later the village invested 200,000 *yuan* to pave village roads. Ren served during a crucial time when Lengshuigou was moving from a "traditional" socialist economy to a modern, market-oriented society.

Liu Chuncai—the present Party branch secretary of Lengshuigou: Liu Chuncai was born in 1952 and earned a junior college degree. Liu joined the army in 1973 and the Communist Party in 1976. After retiring from the army in 1977, he first worked at the Licheng Movie Theatre and returned to the village in 1983 to run the dairy-cattle business. In October of 1993, he was elected and then was reelected as Party branch secretary of Lengshuigou. During his tenure, he was elected as the vice president of the Licheng Cow Association, Licheng NPC (National People's Congress) member, and Jinan CPPCC member.

Before becoming the secretary, Liu Chuncai was a very successful dairy-farm specialist. He represents a new type of village elite as an individual who began with economic success and only afterward got involved in village politics. He combines entrepreneurial experience and a spirit to challenge problems, which he learned through military service. As Party secretary, he devoted much time to reforming land management in the village, leasing land to firms that wanted to set up operations. Beginning in 1996, the village leased over 1,000 *mu* to nearby factories: leasing land not only gave the village a steady source of income but has also opened up many employment opportunities. Under his leadership, Lengshuigou has further developed its dairy business, setting up in 1999 a dairy center with seven modernized milking halls. Using his technical knowledge, Liu assisted village dairy farmers in improving their breeding techniques, and the improvements have led to closer relations with various milk companies. Lengshuigou has become a dairy center for one of Jinan's largest dairy firms, Jiabao.

The profits from agriculture and land leasing have been reinvested in building the village infrastructure. Between 2002 and 2007, the village invested 800,000 *yuan* to build a village committee office building and 5,500,000 *yuan* to construct the asphalt Baicai Road and to pave other village streets. An additional 210,000 *yuan* was used to build the Culture and Sport Square covering 7,000 square meters, with recreational equipment, greatly enriching villagers' lives.

In the three-plus decades since the beginning of the reform policies, the political elite in Lengshuigou has been transformed from the political elite of the socialist era that acted as agents for state power to a modern political elite that is entrepreneurial and innovative, striving to represent villagers' interests. There is no question, however, that this transformation has been accompanied by a growing gap between the poor and the rich. Although the village now has more efficient management, there has also been a decline in trust. We believe that these are problems of a transitional society and that they will ultimately be resolved.

Economic Elites: Seizing Opportunities and Achieving Personal Success

Although village management was still in the hands of the Communist Party branch and the village committee, which was also dominated by Party members, the post-reform economic system created space for a new kind of elites who influenced village development but were not members of the formal village governance structure. This included individuals who gained economic success as well as those who came to play important roles as members of the cultural and social elites.

With the beginning of the reform policies, the state loosened its control over rural society, allowing villagers to seek new development possibilities. Close proximity to Jinan gave Lengshuigou villagers an advantage in exploiting such opportunities. Among the first to try new paths were the young who did not want to follow their parents in toiling in the fields. Some of the young found jobs in factories or other enterprises, some were successful in starting their own businesses. Let us look at the career of Cheng Kehong, Lengshuigou's most successful entrepreneur.

> Cheng Kehong was born in 1960 and earned a degree from a junior college. He joined the Communist Party in 1994. In 1998, he resigned from his position as deputy general manager in the Yuquan Group and started his own enterprise, Hongteng. Now he is a member of the standing committee of Licheng's National People's Congress (NPC), a member of the CPPC in Jinan, vice president of the Association of Industry and Commerce in Jinan, Executive Committee Member of Shandong Association of Industry and Commerce, vice chairman for Jinan Chamber of Commerce, vice chairman for Association of Private Enterprise of Jinan and vice chairman for Association of Private Enterprise of Shandong. He has won numerous awards (LCZ 2010, 191–97).

Cheng Kehong is the pride of Lengshuigou. After graduating from middle school, he worked as a carpenter for a short time before taking a job in 1988 with the Yuquan Company where he advanced, eventually becoming vice-manager. Through this work, he gained managerial experience as well as a crucial network of connections that would help when he started his own company. In 1998, he resigned from Yuquan, and with over 100,000 *yuan* in borrowed capital, started Hongteng, which specializes in hotels and fast food. He gradually added other businesses to his industrial group, including firms that specialize in interior decorating, furniture manufacturing, and aluminum alloy manufacturing. In 2002, he began a new venture, investing over 10,000,000 *yuan* in developing the Hongteng Science and Industrial Development Zone in Wangsheren. The development zone covered over 230 *mu*, with a total floor space of over 50,000 square meters. Cheng's venture was the first private industrial park in Jinan, and in the first round of leasing, forty-nine enterprises settled in the new development zone. As a result of Cheng's hard work, his group's firms now hold over 60,000,000 *yuan* in assets and employ more than six hundred people in more than ten related firms.

When we look at the career of Cheng and other members of the village's new economic elite, we can identify certain common characteristics. First, almost all of the members of this elite have received some form of postsecondary education, and they are all fast learners. Education has helped them to clearly analyze the intense market competition that characterizes the contemporary Chinese economy. Second, this group has successfully developed skills in getting along well with other people, building *guanxi* networks that helped them to get assistance from friends in the years when they were first getting a start, reducing mistakes in decision making, lowering risks, and helping to make things go smoothly. Third, they are willing to take risks and have good managerial skills. Most of them gained experience working in other companies before setting up their own companies. Like successful entrepreneurs in other countries, they are willing to take risks that others cannot imagine, and this has led to their success.

While the first generation of Lengshuigou entrepreneurs was willing to take risks in setting up their own firms, more recent members of the economic elite have had fewer choices. Once the village land had been leased out, they could not engage in farming. As a result, the more ambitious among them have had little choice but to get involved in commerce and service industries. Those who have been willing to take entrepreneurial risks have received greater economic benefits than less adventurous fellow villagers. While both the first generation of entrepreneurs and those in the second generation are people who have good business sense, the first generation took greater risks at a time of uncertainty and as a result have gained greater wealth than those who followed.

Cultural Elites: Inheritors and Recorders of Rural Culture

Most members of what we have termed the "cultural elite" in Lengshuigou made their careers in education. Their influence in contemporary Lengshuigou is not directly in village administration, but rather in preserving and passing on traditional culture. Lengshuigou, unlike many neighboring villages, has a long tradition of supporting education, and as a result, many villagers became teachers. According to the *Lengshuigou Village Records*, 157 people from the village were engaged in education, including 31 senior middle school teachers, 42 senior elementary school teachers, and 91 college graduates. These retired teachers are the core members of the village's cultural elite.

Retired teachers: Li Xingwei was born in 1932 and earned a college degree. He is a retired teacher from Jinan Railway Middle School and won the title of Distinguished Teacher. Li enjoys writing poems and has a collection of five hundred poems in seven volumes. After retiring, he participated in compiling the *Lengshuigou Village Records*, and has made important contributions to passing on the cultural inheritance in Lengshuigou.

Li Tingfu was born in 1934 and holds a bachelor's degree. He began his career in July 1954 and has devoted all of his life to teaching Chinese in middle school, retiring in 1994. He was awarded the title "Advanced Worker" in education many times and also the title "Distinguished Class Adviser in Jinan." At present, he is the chief secretary for Lengshuigou Huanian Association, a column writer for "World Literature," and a member of the Jinan Writers' Association.

After retiring, together with friends in Lengshuigou Huanian Association, he compiled the "General Situation of Developments in Education in

Lengshuigou" and "Materials on Lengshuigou Culture and Sports Development." He published "Xue Bu Ji," "Poems and Essays by Li Yanfu," and "A Decade." From 2009 to 2010, he was in charge of compiling the *Lengshuigou Village Records* and published "Celebrated People and Well-Known Events in Lengshuigou" in 2012. He has done a large amount of work both in developing culture and education in Lengshuigou and in organizing and recording village history.

Li Yanhe—a representative of the new peasants: Li Yanhe was born in 1949 and has a middle school diploma. Currently he is the managing director of the Huapei Calligraphy & Painting Club of Licheng and a standing committee member in the Lengshuigou Huanian Association. He graduated from Jinan No. 18 Middle School and then returned to the village and worked as a commune member doing farm work. From 1972 to 1980, he was the leader of a work team and an accountant, and afterward he was a clerk, an accountant for a construction team, and a member of the managerial team for the Lengshuigou Guanliqu. In 1986, he joined the Communist Party and assumed the position of assistant factory leader of Lengshuigou Leather Shoe Factory and later worked as an accountant for a private enterprise. He returned to the village in 2002.

In the age when far-left thought prevailed, Li Yanhe was one of those who was criticized; in spite of the difficult times, he seized the opportunity to read a lot of books about politics and Chinese and foreign classic novels, broadening his perspective and learning much new knowledge. Later he studied civil engineering on his own and learned how to make budgets for construction projects and also mastered accounting. In recent years, he has enthusiastically participated in various village cultural undertakings. Since 2006, he has participated in compiling "Huanian Selected Poems," "Materials on Lengshuigou Culture and Sports Development," *Lengshuigou Village Records*, and "Celebrated People and Well-Known Events in Lengshuigou." He is a native rural intellectual, a representative of the new peasants.

Social Elite: Earning Trust through Mediation

With the polarization of villagers' economic interests and social interests, trust among villagers has weakened, and disputes have become more common. Originally, the village committee was responsible for mediating disputes, but as knowledge of the law has risen in recent years, some fair and honest villagers have undertaken the task of mediating disputes. Villagers respect these mediators, and they have come to form a new-style elite that we refer to as the "social elite." Xie Zhaoyi, who was elected to serve on the village committee, is a leading member of this new social elite.

Xie Zhaoyi was born in 1957 and earned a high school diploma. He was a member of the village committee and a secretary for the League branch from 1985 to 1995, and he joined the Communist Party in 1987. He was a workshop supervisor and later manager of the bristle-processing factory. Following the closure of the factory, he worked as manager of the Jinan animal by-products import and export factory. He was once a head of the village militia and now is a member of the village Party branch and also the director of the People's Mediation Committee and director of Security and Protection, in charge of security and mediating disputes.

Xie Zhaoyi is representative of the new-style social elite. In his case, he first earned respect by successfully mediating village disputes and after that was elected to the village Party branch committee. Xie has a reputation for fairness, and it was this reputation that led villagers to elect him as a member of the Party Branch Committee in 2007.

Xie Zhaoyi's prestige built up gradually. His reputation for fairness was first established when he worked at the bristle-processing factory and held the office of League branch secretary. He has helped villagers mediate all kinds of disputes, including conflicts among family members and disputes over housing lots. He successfully represented villagers in a civil lawsuit against the Jiabao Dairy over failure to make milk payments. Xie Zhaoyi's reputation was built through these efforts and he won strong support in the election because of his record for honesty and enthusiastic work on behalf of the public.

Situation of Village Elites in the Present Day

Elites have changed dramatically over the last hundred years, moving from earlier periods, when there were single criteria for determining the elite, to the contemporary scene with a much more diversified elite. The greater diversity in the contemporary village has opened opportunities for a variety of styles of elite behavior, but there are still gaps between individual development and the overall progress of village development. Among economic elites in Lengshuigou, there are many who are very distinguished in their own line of work. However, they have not been able to move beyond their own family to influence village development. The village needs to find a way to incorporate the skills of these people in pushing economic development.

From talking with villagers, we learned that although ordinary villagers acknowledge the contributions of the village cadre, they also are dissatisfied with their performance and feel that they have not lived up to expectations. According to villagers, many measures have been proposed, but have not been implemented. Villagers are particularly unhappy with questions about the use of land rent income and the low level of old-age pensions.

There is a more serious problem in Lengshuigou's elite composition: the shortage of young or middle-aged recruits for the village elite. Whether this problem can be solved will greatly affect future development of the village. Educational levels in the village are rising, and every year many young people pass entrance exams for college. However, few in this young educated cohort are interested in village affairs. The majority of younger villagers work in factories or offices outside the village, and they have no sense of responsibility toward village development. When elections come along, they rely on advice from their parents about the candidates and how they should vote. This problem is not peculiar to Lengshuigou, but rather is common to villages all over China. As the middle-aged elite becomes older, it is difficult to see who will emerge as managers of rural society in the future.

NOTES

1. The *baojia* was a system of collective responsibility, imposed by the state, that organized households into ten family units to form a *jia*, and ten of the *jia* into a larger one hundred–family unit called the *bao*.

2. The district (*qu*) was set up as an administrative unit under the new government policies between 1908 and 1911; a sub-county administrative office was established in relatively larger towns. A district had an elected director and was supposed to be a fundamental unit of self-government.

3. Collective security organizations at the village level were used throughout the Republican period, including the period of Japanese occupation. Internal organization varied, sometimes using the *lülin* with subunits of 5 and 25 families, sometimes reverting to the *baojia* with its subunits of 10 and 100 families.

4. The *Kankō Chōsa* records include a list of all of those who served as *jia* heads and *bao* heads.

5. This term *fanshen* was used by William Hinton as the title of his well-known book on Land Reform (William Hinton, *Fan Shen: A Documentary of Revolution in a Chinese Village* [New York: Vintage, 1966].) To "*fanshen*" meant not only to undergo an economic transformation through acquisition of land and other means of production, but also to accept a new understanding of class and its operation in past forms of exploitation.

6. Regulations with regard to this change were issued in December 1950. These regulations established the administrative village and laid out regulations for popular representation at the village level. See the General Principles of the People's Representative Conference in Xiang (administrative village) and the General Principles of the People's Organization in Xiang (administrative village).

7. Martyrs were people who had died fighting during various stages of the revolution.

8. The campaign to criticize Lin (Biao) and Kong (Confucius) began in 1973 and came to an end with the end of the Cultural Revolution. The campaign, which was

part of the factional struggles of the latter part of the Cultural Revolution, featured attacks on Confucian thought. A second target of the campaign was Lin Biao, who had earlier been designated as Mao's successor. He was accused of plotting to assassinate Mao Zedong and, when the plot failed, of trying to escape. The Chinese government later stated that the airplane carrying Lin and his fellow conspirators crashed in Mongolia in September 1971.

9. The campaign to learn from Dazhai was launched in 1964. Dazhai was a poor mountain village in Shanxi province, which overcame great difficulties to become the model for Maoist-style agricultural development, based on hard work and egalitarian distribution.

10. Ethnic townships were created in areas where non-Han minority groups made up the majority of the population.

11. Zhang was governor of Shandong from April 24, 1925, to May 3, 1928.

Chapter Three

Lineage and Family Relationships

The family is the fundamental building block of social relations in almost all societies, and China is no exception. In rural Chinese society, the family—made up of two to four generations of those closely linked by blood relations—is also a sub-group of the lineage, a large patrilineal kinship group that includes members who trace their relationship to a common ancestor. Both the family and the lineage played important roles in organizing economic and social activity in the village. Moreover, in traditional Chinese thought, the family was viewed as a model for the state, and it was assumed that in some ways the state acted as a large family: we can see this in the practice of referring to the county magistrate as the "mother and father" official, watching out for the people.

Wars and conflicts, political movements, and reform policies over the last century have had a major impact on the lineage and the family. The first section of this chapter will look at the changing roles of the lineage, which came under sharp attack during the first three decades of the PRC, and the latter half will turn to the family, examining the ways in which social change has altered the roles and meaning of both family and lineage.

CHANGING ROLES AND MEANINGS: THE LINEAGE IN RURAL CHINESE SOCIETY

The history of Chinese society is, to some degree, the history of the development of hierarchical relationships within family and lineage groups. Over the last millennium, North China rural society was characterized by a self-sufficient peasant economy in which people lived in groups based on kinship ties, interacting with each other in a system shaped by village norms. People shared a value system in which age hierarchy and distinctions in status guided their daily lives, including their political lives. In village China, there were two principles with regard to lineages that were preserved throughout. First, the lineage is based on the patrilineal line. Although women who enter the family through marriage are included, maternal relatives are excluded. Second, the core members of the lineage are men who share the same paternal ancestors and are members of a "mourning network" with clear obligations based on the degree of kinship (Xu and Yang 1994, 286). Lineages within the village determined the basic social structure of a village and framed the scope of individual interactions. Without an understanding of the relationship between family and lineage, we cannot understand the logics of action and the value system. Hence for us, as for generations of social scientists, study of the lineage is the starting point for our research on rural society.

Much of the theoretical work on Chinese lineage has been based on ethnographic work in central and south China, where single-surname villages were common and where lineage boundaries coincided with the village boundaries. In those settings, village political and ritual affairs were also the affairs of the lineage, and leadership in the lineage often—though not always—overlapped village leadership. Lengshuigou, on the other hand, is a typical multi-lineage North China village. Unlike the single-surname villages of south China, multiple lineages shared the same village space. Thus, there are clearer dividing lines between the ritual and economic activities of the lineage and those of the village and complex patterns of interaction between the various lineages.

Before looking at changes over time, it is important to clarify some basic terminology, particularly the distinction between lineage and surname. While members of the patrilineal lineage all share the same surname, not all of those in a village who share the same surname are members of the same lineage. In Lengshuigou, as in other North China villages, it was quite common to "share the same surname but belong to different lineages" and to "have the same surname but belong to different families." In these cases, although the surname was shared, there was no blood relationship among different lineages of the same surname. At the end of 2010, there were 1,450 households in Lengshuigou with a registered population of 4,271, with the villagers divided among twenty different surnames. The largest surname group in the village, the Li, was divided among twelve lineages sharing the Li surname. The Lis' three branches traced their families to a common ancestor, Li Jin. This Li lineage was the largest in the village, with 185 households and 685 people. The second largest lineage, the surname Xie from Zaoqiang County, Hebei province, included 86 households with 420 people.

Distribution of Major Surnames

In Chinese villages, members of the same lineage usually live near each other; as a result, when we look at a village map we can identify areas where members of the same lineage have their homes. In the south China villages studied by famous anthropologists like Lin Yaohua and Morris Freedman, there was a complete overlap between lineage space and the village boundaries. Lin noted this connection: "A lineage village is one village type. The lineage is an extension of a family formed by the descendants of a common ancestor; the village is a natural unit created by those who live in contiguous space, and together with townships and markets it is one of the building blocks of political units." (Lin 2000 [1935], 1) The British anthropologist Morris Freedman, who is well known for his study of lineages in southern Chinese villages, also noted that sharing a common living space was one of the characteristics of the lineage.

According to the *Kankō Chōsa* materials, one of the things that distinguished Lengshuigou from other villages was the pattern of contiguous residence of lineage members. The Li lineage even had an ancestral hall in honor of the Li family ancestors. "The Li surname group is the largest surname group in Lengshuigou; there are 188 families surnamed Li out of the total of 376 households. They are also related to the Lis in Lijiazhuang, 200 meters to the southeast" (KC 1955, 55). According to the records gathered by the Japanese survey, the Yang surname group stood in second place with 48 households; the Xie surname group was third with 40 households; the Zhang surname group was in fourth place with 18 households; and the Ren and Liu surnames were both in fifth place, with 17 households; there were fewer than 15 households with the surname Cheng (KC 1955, 76) (table 3.1).

Table 3.1. Distribution of surnames in Lengshuigou, 2010

Surname	*Lineage number*	*Number of households*	*Number of individuals*
Li	12	370	1,341
Yang	5	226	755
Xie	1	86	420
Zhang	8	65	255
Ren	1	64	228
Liu	6	52	188
Cheng	1	34	156
Du	1	30	117
Wang	5	31	98
Gao	2	25	91

Source: LCZ 2010, 23–27.

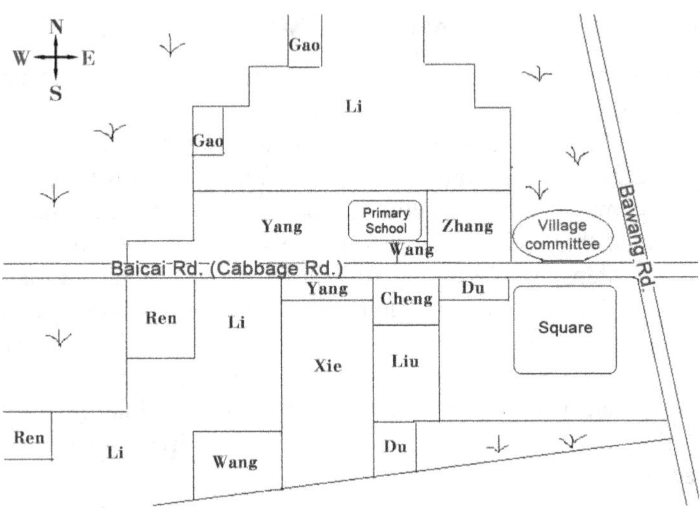

Map 3.1. Spatial distribution of major surnames
KC 1955, 56.

While villagers of the same surname were living in clusters at the time of the Japanese survey, there have been major changes over the last ten years. As we can see from map 3.1, only two of the largest surname groups, the Li and the Yang, still have concentrated areas for their families' homes. Reasons for this include the growth in population but also patterns of expansion of the village, including construction of a wide road through the middle of the village. Rapid urbanization of the region has brought external pressure to bear, breaking up the traditional internal spatial organization of residence patterns in the village.

Rise and Fall of Lineages over the Last Century

The lineage has gone through several cycles of rise and fall over the last century. Before 1949, the lineage played a stabilizing role, helping to integrate the village while supporting the families and individuals who were its members. Beginning with land reform in the early 1950s, the lineage came under attack as the new state strove to create an institutional framework in which loyalty of individuals and families was transferred to the collective and to the state. The loss of lineage land during land reform took away the major economic foundation for lineage activities, and subsequent political movements attacked the hierarchical and particularistic principles of lineage leadership, replacing it with new forms based on class. During this first cycle of lineage decline, state pressure played a major role in producing change. A second cycle was initiated with the breakup of the commune and the return to household-based economic activity in the early 1980s. Over the last three decades, we can see a revival of interest in the lineage followed by a slow, steady decline in its importance, this time propelled not by state action but by changes that grew naturally out of the social changes accompanying rapid urbanization and the shifts it has brought in occupational structure and marriage patterns.

Lineage was, however, not just a functional structure operating in village society, but also a mental and emotional construct, and so we also need to pay some attention to lineage consciousness as a factor in individual and family identity. Lengshuigou villagers, like residents of many villages on the North China plain, believe that their ancestors migrated to the region from the northwest. Stories throughout the region report that migration began in northwest China in Hongdong County, Shanxi province, where migrants gathered under a large ash tree (*da huaishu*). While the legends speak of migration from Shanxi, inspection of the genealogies of the Li, Xie, Ren, and Wang lineages and interviews with older villagers revealed that the ancestors of most of the families in Lengshuigou migrated from Zaoqiang County, Hebei.[1] Villagers share a relatively high level of consciousness of this account of the origins of their lineages and village, and this common lineage memory enhances cohesion and facilitates social relations.

Lineages as Stabilizing and Integrating Forces in the Village before 1949

Ideas of integration of family and nation, and unity of state and family, have long been central to Chinese culture. However, in the years before the founding of the PRC, rural society was in crisis as a result of wars and natural disasters. Lengshuigou, like other villages on the North China plains, was affected by these disasters. During those difficult years, lineages played a significant role in maintaining village order. According to the *Kankō Chōsa* materials, during this period, lineages in Lengshuigou possessed not only symbolic meanings as expressed in family ancestral altars, in the lineage hall, and in the compilation of genealogies, but also exercised important functional roles through the authority of the lineage head, the protection of ancestral tombs, and the use of marriage alliances between lineages as a way of strengthening lineage power.

We can see the connections between village power structures and the power of lineages by examining the village's temples. In the 1940s, there were four temples in the village: a Yuhuang temple, Guandi temple, Sansheng temple, and Guanyin temple. Various institutions of village governance were located in the different temples: a Sanguan temple was located inside the Yuhuang temple compound and a Tudi temple was inside the Sansheng temple. The district (*xiang*) office and the office of the young men's association were set up in the Sanguan temple, the village office was in the Sansheng temple, and the elementary school was in the Guandi temple. This arrangement followed historical precedent since from ancient times, lineage buildings and village temples had been used for administrative and educational purposes.

Before 1949, the Li lineage in Lengshuigou was engaged in a number of activities such as worship of ancestors and compilation of an updated genealogy, cultivating deep-rooted respect for seniority and family pride. People in the Li lineage recall that the Li lineage temple was built in 1922; a plaque for Li ancestors hung in the temple hall and a stone stele in the yard recorded information about the temple's construction. According to Li Xingyu, an eleventh-generation descendant, the Li ancestral hall was a traditional Chinese courtyard building, fifteen meters long and twelve meters wide, located on a narrow lane one street east of the main road. In the courtyard, there were three rooms on the north side of the compound and three on the east side. The buildings were all made of unbaked mud bricks, with stone bases and brick pillars. The rooms on the north side were used for the temple, and those on the east side housed the caretakers. Several pine and cypress trees grew in the courtyard (Li 2011, 24). We learned more about lineage activities through interviews with elderly people in the village.

Li Xingyu (eighty-four years old, chairman of Huanian association of retired school teachers; he is also supervising the most recent updating of his lineage's genealogy):

> Q: Was there a temple for the Li lineage? What were the lineage activities?
>
> A: The ancestral temple for the Li lineage no longer existed after 1949. Before 1949 there were 3 rooms in an ancestral temple and there were caretakers for the temple. Every year at the Lunar New Year and Qingming festival (tomb-sweeping day), we gathered there to worship our ancestors. There was a graveyard for the ancestors in the east of the village which was quite large.

Li Tingfu (seventy-six years old, retired teacher, editor of the village gazetteer):

> Q: Was Li an influential lineage before 1949? What were lineage activities?
>
> A: There were 8 branches of the Li lineage in Lengshuigou, and our branch was the biggest. The family head at that time was Li Changnian, who has passed away. I am the third generation. The Li lineage was quite influential. Many families were landowners and many had good education levels so the Li lineage was quite famous in Lengshuigou. There used to be ancestral halls. Li Xiangling from our branch was very strong, almost as if he were a civil official like a

> prefect. Every year at the Lunar New Year, those of us who lived in this part of the village paid a ceremonial call on the Lis in the northern part of the village to wish them a Happy New Year.

From the *Kankō Chōsa* materials, we can see that the big lineages in Lengshuigou had ancestral graves and guards guarding those graves. Francis L. K. Hsu, in his book *Under the Ancestors' Shadow*, gave a detailed explanation of how people believed the spirits of the ancestors protected their descendants. In Xizhou town, the subject of Hsu's study, social activities were all carried out around this belief. An individual's value and fate were not only connected closely with the ancestors but were also in some way a reflection of the ancestors' activities. In Hsu's view, everyone was living under the protection of the ancestors. "The father-son identification and the big family ideal support each other. Together they are responsible for a social system which deprives the younger generation of any feeling of independence, while at the same time it enables them to share whatever wealth or glory is due to their immediate or remote ancestors." The idea of the unity of father and son and the ideal of a large family mutually supported each other, creating a social system (Hsu 1948, 10). Lengshuigou people also believed in the protective power of the ancestors. In places where ancestor worship had a long history, the authority of the father was strong and inter-lineage relationships were close. To a great extent, strong lineage belief guaranteed the prosperity of a lineage. "Preference for sons" and adoption of boys to continue the family line demonstrate people's attachment to lineage, which was documented by adoption papers and other documentary materials included in the *Kankō Chōsa* materials (KC 1955, 100).

So far we have looked at lineage activities that played an important role in maintaining solidarity among the lineage members and enhancing lineage identity. Now we will turn to look at activities that will help us understand the lineage as a social force.

Li Xingyu:

> There were old-style private schools when the Japanese invaded. The Li lineage possessed a private school, which was among the 7 or 8 private schools in the village. Not only were members of the Li lineage accepted but also members of other lineages.

Xie Zhaokui (eighty-four years old; his family had produced three generations of school teachers):

> Q: The *Kankō Chōsa* materials show that the Xie lineage inter-married with the Wang lineage in order to enhance lineage influence. Do you have any recollection of this?

A: I don't remember this. But I heard from the elders that Xie and Li were on very good terms. One of my great aunts was married to a member of the Li family (Li Xiwu). Li and Xie were closely connected. The Li lineage was quite influential and wealthy while the Xie lineage was not. After this marriage, Xie and Li had much better relations.

As we can see from the above interviews, lineages also had important social functions in Lengshuigou, helping to provide education for lineage members as well as playing an important role in marriage alliances. The lineage helped to shape the contours of daily life, and it was impossible for anyone to break away from lineages and live independently. Families strove to carefully protect their own interests, all of the time under the benevolent protection of their ancestors.

Political Movements and Lineage after the Founding of the PRC

After the founding of the PRC, lineage came to be viewed as one of the fundamental building blocks of the feudal order, and efforts were made to destroy it. State pressure increased through a series of political movements, shaking and gradually weakening Lengshuigou lineages. In the following sections, we will trace the attacks on lineage in four steps. First, during land reform, lineage land was confiscated, removing the economic support for lineage activities. Second, early cooperatives strove to create new organizations to provide support to families, weakening the role of the lineage: however, while these new organizations were not based on lineage, because of spatial living patterns in the village, there was significant overlap between membership in the new socialist work units and previously existing lineage organization. During the third stage, under the commune, the lineage's economic functions disappeared, but it still continued to handle family matters like weddings and funerals. In the final stage, during the Cultural Revolution, stress was placed on consciousness of class status, and this led to a fundamental fissure among lineage members. Hierarchy within the lineage had been based on principles of generation and age, and each lineage included both better-off and poorer families. The Cultural Revolution discredited the lineage's organizing principles, leaving the lineage with little role to play in village society.

Land Reform—the first confrontation: Land reform in the early days of the PRC shook the base of the systems based on kinship and land. This movement, which aimed to transform what was at the time referred to as the "feudal land ownership system" into a system based first on household and subsequently cooperative and collective ownership, initially confiscated the land of landlords and divided it evenly among the peasants, thus overthrowing the landlord regime and replacing it with a new system of peasant associations (*nong hui)* controlled by the poorer peasants. Lineage temples and lineage land were confiscated, and genealogies were burned. Taken together, these acts represented an attack on both the material and symbolic bases of traditional lineage power.

According to the *Kankō Chōsa* materials, relations between landlords and peasants in Lengshuigou were not as hostile as they were in some places and, in fact, might be described as relatively harmonious. Before 1949, the gap between the rich and the poor was small, and during land reform only thirty-two individuals were labeled as landlords, with the larger landlords coming from the Li and Wang lineages. Land reform in Lengshuigou took place after liberation, with little active struggle against the landlords, reflecting the generally harmonious relations that characterized relations between the village rich and poor. Lineage land was treated the same way as privately held land and was added to the pool of confiscated land to be redistributed. Although land reform in the village involved little hostile struggle, lineage activities, including lineage sacrifice, were weakened to some extent.

Li Xingyu:

> My family was classified as landlord. At that time, we had more than 10 mu of land and 5 or 6 mu were taken away, leaving only a little more than 8 mu. Every peasant had a piece of land. We didn't have enough people to cultivate the land so long-term workers were hired. Family members didn't have to work. Four girls in our family all went to school.

Li Tingfu:

> In 1949 the temple was gone, mainly because a poor guy in the Li family took the temple as his living place. After 1948 the old order broke down. Since our village is close to the provincial capital, all of the political movements were carried out very thoroughly.

Xie Zhaokui:

> Unlike the Wang and Li families that owned a huge amount of property, there was only one landlord in the Xie family. The only lineage activity left was to continue compiling the genealogy while other activities disappeared.

After land reform, every peasant owned a piece of land. At the same time, land reform had a strong impact on lineage activities and on the mechanisms that had maintained village order. Confiscation of the lineage temple led to the end of ceremonies honoring the ancestors. This was the first strong attack mounted by strong political pressure on the power of the lineage as a major force in preserving village order and harmony. However, this first attack only led to the disappearance of material symbols such as rituals or ancestral temples; family consciousness still played a central role in shaping people's identities.

Transition from "dividing" to "combining"—blurring of lineage boundaries: The movement to establish agriculture cooperatives replaced family-based economic activity with collective production; this transition greatly diminished the role of the family as an economic unit and led to a great decline in the authority of the lineage. As a result of this movement, peasants were for the first time incorporated into units that cut across lineage boundaries. This new system replaced production groups that relied on individual family endeavor or cooperation with members of the same lineage with new, strong administrative units that were no longer based on kinship ties.

However, unlike many other northern rural villages, in Lengshuigou, the new cooperative units did not completely replace lineage units. In the first stage in 1952, which involved the formation of voluntary mutual-aid groups, most of the teams were built on relationships with people of the same lineage or with neighbors. Although there is no question that the mutual-aid teams introduced new forms of production relations that weakened some of the mutual-assistance features of the lineage, these were not completely replaced, and people still experienced a close relationship between the lineage and daily activities. During this movement, some of the larger lineages also began to build new forms of alliance. We can see this very clearly in the development of the East Is Red Collective Farm, which grew out of a mutual-aid team involving nineteen households, then grew to include fifty households, and eventually came to encompass the whole village. This mutual-aid team was cofounded by the Li and Xie lineages, with an elder from the Li lineage as the president, and eventually developed into a force that influenced the entire southern village. This alliance between the Li and Xie lineages was built on their tradition of intermarriage and the fact that members of the two lineages lived in close proximity. In some senses, the cooperative movement brought new energy to lineage alliances based on kinship and neighborhood, while at the same time blurring the boundaries between lineages.

People's Commune movement—further weakening of lineage forces: The People's Commune movement, which started in 1958, reinforced the status and function of collective organizations, further restricting the functions of families and lineages, limiting the role played by kinship in maintaining the order of the village community, and thus weakening the survival base for lineages. As control over economic resources became even more concentrated at the national level, villages like Lengshuigou could not escape from the pressure to conform. As collectivization reached higher levels, lineage forces were weakened, and lineages that used to be on very close terms gradually grew apart due to the intervention of new forms of organizations. At the same time, new forms of integration among lineages developed. As the role of administrative authorities strengthened, the lineage came to act as a supplement to administrative power, handling such tasks as family divisions, weddings and funerals, and mediation of interpersonal conflicts.

In a word, changes in rural politics and economy led to changes in social structure and social organization. The establishment of public ownership broke the mutual assistance based on lineages, placing the individual in an atomized state. Collectivism came into being and overwhelmed the lineage as an organizing principle.

The Cultural Revolution—distinction by class status: During the Cultural Revolution, class struggle smashed kinship-based relationships, in some cases triggering splits within families and delivering a lethal blow to the rural lineage tradition. Symbols associated with the lineage such as the genealogy were categorized as "four olds"— representations of the old "feudal" culture that were targeted for destruction. The idea of class struggle was so deeply implanted in the minds of villagers that both the consanguinity-based relationships and neighbor-based relationships that had been the bonds to maintain the village community for thousands of years were forced out of the picture. Class status was the only criteria to distinguish between family and outsiders. Lengshuigou, due to its proximity to the city of Jinan, was greatly influenced by the urban Cultural Revolution.

Li Xingyu:

> I was categorized as a landlord during the land reform and had always been regarded as such, and I had to do self-criticism. At that time only class status was taken into consideration, no more lineages. Within the lineage nobody talked about these political affairs, this was only a matter for discussion between the leaders and the ordinary people. Weddings and funerals were simplified, and the production brigade was put in charge of managing them. Things that used to be done by family members—weddings and funereals—were now in the hands of production brigades. However, the peasants still had to pay the costs.

Li Tingfu:

> Compared with lineage and kinship ties, class relationships were more important because the brigade leader was in control of your life. In many landlord families, the son—burdened by his family's class status—would arrange a family division, separating himself from his father. But even after separation,

> the Communist Party would not give the son a different class status. So people didn't trust each other anymore. Under the special characteristics of those times, people had no choice but to accept the class perspective and act accordingly.

The lineage system that had supported all aspects of rural life was destroyed. Under the intense political pressure of the Cultural Revolution, class status surpassed consanguinity-based relationships and lineage relations to become the main criteria for determining identity and served as a guide in determining how to treat other people. However, in the interviews, we found that elderly people all reported that even under intense political pressure, people still were aware of mutual assistance and communication within the lineage. Some lineages were able to hide their genealogies and so they survived. The discretion and frustration demonstrated by the villagers we interviewed indicate that, at least on one level, the political movements proceeded in a formalistic manner, and the internal bonds and latent power of the lineage tradition still survived. We can see this in the revival of lineage activities following the reform policies, which brought an end to the state's attacks on the lineages.

The Revival and Decline of the Lineage under the Market Economy

We believe that the Reform and Opening Up Policies, which began in the 1980s, initiated the most important social changes of the twentieth century in China. The opening-up policies reconnected China with the outside world, while the reform policies transformed social mechanisms within China. Social structure was reorganized, leading to the emergence of new organizational forms and new identities. These new policies presented an opportunity for the reemergence of the village lineages.

The household responsibility system—revival of lineage power: The household responsibility system broke up the system of collective production, contracting land to individual households. Under this reform, the household once more became the basic production unit. The key to a household's success in the new economy was finding a way to most efficiently use its labor resources and above all to tap into expanding markets. As families sought to raise the productivity on their assigned plots, they turned to new forms of cooperation; consanguinity-based relationships and lineage bonds became major tools for coordinating production and arranging mutual assistance, as well as becoming important ways to integrate the community and share resources.

There has been much academic interest in the revival of lineage power after the Reform and Opening Up Policies. For example, Han Min, a social anthropologist, who has studied a single-lineage village in northern Anhui, has argued that continuance of the lineage provides the basis for lineage consciousness, which in turn has led to the revival of traditional practices and beliefs (Han 2001, 3). Zhou Daming, an anthropologist at Zhongshan University, has suggested that the notion of lineage, a concept that encompasses kinship, identity, ritual, religion, ethics, and law, has already become a core part of Han ethnic consciousness. While lineage practices may be suppressed for a time, they will reappear once the environment permits (Zhou 2002, 5); and Cao Jinqing has argued that peasants who now engage in independent cultivation under the household responsibility system have turned to the lineage in their efforts to create a new "force. This new force is a form of self-protection in the face of the challenges of a strange and risky market economy (Cao 2000, 555). Although many questions related to lineage identification, lineage conceptualization, and lineage protection can be reasonably explained by the above research, through our study of Lengshuigou, we have come to believe that the most important factor in explaining the revival of the power of the lineage is the weakening of political pressure, leading to a system that makes room for instrumental needs within the new economic system.

Li Xingyu:

> Lineage relationships were closer. Matters once managed by the brigade were in part brought back to families and lineages. However, we no longer have activities that involve the whole lineage. Because I still identify with the lineage I took the lead in revising our lineage's genealogy. Although there was no payment, I was happy to revise the genealogy and so everyone was willing to follow me. That does not mean that I could control the whole lineage.

With the weakening of political movements and control after the beginning of the reform policies, major lineages in Lengshuigou decided to revise their genealogies; these efforts were led by literate senior members of the lineage. This practice of revising the genealogies is, on the one hand, a reflection of nostalgia for the more stable lineage solidarity and consciousness of the past and, on the other hand, provides a basis for naming and ranking new lineage members, leading to respect for seniority. We can see this clearly in the efforts to revise the Li and Xie genealogies.

Although the lineage tradition has experienced some degree of recovery, and there is a somewhat stronger identification with the lineage—especially among the elderly—this does not mean that all of the members of the lineage now share the kinds of close connections of an earlier day. Following the several decades of political movements and attacks, the core of the lineage system and its behavioral logics has been blurred. What remains are vestiges of the system: rules stipulating the scope of intermarriages, mechanisms for mediating disputes between lineage members, efforts to provide psychological support for members, and mild levels of inter-lineage competition (Xu and Yang 1994, 287–88).

Rise of the market economy and decline of lineage power: Over the last three decades since the launching of the Reform and Opening Up Policies, urbanization and industrialization have proceeded at a rapid pace, and modern lifestyles and values have gradually permeated Lengshuigou. As a result, acquired status has come to play a more important role than ascribed status, giving villagers new possibilities for creating their lives. Ideas about equality, modern contract institutions, and village autonomy have broken the traditional lineage modes of respect for seniority and the authority of the senior generation, leading to the decline of the traditional lineage system. Even seniors in big lineages express their helplessness:

Li Tingfu:

> Just let nature take its course. It is meaningless to continue the genealogy. A single person can't stop the wheels of history. But emotionally, it is fine to continue the genealogy because, after all, lineage has its advantages. At least, it has no bad influences for society. Why not continue?

Li Xingyu:

> The concept of having a grandson to continue the family is still important. Nowadays people still want to have boys, to have a son to continue the Li family. It is natural. But there are few people who don't like girls.

It is worth noticing that this wish to maintain the lineage can only be found among the senior generation in thriving lineages like the Li and Xie, while in some minor lineages, these ideas have disappeared. Thus, we can see great differences among the lineages. While lineage loyalty is fading, fictive kinship, which is a more adaptive practice, has become increasingly popular.

Xie Zhaokui:

> My great-grandfather had four brothers, and they took the four brothers of the Li lineage as fictive brothers. They look out for each other in everything and still enjoy a good relationship. Li and Xie are a family.

The Xie lineage, which had been strengthened through intermarriage with the powerful Li lineage, continued to increase its reach through fictive kinship. On the one hand, fictive kinship provides emotional comfort; on the other hand, it can expand social capital, leading to the acquisition of greater social resources and protection. This suggests that the decline of emotional links to the lineage opened up opportunities for a new-style fictive kin relationships, which came to play an important role as a source of mutual aid.

Reflecting on changes in the lineage over the last hundred years, we can see that the kind of moral instruction that used to play a vital part in family ethics, the lineage system, and family identity has changed dramatically. As a result of the attacks during political movements, as well as the changes brought about by the transformation of the economic system and the entry of modern ideas following the launching of the reform policies, the old-style morals have lost their central role as a source of behavioral logics underlying village order. The decline of the lineage has led villagers to search for emotional support and instrumental rationality through other organizations and institutions.

CHANGES IN FAMILY STRUCTURE

Family Structure before 1949

Traditional Chinese values regarded the large extended family in which brothers and their family members lived together in harmony as the ideal family type. In the pre-1949 period Lengshuigou families strove to realize this model: joint and stem families were common, with only a few nuclear families. This family structure reflected the values of *he,* which can be literally translated as "joining together," but also has suggestions of "harmony."

Before 1949, children lived with their parents after marriage. When one of the sons wanted to divide the family and live separately, he had to get permission from his parents, and parents had the authority to refuse a request. The eldest son was expected to live with his parents and care for them. These ideas about the extended family were very strong; if a family decided to divide, the matter was usually handled very quietly since it was assumed that the decision to divide was the result of conflict between family members. Since familial ethics stressed the importance of harmony in the family, which was a major support of the patriarchal system, senior members of the family often tried to block proposals for family division. According to the *Kankō Chōsa* materials, the most common reason for family division in Lengshuigou was conflict between daughters-in-law; other reasons included conflict between daughter-in-law and mother-in-law, between brothers, and between father and son (KC 1955, 92). It was commonly said that harmonious families did not divide even after five or ten generations.

We can find the following accounts of "family and property division" in the *Kankō Chōsa* survey (KC 1955, 121):

Q: When did you divide your family?

A (Li Yongxiang): Five years ago I separated from my brother Li Yongzhang.

Q: How did you divide up the family property?

A: We split the two-and-a-half mu of land (dry land) in the north of village, two mu of dry land in the west of the village, two mu (one mu of dry farm land, one mu of paddy farm land) in the southwest of the village. About the three mu (eight fen of dry farm land, two mu and two fen of paddy land) in the southwest of the village, Yongxiang had the dry land and we split the paddy land. Two mu of paddy land in the south of the village were divided evenly. About the four mu and half of dry land in the south of the village, Yongzhang had two mu and a half, and Yongxiang had two mu. Yongxiang had one mu of dry land in the east of the village.

Q: What about land around the house?

A: My brother got 6 *fen* of land around the house, I didn't get any.

Q: Why did your elder brother get a bit more land than you?

A: The house I received [the family had two] was better than the one he got, so my elder brother got a bit more land.

Q: How large was the plot your house was built on?

A: My house was built on 3 *fen* of land, my older brother's on six.

Q: So even though your house was built on less land, it was better than the house your brother received?

A: Yes.

Economic conditions of the family also influenced family divisions. "Poor families find it hard to support themselves. When the family head can't be of much use and there are a lot of boys, family members split to work separately and properties are divided" (KC 1955, 69). Poor families found it hard to sustain the large-family ideal so parents had no choice but to let their children live independently in order to lessen the burden. Although it is easier for financially advantaged families to maintain the extended family, special circumstances can lead a wealthy family to choose to divide. For example, "in a rich family, if three or four children think that the property should be commonly shared, each may think they have a right to all of the income—and this can lead to a decision to divide the family" (KC 1955, 69). This is what is commonly referred to as "family and property division." Although there were many cases of family division before 1949, the large extended family was held up as the ideal. The preference for this family type was closely linked to the level of social development at that time.

Before 1949, Lengshuigou was a self-sufficient natural economy in which agricultural production was the main source of goods for household consumption, and a management system based on the extended family was most suitable for this kind of small peasant economy. In this period, the major crops in Lengshuigou were rice, gaoliang, and other grains. Under the technological conditions of the time, production of these crops required coordination of a large supply of labor to deal with the short turnaround time between crops and the relatively backward level of technology. Large families had an advantage in organizing labor and other production factors so that they could guarantee the successful operation of household agricultural production. Hence, villagers tended to choose to maintain large families.

The family also was the core and basis for social life in traditional family-centered Chinese society. Without a family for support, individuals had no sense of safety and security. As a result, Lengshuigou villagers regarded the extended family as a natural choice.

In this system, the family head was responsible for maintaining the integrity of the family. The family head was the master of the house, usually the eldest, according to seniority in the family. He was responsible for supervising, protecting, and instructing family members. He managed the income and daily expenses: income earned by family members was pooled and shared by the whole family. Family members who earned income from non-farm jobs were expected to turn over their earnings to the family head and request funds to cover their expenses. The family head fulfilled his responsibility of guaranteeing the livelihood and development of family members through his management of family property.

When a family divided, the property was divided among family members. This resulted in a weakening of the family's ability to protect its members since each of the smaller units had less labor power and property. In the interests of maintaining production and protecting family members, the family head usually tried to sustain the large family and avoid family division. Since the family head controlled the family's economic resources, children would usually comply with the demands from the large family.

In the Chinese village, labor assignments in agricultural production were based on the gender, physical capabilities, and age of family members. Male adults were regarded as both the primary source of labor and as the primary earners of income. A folk saying that "men managed the outside, women the inside," described this gender-based division of labor, one in which the control of the family was in the hands of men. In an economic system in which agricultural production was the chief source of income, this seemed like a natural outcome. Under the patriarchal system, men were the sole inheritors of family property, hence the preference for male children. In a rural family at that time, the birth of a baby boy was significant for the whole family since it 1) added to the family labor supply and provided a replacement for older male laborers, 2) provided an heir to inherit family property, 3) insured there would be someone to support the elderly, and 4) guaranteed continuation of the sacrifices for ancestors (Lei 1994, 19). These reasons were the origin of popular sayings like "to carry on the family line," "to have a large family," "to have a big household," "more sons, more blessings," and "to have many children and grandchildren."

Ideas about childbirth also influenced marriage patterns in Lengshuigou before 1949. Men and women married early, usually becoming engaged at twelve and marrying at fifteen. One reason for early marriage was to bring the woman into the man's family to share the work and serve his parents. But early marriage was also encouraged as a way to insure the birth of male offspring to carry on the family line. Marrying early increased the chances of having many children. From the *Kankō Chōsa* survey, we know that if a wife did not give birth to any children, her husband's family might use one of two measures to deal with this problem. One approach was for the man to acquire a concubine. "Generally, the husband would take a concubine if the wife couldn't give birth to a child. It was quite rare for a man to take a concubine unless his wife failed to have a child" (KC 1955, 65). An alternative approach was to adopt a child, usually from relatives in the same lineage. "When a family has no child, they adopt a child from relatives. If there was no child available in the lineage, they have to adopt from other lineages" (KC 1955, 67). In rare cases, a family might appoint a joint heir (*jian tiao*); this happened when there were two brothers, but only one had a son. That son would be appointed as the heir to both his father and his uncle (KC 1955, 68). Basically, all these customs were developed in response to the wish to have "more sons, more blessings" and the imperative to "carry on the family line." The large family, however, was not only favored because of such traditional ideas but also because it provided a stronger material base for reproduction. Thus, we can see that the large extended family had developed in response to these ideas about the importance of having many children.

In his book *Institutions for Reproduction* (*Shengyu Zhidu*) Fei Xiaotong argued that one of the main aims for human life is to carry on the race (*zhongzu*), and marriage is the route to guarantee this (Fei 1999 [1947], 29). For this reason, marriage was of vital importance in traditional society. Marriage served a number of purposes: on the one hand, families were able to expand their social networks through marriage alliances, and on the other hand, marriage created the fundamental unit for reproduction, giving birth to new family members who would work in economic activities and also care for the aged. In choosing marital partners, stress was put on fulfilling family responsibilities; little attention was given to the personal wishes and emotions of the individuals involved. This was true of marriage in Lengshuigou before 1949. Husbands were usually younger than their wives since families sought a daughter-in-law who would be able to take care of her parents-in-law (KC 1955, 62). When parents chose their future son-in-law or daughter-in-law, they tried to find someone who would be able to take care of the parents, give birth to children to carry on the family line, and take responsibility for supporting the family. Since the marriage was designed to serve the interests of the family, whether the man and woman had feelings for each other was of no concern. Parents usually asked the newly married couple to live together in the large family since this maximized the benefits brought by the marriage, that is to say, the advantages gained by connecting two large families. The family head encouraged all of the daughters-in-law to work together to serve the family. Thus, most children continued to live in extended families with other family members after marriage.

Children were expected to follow their parents' wishes and heed the matchmaker's advice in selecting marriage partners; there was no room in the system for what we today know as "love marriage." "When it comes to marriage children must obey their parents' orders. Even when they are unhappy and complain after marriage, parents will persuade them by saying it is their destiny. Even if a son or daughter indicated a preference for a specific marriage partner, they would not be allowed to marry unless their parents agreed" (KC 1955, 65). Needless to say, not all marriages were happy, but even if the couple were in conflict, divorce was not an option. Children who rebelled against their parents' wishes would be criticized as unfilial, violating one of the most fundamental moral standards in the traditional Chinese value structure; moreover, divorce was regarded as shameful, and even rumors of divorce would lead to ridicule by fellow villagers. Even when the couple were unhappy or had conflicts with other members of the family, they would not divorce or break away from the big family since it was commonly believed that the economic benefits marriage brought to the whole family outweighed personal interest. Since parents were the only arbiters of marital problems, daughters-in-law usually buried their complaints against husbands and put up with them for the greater good of the family. As a result, there were few divorces in Lengshuigou before 1949.

Needless to say, there were close links between the form the large family took and the overall economic situation of the village. A family's economic conditions determined how many members a family could support, while at the same time, the number of family members was related to the type of family structure (Wang 2006, 206). The clearest indication of a family's economic status was how much land they owned. More land was associated with higher levels of production and so, naturally, such a family could support more members. If a family was poor—owning insufficient land to support an extended family—they might be forced to divide the family and let their children move out of the family to lessen the burden. In such cases, family division was unavoidable. As we have seen, Lengshuigou was a relatively rich village, and the gap between the rich and the poor was not so sharp. Villagers all owned some land and lived a comparatively wealthy life, and these economic advantages helped to sustain the pattern of large extended families.

While there is no question that the extended family was the ideal—both as a value and for its practical results—there is also no question that many household units were considerably smaller. The *Kankō Chōsa* survey shows that the average household included 4.8 people. When we look to see what factors influenced this gap between the ideal and practice, we can identify several factors. First, by the second and third decades of the twentieth century, new ideas introduced as part of the "family revolution" led some young people to put greater stress on ideas about individual choice. Moreover, while families lived together as long as the parents were alive, it was quite common for brothers to divide the family property after the death of the older generation, and the *Kankō Chōsa* materials have many references to family division. Thus, in Lengshuigou, although the large family was the ideal, there were also a number of nuclear families before 1949.

Family Structure: From 1949 to the Reform Period

The many political and institutional changes after 1949 brought about great changes in family structure. The large family, which had worked well for the traditional economy, was challenged as a result of land reform, the establishment of the people's commune, and various political movements. This led to the decline of the large, extended family and the shift to the nuclear family. Among the factors contributing to this shift were the overall rise in the status of women and the weakening of the economic functions of the family. Stem and combined families survived for increasingly short periods of time, and the nuclear family became the dominant form in Lengshuigou.

Transitional Period in the Early Phase of the PRC

During the early years of the PRC, there was a radical change in landholding, which led to changes in family structure. Land reform transformed the landholding system: land and buildings of landlords and rich peasants were confiscated and divided among the peasants. While the household was still the basic production unit, individual households now held rights to their own plots, and the larger holdings, which had once supported large extended families, had been broken up. These changes eliminated many of the advantages of the extended family, and as a result, combined families began to break up, and the number of nuclear families increased.

A second major factor was the promulgation of the Marriage Law on May 1, 1950. This law abolished arranged marriages and the assumption that "men were superior to women" and strove to establish freedom of marriage, monogamy, equal rights for men and women, and legal protection of women and children. This law brought great changes to traditional large families by advocating equality of men and women and raising women's social status.

Weakening of the Family during the Period of Collectivization

Through collectivization and the establishment of people's communes, land once owned by families was consolidated, and ownership rights shifted from the individual family to the collective. Agricultural production methods changed from scattered household cultivation to collective cultivation. The production brigade became the basic unit for agricultural production, and the family role in production faded. As a result of this transition in the economic system, the foundation for the existence of traditional large families was weakened, and a new family pattern began to take over from the old. In this period, the percentage of stem families and combined families decreased while nuclear families increased, leading to three major changes in the family structure.

First, family-based capacity was weakened. Before 1949, the family was both a production and consumption unit. The family supported family members, and an individual depended on the family. After establishment of the people's commune, production was organized and carried out by the collective. Since the family was no longer responsible for supporting its members it had less control over them, and family members did not feel the need to maintain the large family.

Second, the authority of the family head was weakened. The loss of control over the land and the shift to collective production led to the weakening of the family head's control. Within the collective, both parents and children participated in collective labor; where earlier the family head had directed production, his role was now more on an equal plane with that of his children. The children became less dependent on the parents, and the parents had less control over the children. Under the collective system, since land and the means of production belonged to the collective, the parents had no leverage to stop children from dividing the family.

Gender roles also began to change. Interviews with elderly people in Lengshuigou revealed that after 1949, many women started to work or study in downtown Jinan. With women's social status improving, daughters-in-law didn't have to be housewives. Instead they could be breadwinners while mothers-in-law managed the house. Hence, once there were conflicts, it was

Photo 3.1. Family portrait from the 1960s

hard for mothers-in-law to constrain daughters-in-law, leading to the inevitable division of the family.

Third, there were great advances in freedom to marry. The 1950 Marriage Law advocated "freedom of marriage," "equality of men and women," and monogamy. During the campaigns to promote the new marriage law, people praised freedom and equality while arranged marriages and marriages involving "bride price" (sale of daughters) were criticized. Since Lengshuigou was located in the suburbs of the provincial capital of Jinan, new values and ideas from the city quickly penetrated the countryside. In this period, young people began to pursue freedom of marriage, and as a result of collective work, they had more opportunities to meet and fall in love. It became increasingly difficult for parents to intervene in their children's choice of marriage partners. Even when parents arranged a marriage, children had the right of final approval. In an earlier day, the bride and groom rarely met before the wedding ceremony. Under new-style arranged marriages, after matchmakers introduced the young couple, the young people were given a chance to get to know each other. Thus, while parents might suggest appropriate partners, they no longer exercised ultimate authority in choosing mates.

In addition, the taboo of marriage within the same surname was gradually broken. "One reason was that in some large lineages the relationship between branches was so distant that although they shared the same surname there was no possibility of incest. Another reason was that the young valued emotional ties and disregarded what they saw as the outdated obstructions of their elders. . . . To young people in Lengshuigou pursuit of freedom of marriage outweighed respect for tradition" (Xu and Yang 1994, 275). Under these circumstances, many young people chose their own spouses. New ideas about and expectations for married life emerged together with the appearance of marriage based on equality and love. For a couple to get married was to pursue love instead of pursuing the benefit of the family. When there were conflicts between family members, they would choose their own happiness and divide the large family. Since the authority of the parents had been weakened, they could no longer restrain children's desire for a freer life. Hence, family division became very common as young people sought freedom and also struggled to escape disputes within the family.

Fourth, a series of political movements also had significant impact on family relations. Especially under the influence of leftist political thought during the Cultural Revolution, politics outweighed consanguinity-based relationships, and generational clashes within some families became very intense. As a result, increasing numbers of parents and children decided to live separately. Our elderly informants reported that many family divisions during this period were related to political issues. The Cultural Revolution, with its rejection of traditional ethics and morals, dealt a fatal blow to the status of parents. Parents had less and less authority over children, and it was hard to maintain a harmonious household.

During this time a new standard emerged for choosing a spouse—concern for the political status of the proposed partner. This trend was heightened as a result of class struggle during political movements. Where earlier standards for choosing an ideal partner had stressed economic competence, class status now became the decisive criteria. Those who came from what were regarded as bad class statuses (landlords, rich peasants, etc.) suffered from discrimination and had difficulty finding marriage partners.

To summarize, there were great changes in Lengshuigou family structure after 1949: the proportion of stem families and combined families shrank and that of nuclear families increased. Changes in the political and economic systems as well as the impact of political movements played a part in transforming both the economic bases and cultural concepts of the traditional large families. Family division became much more common. By 1978, the average household in Lengshuigou had 4.06 members, slightly below the Shandong province average. By comparison, the Shandong averages were 4.6 people per household in 1964 and 4.2 people in 1982. However, despite the fact that some large families dissolved and disappeared, a certain proportion of stem families and combined families still survived, even after land reform and the political movements. Although, as we have seen, the authority of the family head was weakened, members of the family still showed some respect for the family head's views and did not completely abandon traditional family ethics.

Changes in Family Structure since the Reforms

Family structure in Lengshuigou has undergone major changes in the last three decades in response to the many social and economic changes that have accompanied the development of the reform policies. In this section, we will use data collected in our surveys to describe and analyze those changes.

One of the most dramatic changes has been a steady decline in the average size of the household. In 1978, the average household had 4.06 members. Three years later (1981) that had shrunk to 3.94 members and to 3.33 mem-

Table 3.2. Household size in Lengshuigou, 2010

Household size (number of individuals)	*Frequency*	*Percentage (%)*
1	5	0.9
2	51	9.5
3	126	23.4
4	122	22.7
5	168	31.2
6	39	7.2
More than 7	27	5.0
Total	538	100.0

Source: Shandong University Survey, 2010.

Table 3.3. Changes in household size in Licheng District, 1982, 1990, 2000, and 2010

Household size (number of individuals)	*1982 (%)*	*1990 (%)*	*2000 (%)*	*2010 (%)*
1	7.6	6.0	8.0	11.4
2	9.6	11.7	18.6	25.1
3	17.7	31.6	38.2	34.6
4	21.3	27.9	21.4	15.5
5	18.6	13.9	10.2	9.8
6	12.8	5.6	2.8	2.7
7	6.9	2.0	0.5	0.6
8 or more	5.5	1.3	0.3	0.3
Total	100.0	100.0	100.0	100.0

Source: Census data for 1982, 1990, 2000, and 2010 in Shandong.

bers in 2008. Our sample of 540 households showed an average of 4.2 family members: 56.5 percent of the households had 4 members or fewer and 12.3 percent had more than 6 family members (table 3.2).

What we can see in Lengshuigou was very similar to developments in the larger Licheng District. Table 3.3 shows that the percentage of larger households with 5 or more family members dropped and the percentage of nuclear families with 2 or 3 people rose sharply. According to the 2010 census, there was also a marked increase in one-person households.

From the census data and our survey, we can see that the nuclear family became the dominant pattern. Our household survey showed that 46.1 percent of our informants reported that they chose to establish a separate household after marriage. From this we can see that the nuclear family has become the ideal for most people. The percentages of divorcee and single-inhabitant households have also increased.

Third, a fairly recent phenomenon is the emergence of skipped-generation households where grandchildren live with grandparents. This reflects the fact that an increasing number of people have sought work in the city, leading to the emergence of households of grandparents with grandchildren and empty-nest families. This new family structure has become quite normal in Lengshuigou.

The household responsibility system, which was a key part of the reform policies, has given peasants freedom to make decisions about agricultural production and allocation of labor. Since the 1990s, industrialization and urbanization have changed family lifestyles, as peasants have migrated from the countryside to cities and suburban areas. Located in the suburbs of Jinan, Lengshuigou has also felt this influence. Many villagers have left farming to look for jobs in other industries. Among our sample households, 84.5 percent have members working outside, and 83.2 percent of villagers claim income from nonagricultural sources—such as working outside (including construction and factory work) and running their own businesses that have become their major source of income. Most (93.9 percent) villagers regard working outside as very helpful to the whole family, and only 6.7 percent still rely on agricultural production as the main source of income. From the above, it is clear that agricultural production occupies an increasingly small position in the family economy and has gradually become a minor side business. As these changes have proceeded, the role of the household in organizing production has shrunk. As a result, individual survival strategies depend more on non-agricultural production outside of the household. Hence, the nuclear family, with its simplified structure and functions, has become the ideal option.

Lengshuigou's proximity to the large city of Jinan has opened opportunities for villagers to work in factories in that city or in the factories that have been built near the village. However, some couples, in order to earn higher wages, choose to work for years in more distant cities, leaving their old parents home alone, a phenomenon known as the empty-nest family. Moreover, under the restrictions of the household-registration and school-district systems, children of migrant workers cannot go to school in the cities where their parents work, so parents have no choice but to leave them in the care of grandparents. This has created the new-style family with grandparents and grandchildren.

The changes in family composition have also given rise to new attitudes toward marriage and family. The younger generation has more freedom in marriage and feelings for each other are the major consideration in choosing marital partners. We found an increasing rate of marriage with partners from outside the village and an increasing number of brides from more distant places. One reason for this is that, because of its proximity to Jinan and fast economic development, Lengshuigou is a comparatively rich village, and as a result, women are attracted to village men as marriage partners; this has included some women from Jinan city. A second reason for the increase of brides from elsewhere is that young people who go to school or work in other places have many more opportunities to meet potential partners from those places, and villagers have been willing to welcome them.

For instance, our sample shows that 36.7 percent of the informants said that they lived more than ten *li* from the home village of their spouses. When we analyze the data on marriage by age cohort, we can see the dramatic change in recent years; the youngest age cohort was much more likely to have married someone from a more distant place (table 3.4).

Table 3.4. Distribution of Lengshuigou villagers' marriage networks across space, 2010

Distance to bride's home	*Under 30 years of age (%)*	*31–60 years of age (%)*	*Above 61 years of age (%)*
Within the village	9.0	18.2	19.6
Within 5 *li* of the village	12.8	24.4	32.7
Within 5–10 *li* of the village	11.5	21.9	29.0
More than 10 *li* from the village	66.7	35.5	18.7
Total	100.0	100.0	100.0

Source: Shandong University Survey, 2010.

In contemporary Lengshuigou, freedom of love and marriage has become quite common, and parents have less and less authority over their children's marriage choices. In our sample, more than half of people over 61 reported that their marriages had been arranged by their parents while only 11.8 percent of younger people gave the same answer (see table 3.5). For the youngest cohort, the most important considerations were mutual feelings, habits, and common interests and hobbies. Thus, we can see a generation gap between parents and children in both attitudes and behavior. To pursue independence, children usually choose to live separately from the parents after marriage to establish their own family. That is also why the nuclear family has become the most common family structure. As more young people work in cities and have families there, independence from parents has increased. There are many cases of parents living in the village and children living in the city. Even in cases where the parents and children live together, they are usually independent financially. In appearance, they keep the life pattern of a stem family but in fact they have formed independent families.

The average age for marriage has also risen; in our sample the average age for marriage is 24. Among people who got married under the age of 20, the

Table 3.5. Marriage decisions by age cohort, Lengshuigou, 2010

Person who made the decision	*Under 30 years of age (%)*	*31–60 years of age (%)*	*Above 61 years of age (%)*
Parents' decision	11.8	23.5	50.5
Bride/groom's own decision	67.1	46.6	26.2
Decision negotiated with others	21.1	26.9	21.5
Other	—	3.1	1.9
Total	100.0	100.0	100.0

Source: Shandong University Survey, 2010.

elderly outnumber the middle-aged and the young (the number for the latter is quite small); among people who got married under the age of 26, the middle-aged and the young outnumber the elderly.

In modern families, wives have a higher status with more decision power in family affairs. No longer limited to work inside the household, more and more women take non-agriculture jobs. In our questionnaire about who should be responsible for housework, 73.5 percent responded that it should be women, 7.6 percent answered "men," and 18.9 percent answered that it should be the joint responsibility of the spouses. Comparatively speaking, an increasing number of men among the youngest cohort are willing to share responsibility for housework.

Since 1949, the Chinese official position has been that men and women are equal, and when we asked our respondents about this claim, 77.8 percent agreed with this statement, while 9.3 percent replied that they think women's status is higher than men's. At present, the conjugal relation has become the key relationship in family relations. Young people increasingly want to make family decisions and reject parental intervention. Couples hope to devote time and energy to their own family without giving much attention to other family members. As the status of the wife has risen, the mother-in-law's ability to control the daughter-in-law has disappeared. Wives hope to be the woman of the house, and their husbands support them without worrying about their parents' authority. Hence, it is usually the wife who initiates a proposal to divide the family, and parents respect their decision.

All of the changes that have followed on the reform policies have also led to new patterns in caring for the aged. Several patterns have emerged. In looking at them, it is important to note that because of the proximity to Jinan, many in the younger working generation commute to the city, returning to the village at night. Some live in the same households as their parents, others live in independent households in the same village.

The first pattern is one in which the children provide for the aged. According to our sample, in 59.4 percent of surveyed families, children provide for their parents. Living with or near their children, the aged are taken care of, and at the same time, they can help their children in looking after grandchildren, doing housework, and managing domestic affairs. In this pattern of children providing for the aged, we should note that although the parents and children live together, the parents have their own financial resources so what their children provide is primarily spiritual support instead of material support.

When we turn to attitudes, our survey found that 68.9 percent of villagers think children should provide for their parents and 66.3 percent believe that raising children to support their parents in old age is important. Although it is commonly said that filial piety has declined along with the authority of the family head, many still believe in the thousand-year-old tradition that children should return the benefits received from their parents. Furthermore, contemporary Chinese law stipulates that children should provide for their parents. Thus, although many pursue independence and the nuclear family, the stem family structure continues to survive. However, among the young, the idea that children should be raised to care for their parents in old age is declining as we can see in table 3.6. The percentage of young people disagreeing with this concept is the highest at 38.5 percent.

In a second pattern, the elder generation lives alone. After their children get a job in other places or establish their own families, parents live on their own resources, work in the fields, or rely on money provided by their children monthly. In our sample survey, 39.7 percent of the older generation were looking after themselves. One reason for this is that parents choose to live alone to avoid domestic conflicts and the other is that children, working in another city, cannot take care of their parents. Many of our elderly informants said that they did not want to live with their children because of differences in ideas and behavior; living separately meant less trouble, making them feel comfortable and happy. This pattern is increasing and gaining increasing acceptance, and as long as the parents are capable of caring for themselves, children usually choose to live separately.

The third pattern is one in which the village committee cares for the elderly collectively, which usually applies to individuals who have no one to support them, a category known as *wubao*.[2] These elderly people have no children and are incapable of taking care of themselves, so they are left in the care of the village committee. The village committee takes over their land and provides them with the food and other things they need for daily life. In the sample, only 0.6 percent of the villagers were in this category. In Lengshuigou, the village committee also gives all elderly residents over the age of seventy a stipend of fifty *yuan* a month.

Table 3.6. Villagers' attitudes regarding "raising children to secure old age," Lengshuigou, 2010

Attitude	*Under 30 years of age (%)*	*31–60 years of age (%)*	*Above 61 years of age (%)*
Totally agree	16.3	33.5	55.6
Agree	34.6	30.5	32.4
Don't agree	38.5	26.2	9.3
Not clear	10.6	9.8	2.8
Total	100.0	100.0	100.0

Source: Shandong University Survey, 2010.

The fourth pattern is in sending the elderly to nursing homes. In the sample, this pattern was adopted by 0.4 percent, and 5 percent of the sample thought that this approach was acceptable. Although at present there are only a few elderly people living in nursing homes, people are increasingly accepting this as a viable option. There is no nursing home in Lengshuigou, but there is one in the Wangsheren district, to which Lengshuigou belongs, and the nursing home is shared by nearby villages. However, nursing homes have certain admission requirements, and only the elderly who meet the requirements can get in. Although there is an increasing acceptance of collective solutions to the care of the elderly—especially in the light of the increase in empty-nest families, this is still not the most popular option. In some cases, the elderly are not willing to leave their homes and move to another environment; other challenges include the availability of such facilities and remaining worries about social criticism of this solution.

In general, in Lengshuigou, families are responsible for caring for the older generation. Although in some families parents and children still live together, they are financially independent, and the children's main responsibility is to provide spiritual consolation. That is why for those who are able to take care of themselves, the option of staying at home is preferred. In the future, improvements in the public support for the elderly may help to resolve the problems in a context characterized by nuclear families and empty-nest families.

From the above analysis, we know that a certain proportion of stem families still exists despite modern society's preference for simplified and small nuclear families. We have identified three explanations for this.

First, there is the reduction in the number of children. After the 1980s, birth control policy limited family size, and people came to accept the idea of "having fewer and better children" and "late marriage and late childbearing." An additional factor was the rise in women's educational levels, which also impacted the birth rate. As we can see from table 3.7, 50 percent of Lengshuigou families have only one child. This is in sharp contrast to the 1940s and 1950s when woman had more than four children on average. When there are fewer children, family members, especially siblings, have fewer conflicts and are less likely to divide the family. One of the major reasons for the reduction in the number of children was the one child policy. If a family had a son and a daughter, after the daughter married, the son would not separate from his parents. Studies by other scholars have shown that "the main reason for the increase in stem families is the rise of the proportion of single-child families in rural areas" (Wang 2006, 528).

In a second pattern, parents who originally had the ability and desire to live separately from their children had to move in with them when the parents lost the ability to care for themselves.

Table 3.7. Number of children per household, Lengshuigou, 2010

Number of children	*Frequency*	*Percentage (%)*
0	15	3.0
1	245	48.2
2	169	33.3
3	50	9.8
4	16	3.2
5	13	2.6
Total	508	100.0

Source: Shandong University Survey, 2010

The third pattern is common among those who might be described as "financially challenged." In traditional rural society, there was a kind of bargain between parents and children: parents were expected to raise and marry off their children, and in exchange, children had a responsibility to care for their parents in old age. In contemporary society, parents still carry out their part of the bargain—which now assumes that the parents will prepare housing for their son in preparation for marriage. Usually this involves paying for new housing, and if the family divides, the new housing is regarded as part of the son's property. In some cases, however, the family is not yet able to provide the new housing, and as a result, the young couple lives with the older generation. While this may look like a traditional stem family, obviously the motivations are quite different, and when the family is able to put aside sufficient resources, the young couple will move into new housing.

Brief Conclusion

Looking back over the last century, we can identify two major trends in the structure of Lengshuigou families: first, the once dominant, large extended family structure has declined as an ideal, and second, it has been replaced by the nuclear family. These changes in the family structure reflect the contemporary choice for family division over the extended family that combined several generations and included married brothers and their families. We have argued that the older extended-family structure helped to sustain family members as a result of its greater ability to mobilize family labor and other economic and social resources. However, as times changed and different forms of ownership of the means of production appeared, different family styles appeared that were better able to deal with the new conditions.

Changes in Lengshuigou reflect the broader changes in Chinese rural society. The rise of the nuclear family and the shrinking of the average household size are common across rural China. These changes came about in response to changes in economic and social organization and also as a reflection of new ideas, including the greater stress on individuality. The family's control over its members has weakened, young people no longer feel such strong responsibility for caring for the elderly, and some old people have been left with no one to care for them. These problems are problems for individual families as well as for all of society, and new social policies and institutions are needed to resolve them. For example, the problem of elderly support demands an improved social welfare system and a family culture that stresses a sense of responsibility. However, since modern society advocates an independent and free lifestyle, every person wants freedom in both marital life and individual behavior. Thus the nuclear family is bound to be the ideal living pattern in the future because of its simple structure and allowance for more personal space.

NOTES

1. Dahuaishu, famous for being the homeland of many immigrants in China in the Ming Dynasty, is located in Hongdong County, Shanxi Province. Now a historical site, Dahuaishu is regarded by many Chinese as the root of their family. We assume that the Wang and Du families originally moved from Shanxi to Zaoqiang, and then to Lengshuigou.
2. *Wubao* (literally, "those without support") refers to the old, to those who are disabled or incapable of work, to those who have no source of income, to those who have no one to look after them, or even if they have someone, this person is not able to provide for them. *Wubao* recipients can be provided with food, clothes, medical care, a living place, and a funeral (and education in case of a child).

Chapter Four

Social Structure and Social Life

This chapter focuses on changes in social structure and social life over the last century. Chapter 3 examined the role of kinship and the family in Chinese rural society. Examination of social strata, which cut across kinship boundaries, provides another opportunity to assess social and power organization in the village. This chapter considers how changes in social strata have been reflected in the daily lives of residents, with special emphasis on the impact of changes in gender relations.

CHANGES IN SOCIAL STRUCTURE

By *stratification* we do not mean categories based on the household registration system or political categories, but rather categories based on occupational career differentiation. Earlier analyses of Chinese society used a model based on a notion of two classes (i.e., workers and peasants) and one stratum (i.e., intellectuals). In recent years, Chinese scholars prefer to use *stratum* rather than *class* in analyzing social structure. Although in classical Western sociological theory, class analysis was based on a consideration of economic circumstances, in China—especially after the land reform of the early 1950s—class was used as a political category. Class statuses assigned to individuals at the time of land reform were recorded on identity documents and inherited by children and grandchildren. This use of class categorization was brought to an end in the early reform period but because of the strong association of "class" with this politicized system, we prefer to use *social strata* as an analytical category. Social-strata analysis uses a variety of standards including wealth, power, and social prestige.

One of Mao Zedong's earliest works was an analysis of Chinese social structure in which he divided the rural population into five classes: landlords, rich peasants, middle peasants, poor peasants and handicraftsmen. Mao's analysis used economic and social criteria as the crucial factors for dividing the classes. Naturally, Lengshuigou, like other villages, had all five classes. Through the processes of land reform and collectivization in the first half of the 1950s, ownership of the means of production was assigned first to individual households within each village and then transferred to the collective. This led to an equalizing of living standards, so that the primary differences between families were derived from the number of laborers in the household and the work points they earned in collective labor. In the course of land reform, the peasantry had been classified on the basis of an assessment of class position as *poor peasant*, *middle peasant*, *rich peasant*, or *landlord* at the same time that the material basis for the classification was eliminated through redistribution of land. As a result of the reforms of the 1980s in which the collectives and the communes were abolished, land was distributed to households on the basis of population, agriculture reverted to the household economy, and rural industrialization occurred in some regions. This produced a very complex situation in the countryside, and a simple division of the peasants based on either economic or political factors is insufficient for our analysis. In assessing contemporary rural society, we need to consider such factors as ownership of land and other means of production, income, position in the market, occupation, access to political power, education, cultural resources, social resources, and reputation.

While we need to consider multiple factors, occupation is one of the most important factors in understanding stratification in contemporary Lengshuigou. Max Weber's three-pronged analysis of social stratification used wealth and income (economic status), power (political status), and prestige (social status) as the crucial factors, but in fact these three were all closely related to occupation. In reform-era rural China with its rapidly diversifying occupational structure, this analysis can give us a rough guide to important patterns of social change.

Before 1949

The Chinese classical tradition used a four-part division of society: peasants, artisans, scholars, and merchants, with peasants making up the overwhelmingly largest group. In Lengshuigou, as in other ordinary villages, production was based on private-land ownership, and most people made their living from the land. The *Kankō Chōsa* survey described land ownership in Lengshuigou as follows:

> The whole village had a total of 42 *qing* and land was divided fairly evenly. There was only one household possessing more than 100 *mu*. Quite a few households (about 10) possessed more than 50 *mu* and only a very few had no land at all. Most households had about 10 *mu*. Most villagers worked on their own land and less than 25 households rented land. (KC 1955, 9).[1]

R. H. Myers, who used the data collected by the Japanese *Kankō Chōsa* research team, disagreed with their conclusions (table 4.1). Myers argued that about two-thirds of the households owned less than 10 *mu*, indicating that distribution of farmland was not as equal as has sometimes been claimed (Myers 1970, 98).

At the time of land reform in 1950, thirty-two households were classified as landlords and eight households as rich peasants (LCZ 2010, 10). In thinking about why the land reform results differed from the situation described by the Japanese researchers, we need to consider two factors: first, changes in land ownership between the early 1940s and 1950s as a result of land sales, and second, the difference in standards for classification. It is important to remember that land-reform standards looked not only at total land holdings but also at how the land was managed. For example, a labor-short household headed by a widow might be classified as a landlord household if the household's income came primarily from renting out land, even if the amount of land was not so large.

However, in general we believe that Lengshuigou can be seen as a community of poor and middle peasants. This conclusion follows from the proportion of poor and middle peasants and the small gap between the rich and the poor.

Although Lengshuigou's landlords were wealthy compared with their neighbors, villagers did not view them as despotic. In response to our questions, Ren Yanting (born in 1938, former Party secretary of the village) remembered:

> I think there were no despotic landlords in Lengshuigou. But during political struggle sessions, some people accused some of the landlords of being despotic.

Table 4.1. Land distribution in Lengshuigou, 1940s

Amount of farming land owned (mu)	*Number of names listed*	*Percentage (%)*
No land	20	4
0–10	302	61
10–20	135	27
20–50	42	8
Total	499	100

Source: Myers 1970, 339.

It is hard to classify them as such because they just had a lot of land and hired some long-term labor but they didn't bully and oppress others.

As for the village's rich peasants, they had good reputations and a reasonably well-off lifestyle and were literate. There were a fair number of middle peasants who led average lives. They worked on their own land, and only a few households rented out land to others. Most households in the village were poor peasants. While some of them owned a small amount of land, they also had to rent from others. Their living standards were low.

There were about twenty households of hired laborers, and most of them were from outside the village. Usually they rented land for three to five years, and most of the harvest was handed over to the landlord as rent. According to the *Kankō Chōsa* survey,

Good paddy land could produce 6 *dou* per *mu*, and 5 of that would be paid in rent; middle quality paddy fields could produce 5 *dou* per *mu*, and 4 would be taken as rent; and poor paddy land produced 3 *dou* per *mu*, of which 2 would be taken as rent. As for dry field land, you could harvest 5 *dou* from a sorghum field, and 2.5 would be paid as rent; and if you planted coarse grain, you could harvest 7 *dou* per mu from grain field, with 2 to 4 taken as rent. Output of coarse grains varied from crop to crop. (KC 1955, 147)

The *Kankō Chōsa* materials include the following comments on the relationship between hired peasants and landlords:

Q: Were there cases of hired peasants living in the houses of landlords?

A: No.

Q: Did hired peasants just pay rent to landlords?

A: Of course.

Q: Would hired peasants pay their respects to the landlords on festivals?

A: No.

Q: When landlords did construction or repairs on their buildings, would hired peasants go and help?

A: They didn't have to go. It was their choice.

Q: Would landlords attend marriages and other ceremonies?

A: There was no need to invite landlords. Just neighbors were enough.

Q: When landlords visited a tenant, how were they treated?

A: More formally than ordinary people.

Q: How did tenants refer to their landlords?

A: They called them "Lord" (*laoye*) or by their names.

Q: How did the landlord refer to tenants?

A: Usually they called them by their names. (KC 1955, 151)

In addition to those engaged in farming, a few villagers engaged in handicrafts, mental labor, or managerial work. Since the number of people in these occupations was quite small, they cannot be called a stratum. Philip Huang observed that the involution of the peasant economy hindered the development of industry and commerce. Involution, in Huang's argument, focuses on the relationship between increases in total output as a result of the investment of additional inputs of labor and stagnation in labor productivity, or output per labor unit. Huang believes that gains in total output were the result of self-exploitation of family labor. By disregarding the costs of family labor, including in handicraft activities that were undertaken to increase total family income, rural households produced daily-use items at costs that could not be matched by industry. From the *Kankō Chōsa* materials, we learn the following about living standards among those engaged in commerce and industry:

> In the past there were four or five people working in a Jinan cement factory. They took up this work because they had only two or three mu of land so they had no choice but to work in factories to make a living. There were a dozen others who worked as apprentices and shop assistants. These people had a lot of family members to support and they were able to get such positions because they had connections to someone in the businesses.
>
> Many peasants wove straw rope as a sideline. In slack seasons when they didn't have to tend the fields large numbers of men went outside to work as coolies. (KC 1955, 2 and 9)

Ren Yanting recalled:

> Before 1949 during the slack agricultural season people went to Jinan to look for jobs. Back then there was no household registration system and hired workers were paid by the work they did, both long-term and short-term.

There were some villagers who were engaged in teaching or other forms of mental labor. In a relatively closed traditional society, the boundaries between strata were relatively clear, and there was little mobility between the strata. The social stratum of a villager was generally determined by the family into which he was born, and usually the person remained in that stratum for the rest of his life. However, in Lengshuigou there was some mobility. The main factors that would allow someone to move into a higher social stratum were joining the army, getting an education, mastering a special skill, or grasping a political opportunity.

Many villagers left the village and found better jobs by joining the army. According to the *Lengshuigou Village Gazetteer*, ten or twenty men joined the army before 1949, and some of them were promoted to officer. For example, Yang Mutao (born in 1923) was born into a wealthy family. He joined the eighth route army in 1939 and studied at the Shandong Anti-Japanese Cadre School. He served in the army during the Anti-Japanese War and the War of Liberation; after serving in the Korean War, he studied at the PLA Political Academy. Later he was assigned to the Jinan Military Region as deputy director of the political department of the engineering corps, director of the *Qianwei* newspaper agency of the military's political department; he was deputy director of the political department of the joint logistics department when he retired. Ren Yanjing (born in 1928) joined the Chinese People's Liberation Army in 1949 and served as a company commander, battalion commander, chief of staff and deputy regimental commander, and so forth. Later he transferred to the Jinan Iron and Steel Company as director of the Security Office and Party Secretary (LCZ 2010, 158 and 160).

Getting educated was another way to achieve upward social mobility. In Lengshuigou, education has always been valued, and there were a number of people who pursued careers in government or education. According to statistics gathered by the village, before 1949 there were more than a dozen people who worked in government offices and companies after graduating from primary school. However, due to limited educational resources and the constraints of the economy, it was still difficult for most people to realize social mobility through education.

There are several other examples of men, who under the political circumstances of that era, seized opportunities to rise in status. For example, Liu Duo (born in 1930) went to Taiwan in 1949 as a military doctor for Guomindang troops, with the rank of lieutenant colonel and as director of a clinic. Li Fengshi (born in 1930) went to Taiwan in 1949 and was principal of a primary school in Jiayi County (LCZ 2010, 169–70).

Generally speaking, although there was some social mobility in this period, the range and scale of social mobility were greatly restricted, and the majority of people spent their lives in the same stratum they were born into. This is not surprising since it is generally assumed that low rates of social mobility and rigidity of the social structure are features of a closed society.

From 1949 to the Reform and Opening Up Policies

The reorganization of rural society after 1949 beginning with land reform and continuing through collectivization and establishment of the people's communes radically transformed the traditional class and status systems. As a result of a series of political movements, many of which used the tactic of struggle sessions, the newly introduced systems of "class status" and class consciousness spread throughout society. Land and property ownership, which had earlier served as markers of status, were no longer important following the leveling that accompanied the establishment of the commune. As for distinctions based on employment, since all villagers were classified as commune members (*gongshe sheyuan*)—which in itself became a kind of occupation category—this also no longer had an influence on social status. Moreover, within the commune, work was fairly similar and there were few distinctions among commune members. Within this system, political factors and expressions of ideological commitment came to play the central role in determining an individual's status. Eliminating privilege and de-stratification were the chief features of this period.

Following the promulgation of the Agrarian Reform Law of the People's Republic of China in June 1950, a peasant association was established under the supervision of the land-reform work team of Licheng County to educate people about this law. In Lengshuigou, as in all rural villages, investigations were carried out to determine how much land and property each household held, and class statuses were determined on the basis of the results. Altogether, there were 400 or 500 households in the village: 32 households were classified as landlord, 8 households as rich peasant, more than 100 households as middle peasant, and the rest as poor peasants and hired laborers. The average landholding for middle peasants was 7 *mu* per person, and those with more were classified as rich peasants or landlords, those with less as poor peasants or hired laborers.[2] In the winter of 1950, there was a movement to deal with those who were opposing land reform, and a small number of people were charged as counterrevolutionaries, and a few of them were executed. Later, some people were labeled as "bad elements." In 1957, the Anti-Rightist Movement was launched in Lengshuigou, and a small number of people were wrongly labeled as "rightist."

Through land reform, land once owned by landlords and rich peasants was distributed among peasants who had little or no land; poor and hired peasants got a piece of land, and land ownership in the village became more equal. However, after establishment of the people's commune, land became the property of the community, and villagers became commune members. Within the commune, there was a new status system based on political categories. We can identify several strata (called "classes" at the time), including production brigade cadres, ordinary commune members, and the three groups or strata of those with "bad" class statuses including landlords, rich peasants, and a third group that included those designated as counterrevolutionaries, bad elements, or rightists. Peasants were divided into four groups, based on their economic status at the time of land reform: poor (hired) peasants, middle peasant, rich peasants, and landlords. The poor and lower-middle peasants were the largest group, and the poor (hired) peasants held the highest political status.

The following is an interview with Li Tingfu (a teacher who was responsible for the composition of the village gazetteer). Li, who collected many materials and interviewed many of the elderly in preparing the village chronicle, made the following comments on social conditions during this period:

> Leaders of production brigades were the core because they could determine your life. . . . Commune members were not entirely equal. If you were labeled as a "landlord, rich peasant, counter-revolutionary, bad element or rightist" then you were not treated as an ordinary member.
>
> Q: Were there three types: leaders of production teams, ordinary members and "landlords, rich peasants, counter-revolutionary, bad elements and rightists"?
>
> A: Yes. The "landlords, rich peasants, counter-revolutionary, bad elements and rightists," had the lowest social status and were treated badly.

The "landlords (*dizhu*), rich peasants (*funong*), counter-revolutionary (*fan geming*), bad elements (*huai fenzi*), and rightists (*you*)," or the so-called five black categories (*hei wulei*), had the lowest status in the village. In fact, Lengshuigou became a core location for political movements in Shandong province, and as a result, these five black categories were continuously criticized, forced to do "voluntary" work, and some did not survive. For example the landlord Ren Yanming was executed. Landlords' social status dropped sharply compared with the past.

Many villagers recall situations from these times. Among them, the former secretary of the Party Ren Yanting said:

> After the land reform landlords' social status dropped sharply and the "landlord" label was not removed until 1983. At that time "landlords, rich peasants, counter-revolutionaries, bad elements and rightists" had very low social status. Ordinary villagers shunned them and very rarely would go to visit them. When people passed them on the village lanes they would usually not exchange greetings, even if the individual were a relative or a former teacher. However, if their families had some crisis, some of the poor peasants would disregard their status and give them assistance.

Li Tingfu, who was responsible for the composition of the village gazetteer described the situation of landlords in the following way:

> At that time, if the father were a landlord, the son would want to divide the family and set up a separate household. This was quite common in the village during those days. Even if you divided the family, the Party would not recognize the change [i.e., the son was still categorized as the son of a landlord]. If you were a landlord, you were not to be trusted regardless of anything else.

Production-brigade cadres formed a new social stratum. Most of them came from families that had been classified as tenants, poor peasants, or lower-middle peasants. The cadres were selected from those who had some education and higher levels of political awareness (a Communist Party or a Youth League member). A man who was born in 1957 and had served as the recorder of work points for the nineteenth production team told us:

> Cadres of production brigades were elected with a family background of poor or lower-middle peasant. People from higher social status were rejected. One had to be literate, at least a middle school or high school graduate, usually a Party member, sometimes a League member. Children of landlords couldn't join the Party because there were strict restrictions back then.

Cheng Kexing (born in 1943, former village head, and head of the Lengshuigou production brigade from 1971–1974):

> Cadres of production brigades were elected from poor peasants and some middle peasants. They had to be capable.

From the above descriptions, we can see that there were distinct differentiations between strata in Lengshuigou, and statuses were inherited. Ascribed factors played a vital part in determining "class status" among villagers. An individual's status was determined by his family's background. In this period, the whole village was immersed in a highly politicized and ideological atmosphere, and individuals had to be very careful about words and actions since they all had political implications. There was great hostility between strata, and "class struggle" was an important aspect of the relationships between strata.

Li Tingzhu (born in January 1940, former accountant of the production brigade) remembered:

> At the time of the Cultural Revolution, one had to pay great attention to one's words. Family background mattered a lot. Even the Red Guards had different groups so one had to be extremely cautious.

Former Party secretary Ren Yanting also said:

> From the time of land reform to 1983, there were constant political struggles. Chairman Mao once said that constant attention should be paid to class struggles. So whenever there was a political movement, these people [of bad class background] would be criticized.

Li Tingfu further commented:

> If you were a landlord and I was a poor tenant, we had different identities. I won't ever forget that period in which Mao Zedong was the leader and class struggle was most important, a struggle against heaven, against earth, and against people. This was Mao's philosophy of struggle. At that time class struggle was quite intense.

The "class status" determined at the time of land reform had a huge impact on social mobility. In this highly politicized social atmosphere, the determining factor in social mobility was this kind of ascribed status, and villagers were categorized by their class status, which was in turn a decisive factor in access to opportunities and chances for social mobility. Villagers born to families in the five black categories had no choice but to move downward.

Xie Zhaokui (born in 1927, in a family that had produced three generations of teachers), cited the following case:

> In the past there was a landlord. . . . He ranked as a senior in the family, had money and power, so it was natural that he became the family head. But after 1949 he was struggled against and overthrown. No one cared [i.e., no one cared that he was once powerful].

Since "class status" and "identity" were inherited, children of the five black categories faced many obstacles: there were restrictions on getting an education, joining the army, joining the Party and the League. Class status even influenced their marriages and giving birth to children. Many people's lives were changed. The former Party secretary Ren Yanting told us:

> There was no way out for these children. There was no chance for them to get education, to join the army, the Party, or the League. The only choice was to stay in the production brigade and earn work points. Whenever you wanted to take an exam, join the army, work in a factory, or go to school, you had to provide information on your family background. As soon as someone noticed that your parents "wore hats" [i.e., had bad class status], it would influence your chances for success.

Under these unusual historical conditions, some children of five black category families had no choice but to cut all relations with their parents in order to get opportunities for personal development. Former accountant Li Tingzhu gave us a well-known example:

> There were those who broke off all relations with parents and sought individual development in Yunnan. They did not come back until a few years ago when labels were finally taken off.

These cases demonstrate that the system, policies, and social structures had direct effects on the lives of individuals, restricting a person's social mobility. In a normal society, individuals have the possibility of moving upward. However, during this period, the highly politicized social environment deprived many people of such possibilities.

On the other hand, to have impeccable lower-class credentials or to be born in a politically advantaged family was a precondition for moving up the social ladder. The following is a part of an interview with the former head of the village committee Cheng Kexing, which illustrates the role of family status in upward social mobility:

> My family background is poor peasant. . . . At the time of land reform, I was eight. I joined the Party in December 1971 along with 12 other people. I had a high school degree and I was the production team leader. Our production team was one of the top in the village so both the team leader and deputy leader were able to join the party.
>
> Li Tingwu, who was the head of the village militia, was also selected. He was born into a poor peasant family, became a Party member, and was quite capable as well.

One not only needed to come from a politically advantaged family but also had to stand up for the Party's policies. For example, Gao Fuxing, once an ordinary villager, was elected head of the Revolutionary Committee of Lengshuigou, which was established in 1967; he was recognized for his active support of Party policies. Some of those who came from less good class backgrounds found other ways to move up in social status. For example, in the spring of 1956, fifteen young people answered a Party call and immigrated to Heilongjiang to open up wasteland; and in the autumn of 1956, some women from Lengshuigou went to Xinjiang to join production and construction corps. In this way, some children of middle peasants and rich peasants were able to move upward in social status.

Another route to social mobility was through military service. During the campaign to resist U.S. aggression and aid Korea in 1950, many villagers joined the army and fought in Korea. Records show that during the three years of the war, forty-five villagers joined the army. While some of them lost their lives,[3] some of those who returned home safely were rewarded with high positions. For example, Yang Chunxiu (born in 1933) joined the Chinese People's Volunteer Army and went to Korea in 1950. After returning home, he was appointed to be a cadre in the military and met Chairman Mao and Premier Zhou during a ceremony honoring those who had rendered meritorious service (LCZ 2010, 159). There were others who received an education from the military after joining the army, giving them an advantage in climbing the social ladder. For example, Zhang Dechang (born in 1937) joined the army in 1954. After graduating from the Military Artillery School in Shenyang, he was appointed chief of staff, battalion commander, assistant regimental chief of staff and assistant regimental commander of the Military Department, and later was transferred to the Shandong province Public Security Department. Besides them, Li Changxun (born in 1943) and Li Qiang (born in 1950) both moved upward in society by joining the army.

In this period, education as a pathway to social mobility was strongly influenced by politics and political movements. In the 1950s, admission to a university offered another path to upward mobility. However, during the Cultural Revolution, those with education were hit hard by a series of political and reform movements. According to incomplete statistics in the *Lengshuigou Gazetteer*, in the twenty-nine years from 1949 to 1978, fourteen villagers entered institutions for higher education. Eleven of those individuals graduated between 1950 and 1958. For example, Wang Jinzhang (born in 1934) got into the Chinese People's Liberation Army (PLA) Institute of Communication Engineering, graduated, and started working in 1953, becoming chief engineer of a military department with the rank of senior colonel. Li Xinghan (born in 1927) graduated from the Shandong Engineering College and was assigned to the Changchun First Automobile Factory after graduation. In 1987, he was appointed as a chief engineer and went to Germany to do some research. Li Xing,[4] Gao Changfu,[5] Xie Baoxi,[6] and others had similar experiences. However, in the following twenty years, only a few villagers got the opportunity to receive a higher education. During the Cultural Revolution, intellectuals became the subjects of struggle, labeled as "Stinking Number Nine," and their social status dropped to historically low levels.

From the interviews, we learned that despite the ideology of equalitarianism, inequality still existed, especially between production teams. One form of upward mobility was largely restricted to women, that is, moving from a poor production brigade to a richer one through marriage. Likewise, marriage was a method to realize mobility between strata, such as marriage between children of poor peasants and rich peasants.

Meanwhile, the Household Registration Law of the People's Republic of China, passed in January 1958 placed further restrictions on the rural population entering cities: "To move from villages to cities, citizens must have credentials issued by the labor department of the city, an admission notice from schools or permission to immigrate issued by urban household registration institutions, and then apply to the urban household registration institutions for immigration." The household registration system and people's commune regulations exercised firm control over movement by the village population, fixing them to areas where they were registered, creating a closed social group and reducing mobility between cities and villages.

In this period, collectivism and equalitarianism were dominant ideas influencing all of society. People firmly believed in the goal of creating a communist society with equality for all and eliminating what they referred to as the "three major differences" (differences between industry and agriculture, between urban and rural areas, and between mental and physical labor). So after 1949 and before the Reform and Opening Up Policies, equality became a national pursuit that achieved some degree of success: the gap between the rich and the poor narrowed, and occupation differentiation became less distinct. However, inequality still existed in rural areas. The "poor and lower-middle peasants" and cadres of production brigades were at the top of the social pyramid, possessing more power and opportunities; while the five black categories were at the bottom of the social pyramid with very low political status.

In conclusion, in the thirty years from 1949 to 1978, transformation of the Chinese social structure was accompanied by major changes in the social-status system. The determining factor of villagers' social status switched from economic factors such as land ownership to political factors. The traditional closed rural society shifted to a society with sharp distinctions between urban and rural society. Due to restrictions of the household registration system, villagers in Lengshuigou had little chance to move out of their rural community.

From the Beginning of the Reforms to the End of the Twentieth Century

Between 1978 and the end of 1983, the system of assigned statuses that had been established during land reform was dismantled; the first step was in efforts to "remove the hats" of those who had been assigned bad class labels and to restore the good names of those who had been misclassified. The theory of class status was strongly attacked, and the impact of political and ideological factors in shaping social strata was greatly weakened. China moved from a system based on planning to greater use of the market, and as those changes deepened, new strata based on occupation became more obvious. Gaps in income also began to widen. As the socialist market economy continued to develop, a new stratification system began to appear that placed greater emphasis on occupation, income, education level, lifestyle, and social reputation. This much more complicated stratification system replaced the "peasant strata" of the preceding period.

In August 1983, Lengshuigou began to implement the household responsibility system. The land of each production team was surveyed and then contracted out to individual households to farm. The contracts were for long-term use, and households were given certificates for the long-term contracts. Individual households were now responsible for making economic and management decisions.

At this time, the government began to encourage a more diversified economy, and villagers were allowed to run their own businesses, leading to a boom in the establishment of village-based enterprises as individuals, newly freed from the restrictions of collective labor inherent in the system where everyone was a "commune member," seized the opportunities presented by the market economy. Among those who started new enterprises were former cadres of communes, ordinary commune members, and children of those who had been classified as members of the five black categories. For example, Li Encheng (born in 1957) was one of the pioneers who became wealthy through participation in the market economy. He is an example of someone who started from within the administrative system, breaking free of the restrictions under the old system, and creating a new career. After graduating from middle school, he had been selected by the commune to work in the Water Resources Bureau. In 1983, when policies were just beginning to change, he grasped the opportunity and invested in a privately owned factory using funds he had raised himself. He recalled his experience:

> I graduated at the age of 17 from No. 18 Jinan Middle School. After graduation I worked as a clerk in the Museum of Class Education for less than two years. It was quite popular then to join the army, but I had high blood pressure and couldn't pass the physical examination, which was very strict. In the third year after my graduation, I took part in the college entrance examination; I passed it twice, but I failed the physical examination because of my high blood pressure. Later I worked as deputy secretary in the village Youth League branch for four or five years, and then I was picked out to work in the Water Resources Bureau as a technician where I stayed for another four or five years until I quit. It was 1984 and political policies had just begun to change. My brother-in-law was in the business of dealing granite, a business that was quite lucrative. So I quit my job and got into the trade in granite. I opened up my own factory. At that time in the village, the only possessions one had were a few pigs and no one dared to do business since it was called "the tail of capitalism." So I had no money to buy

the necessary machine, which cost 3–4,000 yuan. I took a loan and borrowed some money from relatives and friends to open up my factory. At that time no one else in the village was in this line of business. Later, when they saw what I was doing was profitable, other villagers started four or five similar factories.

The following is an interview with a person who had been responsible for recording work points. From this interview, we can see that the children of those with bad class status (landlords, rich peasants, counter-revolutionaries, bad elements, and rightists) were able to break away from the restrictions that had come from their former "identity":

> Children of landlords and rich peasants now are doing well. It all comes down to personal capacity. You can be successful by running a factory manufacturing parts, being a labor contractor, or working in the construction business.

In response to national policy, Lengshuigou developed village industries. Among the village enterprises were a factory that processed bristles, a fertilizer factory, and a chemical plant. The new enterprises gave individuals with managerial skills opportunities to change from being "commune members" or "cadres of production brigades" to executives of rural enterprises. Another group of commune members worked in those enterprises and became part of the employee stratum.

Meanwhile, great changes have taken place in the national economic situation. With the rapid development of the Chinese economy and expansion of the industrial and service sectors, villagers had opportunities to find employment outside the village. The loosening of the household registration system facilitated movement from agricultural production to the industrial and service sectors. In this period, we began to hear about those who had "left farming but not left their native place," and of others who had "left both farming and the village." Among the latter were those who took up employment in Jinan or in more distant places. In this period, crucial factors in determining an individual's economic status were not only personal skills but also the ability to grasp market opportunities.

Overall we can see that with the removal of political status as an important consideration, a new system of stratification appeared, which was based on occupation. The leading sociologist Lu Xueyi divided rural dwellers into eight strata: agricultural laborers, rural migrant workers in cities, hired laborers, rural intellectual workers, individual laborers and individual businesses, private entrepreneurs, township enterprise managers, and rural administrators (Lu 2001, 444). When we apply Lu's model to early reform-period Lengshuigou, we can see that with the exception of private entrepreneurs, all of these strata had already made an appearance (Xu and Yang 1994, 243–46).

Agricultural labor occupied 30 percent of the total work force. This stratum included those who engaged in agricultural production while also engaging in housework and looking after children. After the implementation of the household contract responsibility system, they were more active in production. The stratum of rural workers (*nongmingong*), which refers to villagers who got most or all of their income from work in state-run or rural enterprises, made up 40 percent of the work force. This group mainly consisted of the young and the middle-aged, with a few seniors close to retirement. The majority of this group worked in the village-run bristle-processing factory, fertilizer factory, chemical plant, or other village-run enterprises; some worked in state-run enterprises in Wangsheren. Although these people were working in factories, most of them still lived in their village homes. Although they spent most of their time and energy on work in the factory, in their spare time or during the busy farming seasons, they helped their family in agricultural production. The hired laborers category (*gugong*) included those who were hired as temporary workers, often on a daily basis.[7] Private enterprises were not very developed at that time in Lengshuigou, and private entrepreneurs did not form a stratum, so there were only a few hired workers, occupying 3 percent of the work force. Rural intellectual workers included teachers, doctors, and technicians; together they made up 7 percent of the work force. One of the comparatively wealthy strata in Lengshuigou was that of individual laborers and individual businessmen, occupying about 15 percent, including carpenters; bricklayers; tailors; barbers; repairmen of household appliances, agricultural machines, bicycles, and motorcycles; and owners of stores, restaurants, and noodle workshops. This stratum included people who reacted very quickly to changes in the economy and had found ways to earn a good income; as their economic status improved, they came to play an increasingly important role in village affairs.

The stratum of township and village enterprise managers refers to managers of rural enterprises, factory heads, and other administration personnel, making up about 2 percent of the workforce. Some of them worked in Lengshuigou, managing factories run by the village, such as the bristle-processing factory, the fertilizer factory, the carbon products factory, and the chemical plant; a few of the managers worked in enterprises in Wangsheren. Since these were not privately owned factories, the managers did not own the companies, but they were responsible for management decisions. In the village, their status, power, reputation, and influence were much greater than that of private businessmen. Finally, the stratum of rural administrators refers to village cadre in Lengshuigou; they also made up about 2 percent of the work force. Some of them were full-time salaried employees, but most of them worked only part-time,, drawing their main income from other productive activities.

In the era before the reform policies, peasants had little chance to move up the social ladder because of restrictions created by national policy. However, as the reforms deepened, individual initiative came to play a more important role in social mobility. Such factors as basic intelligence, ability, and knowledge played an important role in social mobility among the peasantry. In this period, those who were able to respond quickly to changing situations and were willing to take risks in the market economy began to move into a variety of fields. For example, Li Encheng gave this explanation of his own success:

> You must have an acute mind and be quick on the uptake. Also you should have a positive attitude and be able to handle pressure. Have the courage to think and act. Don't be timid. Because we are all equal and we have done nothing wrong. . . . It won't work to just stay at home and not see the world. After working for a few years, you can feel the difference. You can learn how to do business through practice.

Education also became a route for upward social mobility. In this period, college graduates were still considered "God's favored ones," and attending college was seen as an honor. The college entrance examination system had been restored in the late 1970s, but enrolment was still small, and so intellectuals were still scarce. At that time, the government assigned jobs to college graduates, so admission to college not only guaranteed a secure job but also represented a path of escape from the village and entry into the larger society. Thus, many children studied hard to get into a college and left the countryside.

At this time, under the policy known as "shifting from agricultural to non-agricultural employment" some Lengshuigou residents who were working outside the village and their dependents were able to change their household registrations from rural to urban. In the village, a small number of villagers were civil servants, logistics workers, managerial personnel in state-owned enterprises and institutions, professionals, and personnel working at jobs that were designated as difficult or dangerous. These people and their relatives were permitted to change their household registration status from rural resident to urban resident. Since there were still sharp distinctions between the cities and the countryside, this policy offered a small group of people opportunities for upward social mobility.

During this period, individual characteristics came to have a greater influence on social mobility. People came to have high expectations about the possibility of changing their status and, as a consequence, worked harder to achieve their goals. Many villagers expressed their appreciation of the reform policies. For example, Li Encheng said:

> Although personal success relies on personal efforts, a good social environment is also necessary. Without the Reform and Opening Up Policy, personal efforts would have been in vain. These people are wealthy because they are able to make the best of their talents since the Reform and Opening Up Policy.

In conclusion, during the early reform period, Lengshuigou began to step out of an enclosed and rigid social structure and step onto an open and dynamic new stage. Differentiation based on occupation became clear. There were new channels for social mobility, leading to a virtuous cycle. However, it is undeniable that some institutional factors (such as the household registration system, the employment system, the personnel system, and the social security system) left from the era of the planned economy are still obstacles to social mobility, leading to the coexistence of the new and old institutions.

New Changes since the Early Twenty-First Century

On entering the twenty-first century, social development in Lengshuigou advanced to a new stage in which occupational differentiation expanded further, and new interest groups appeared. There was an increase in the number of private entrepreneurs, and they now form an independent social stratum. We can also identify changes in other rural strata.

Occupational Differentiation

Agricultural laborers: This stratum includes rural workers who are engaged in agricultural labor on land contracted from the collective. In present-day Lengshuigou, about half of the village population belongs to this stratum (our survey showed 56.6 percent). Middle-aged women and older men do most of the agricultural work. Younger men are reluctant to enter this field and even those who are temporarily without employment usually find something else to do. People in this stratum are older, with a lower level of literacy, and their earnings from agriculture are only sufficient to make ends meet. On the whole, they are old-fashioned, conservative, and inflexible, regarding cultivating land as the appropriate occupation for those born in the countryside. Among the 302 agricultural laborers that we surveyed, 188 (63.3 percent) said that although income was low, cultivating land guaranteed survival. This is a group that has been unable to keep up with the changes of the market economy and the group that most strongly complains about the loss of cultivatable land. The majority of these people have a certain feeling of nostalgia for the collective activities of the planned economy. They would much prefer to rely on a system rather than the market. In daily life, they mainly work in the fields and look after family members (the elderly and children). Agriculture provides their major source of income.

Rural workers: This stratum includes those who are engaged in non-agricultural labor in township and village rural enterprises. They are workers who are formally employed by the units for which they work and, in the case of collectively owned enterprises, share certain rights with regard to the ownership of the means of production and the management of their factory. From the 1990s, the number of people in this stratum greatly increased. In 2010, there were some five hundred people in this category, most of whom are employed by privately owned firms in the industrial park located on Kaiyuan Road. Compared with hired laborers, rural workers have a comparatively steady income and regular working hours.

Hired laborers: This stratum includes those who are working for private enterprises or individual businessmen and earning salaries. They can choose where to work and can move from job to job with a comparative degree of freedom. Despite the fact that the hired laborers do the same or similar jobs as urban workers, they are not regarded as regular workers. There are two categories among hired laborers: most are in a group described as having "left the farm but not the village"; the second—and smaller group—includes those who have "left the farm and left the village." The construction of the industrial park and reconstruction in the village opened up many opportunities in the building trades, transportation, and service industries. This led to a high demand for hired labor, but the individuals employed in this way do not have the same security as regular factory workers. Companies hire people when they need them and let them go when the job is done. So there is no guarantee, either to the employer or to the employee.

Rural intellectuals: This stratum includes those who have skills and are engaged in education, science and technology, medical care, arts, and other intellectual occupations. In the past, people belonging to this stratum were teachers in local schools and doctors and technicians in factories. Although teachers still make up the majority of this stratum, the proportion of technicians is on the rise. In recent years, innovation has become a key factor in industry; a great number of technicians are needed in construction and interior design in factories and other enterprises. In an effort to encourage people with these skills to come to the village, the village committee has worked together with village residents to help them find housing. Individuals in this stratum have influenced the lifestyle and thinking modes of local villagers. However, within the household registration system, most of them are classified as "non-agricultural households"; they have come to the village temporarily to carry out specific tasks and have little contact with local people.

Independent laborers and independent small businesses: The number of people in this stratum has increased significantly since the 1990s. Many of the people whose houses front on the main street—Baicai Road—have renovated their houses and opened small businesses, including butcher shops, small miscellaneous-goods shops, a barbershop, auto repair shop, a workshop fluffing cotton padding, and so on. The sides of the road are crowded with trucks and carts waiting to deliver cargo. On the eastern edge of the town, there are many restaurants on both sides of the road. To ordinary villagers, people in this stratum are smart and open-minded, have a high income, and lead a high-quality life. They belong to the wealthy stratum of the village.

Private entrepreneurs: With development of the market economy, the construction of industrial parks, and infrastructure-building activities in the village, a number of private enterprises have sprung up in these fields, leading to the formation of a stratum of private entrepreneurs. In the village, they are the most economically powerful, with personal holdings exceeding a million dollars. Most of those in this stratum left agricultural production in the early stage of the reforms and began to engage in businesses of various kinds. Some were formerly rural workers who shifted to work in business. In a word, this is a new stratum.

Rural enterprise managers: Rural factory directors, managers, accountants, directors in major offices, and salespersons all belong to this stratum. They have management and decision power in enterprises. However, the number of people in this stratum has decreased in recent years. The main cause of the decline has been the poor performance of many collective enterprises. Many of the village-run factories were ordered to shut down or to transform their activities, and people who held management positions lost their jobs.

Rural administrators: This stratum includes the members of the village committee and village Party committee and village team leaders. They are organizers and managers of village affairs. Our survey showed that 88.5 percent of them think that important decisions about the village are made under the influence of the village committee. When the village committee and other cadres were mentioned in interviews, villagers expressed their admiration for them and their work. This is a stratum that has wealth, power, and reputation.

Social Mobility

Although ascribed factors still influence social mobility in the village in the twenty-first century, their impact has weakened. As a result of urbanization and penetration of the market economy, social and economic structures have been transformed, and society is increasingly open. We can see this illustrated in table 4.2, which measures cross-generational mobility. The table shows that the immobility rate among peasants and part-peasant part-businessmen is quite high (56.6 percent for those who are peasants and 38.2 percent for those who are part-time farmers, part-time engaged in other business). The people in these categories can be seen as inheriting their status from their family. When we look at the table, we can see, for example, that among those whose fathers were peasants, 30.6 percent in the children's generation are half-peasant half-worker, 7.3 percent are enterprise employees, and 2.9 percent are personnel in science, education, and other such undertakings (table 4.2).

Further analysis can be made about the mobility within generations of villagers in Lengshuigou by looking at changes from the first job to the present job. Generally, mobility within generations is small compared to that between generations. Our survey shows that there is very strong stability lasting from the first job to the present job (table 4.3). Of those whose former occupation was farm work, 81.8 percent are now still in the same line of work. Similarly, 68.1 percent, 60.9 percent, and 62.5 percent of people who previously were half-worker half-peasant, employees of rural enterprises, and personnel in science, education, and other social undertakings, respectively, have not changed their careers. However, compared with traditional society and the collective era, mobility within generations has gone through some obvious changes.

Overall we can see that compared with earlier eras, social mobility in rural areas is more diverse, and the routes to upward mobility are more open. We can summarize the situation as follows.

First, there are more public and private schools with increasingly comprehensive specialties drawing students from a wider area. Social mobility based on education has rapidly increased. According to incomplete statistics, during the nine years from 2000 to 2009, forty-one Lengshuigou residents were admitted to colleges and universities.

Second, the market has come to play an increasingly important role in social mobility in Lengshuigou. After the initiation of the reforms, many villagers seized opportunities presented by the market economy and moved up the social ladder. Many of them have successfully moved from being peasants to operating as independent craftsmen or entrepreneurs of small businesses. In making this transition, personal effort and skills have played a major role.

In sum, the social structure of Lengshuigou can be described as what Chinese scholars refer to as onion shaped. We use this term to describe a Chinese society that was originally pyramid shaped, with a few at the top and many at the bottom. An onion-shaped social structure is one in which the largest part of the population is in the lower middle section, with a small minority at the very bottom, a larger middle group than in the pyramid, and clear hierarchical tendencies at the top.

Table 4.2. Intergenerational mobility, Lengshuigou, 2010

Father's occupation	*Peasant*	*Half-worker half-peasant*	*Employee of rural enterprises*	*Personnel in science, education, and other social undertakings*	*Total*
Current occupation					
Peasant	56.6	51.3	66.7	68.8	56.6
Half-worker half-peasant	30.6	38.2	12.5	0.0	29.8
Employee of rural enterprises	7.3	6.6	12.5	6.3	7.4
Personnel in science, education, and other social undertakings	2.9	3.9	0.0	12.5	3.2
Total	100.0	100.0	100.0	100.0	100.0

Note: N=530
Source: Shandong University Survey, 2010.

Table 4.3. Occupational mobility, Lengshuigou, 2010

The first occupation	*Peasant*	*Half-worker half-peasant*	*Employee of rural enterprises*	*Personnel in science, education, and other social undertakings*	*Total*
Current occupation					
Peasant	81.8	27.7	26.1	31.3	56.6
Half-worker half-peasant	14.0	68.1	4.3	6.3	29.9
Employee of rural enterprises	1.4	3.0	60.9	.0	7.4
Personnel in science, education, and other social undertakings	1.4	0.6	0.0	62.5	3.0
Total	100.0	100.0	100.0	100.0	100.0

Note: N=530
Source: Shandong University Survey, 2010.

CHANGES IN SOCIAL LIFE

Material culture is an important reflection of social and economic development. The ordinary events of our daily lives—what we wear, what we eat, how far we travel from home, how we find marriage partners, whether we have leisure time and, if so, how we spend it—provide important clues to understanding the most fundamental changes that have transformed individual lives. In this section, we will examine such changes in daily life as food, clothing, housing, and transportation as a window to broader social changes over the last century.

Traditional Rural Life

Before 1949, most residents of Lengshuigou made their living in a self-sufficient economy that was commonly described by the formula "men farm and women weave." Life was quite simple, with most activities centered within the village. There were few who were really wealthy but also very few who could not make ends meet. Cultivating the land was the major occupation and was regarded as the proper line of work. Although women spun and wove to make clothes for their families, this did not develop—as it did in other regions of rural North China—into a handicraft industry producing for the market. Families with surplus labor might send some of their members to work as seasonal laborers. During the busy agricultural season, men could hire themselves out as seasonal laborers, seeking work at the labor market in front of the Guandi temple of Yangjiatun. Depending on the season, there would be from twenty to eighty men a day who were willing to hire out. Wages for seasonal labor included food and payment in cash—on average 0.5 *yuan* per day in 1939. Even those who wanted to work more were rarely able to work more than a total of four months a year (KC 1955, 152–53).

During this period, rural people pursued practical results. Although they lived in a small closed society close to their neighbors, most people were inclined to mind their own business. Although people participated in the normal social interactions, most people tried to confine their lives to the realm of their own households. This produced what we might call a "small peasant enclosed lifestyle."

In the early twentieth-century, as we have seen, Lengshuigou was a village where the majority of the villagers were landholding peasants. In the face of military unrest and the Japanese invasion, Lengshuigou chose to seek protection by closing in on itself. The combination of domestic and foreign threats left villagers with the feeling that they were treading on thin ice, fearing that war would come to the door. Women were particularly endangered and to protect themselves, they put their hair up and wore dark and baggy clothes when they were working in the fields so that their gender could not be identified from a distance. The men usually wore unlined long gowns through all seasons and stripped to the waist in summers. Some men had only one or two sets of clothes, but men who came from wealthier families paid more attention to their clothing. For example, the village head seldom wore shorts in front of other people and would always wear a decent long gown if he planned to travel. When villagers met acquaintances on the village streets, they usually nodded in greeting but would not acknowledge those from outside the village. Philip Huang, in his book comparing North China villages, suggested that the degree of insularity varied from one stratum to another within a given village (Huang 1985, 222). The village head and others with economic power and social status had much wider social networks, and it was quite common for them to visit Jinan.

Agricultural techniques at the time were relatively backward, and the grain harvest was just enough for families to pay the rent and leave enough for family consumption. Most villagers mainly ate millet and steamed cornbread; only a small group of wealthier villagers ate the rice that grew in village paddy fields. However, this living standard was much higher than that of nearby villages. There were some poorer households, and it was not uncommon among them to gather leaves and edible wild herbs to supplement the grain. Steamed buns, dumplings, and noodles made from wheat flour, vegetables, and meat were special treats even for the comparatively wealthy families who only ate such items during the lunar New Year and on other festive occasions. Most families used peanut oil for cooking, exchanging grain for peanut oil in the town.

In the 1940s, there was a large-scale famine in neighboring Henan province and some female refugees came to Lengshuigou. These women, who were referred to as "Henan wives," would stay with whomever gave them food to eat. This influx of refugee women temporarily solved the problem of poor men in Lengshuigou who had not been able to marry because of poverty. However, when the famine was over, most of the "Henan wives" went back to their hometowns. Only two stayed in Lengshuigou; in both cases, they had given birth to babies.

Housing in Lengshuigou before 1949 was quite different from what we see at present. Most households had only three rooms connected in a row, a simple yard, and rough walls and a gate. The costs of housing together with the preference for the extended family meant that most households included three generations, who were crowded together in the three rooms. Generally, the center room (*tangwu*) was the biggest and was the room to receive guests; sometimes a wing room was attached to the *tangwu*, referred to as the

Photo 4.1. Old adobe houses built before 1949

"inner room" (*lijian*), where the parents lived. The room to the west was called the "small western room" (*xiaoxiwu*) and was used to store grains or as the residence for the parents. The room to the east was called the "small hall" (*xiaotangwu*) and was for storage and also the place were the children lived. The kitchen was outdoors, next to the gate; the toilet was on the opposite side of the courtyard.

Houses were constructed of adobe, that is, unbaked brick. The bricks were made by mixing clay and wheat straw together and then using a mallet to tamp it into a wood frame. The bricks were then dried in the sun. Because at that time, paper, which was used to cover the windows, was rare and expensive, village houses usually had small windows with two mobile panels that could be opened or closed. Roofs were thatched with a thick layer of wheat straw or sorghum stalks, giving the houses the name "straw house." In later years, people began to use tiles for the roof, which were better-looking and also provided greater protection from rain and snow. A tiled roof was described as looking like fish scales.

Before 1949, there were no teahouses or public squares for entertainment in the village, so after supper, people just gathered in the streets to chat, exchange gossip, and talk about their farm work. Lengshuigou villagers were reluctant to communicate with the outside world; this was in part a reaction to the social chaos of the time, but also reflected attitudes that were common in Chinese rural society. Having said that, since Lengshuigou was near the provincial capital of Jinan, it was more politically advanced than more remote rural areas. The village began to change as it went through the process of land reform, which brought in new forms of association, broke down the traditional reserve of the peasants, and gave them entry into an expanded social world.

Overall, we can see that all forms of economic and social capital were in short supply. Although social capital was in relatively short supply, its relatively equal distribution meant that conflicts were rare. Traditional ideas made villagers very conservative, with little interest in anything other than the concerns of daily life. In this period, the pace of life was slow, and villagers were highly homogeneous, leading a very simple life.

Changes in the Life of Villagers between 1949 and the Reforms

In the early years after the founding of the PRC, although poor peasants acquired more land, there was little improvement in living conditions. During the 1950s, the socialization of commerce and industry converted previously privately owned factories and businesses into state-run concerns. Productivity in many of the factories was low, and articles for daily use were in short supply. Grain was also in short supply, and villagers—worried about having enough to eat—stockpiled grain, thus aggravating the situation. Without cash income, they could not purchase manufactured goods. At that time, the movement to set up mutual-aid teams had started. Villagers came to see that the land tax was a heavy burden, and the more land a family had, the more they had to pay, and so eventually people realized that it was better to join the cooperatives than to try to go it alone. Villagers began to turn their land over to the cooperatives and joined in collective production. Mutual-aid teams were set up in the spring of 1952, and over time more villagers joined.

One of the most striking changes in this period was the incorporation of women into various social movements. Up until this time, most women had been unable to go to school. In the early 1950s, the village organized literacy classes, and both young and middle-aged women enthusiastically joined. It was quite common when night fell to see children and women setting off to attend literacy classes, or to study groups or meetings, leaving the men at home drinking tea and smoking with a few friends or relatives.

After the launching of the Great Leap Forward and the establishment of people's communes, the higher level cooperatives were merged into big communes, and peasants devoted more of their time and energy to collective life.

Villagers lived together, ate from the commune canteen, and enjoyed a supply system based on egalitarian principles. The collective life in this "socialistic family" gave villagers an unprecedented sense of belonging. This collective life was of high social value in helping establish new social connections and adjusting social relations of all kinds.

During the initial stage of the People's Commune, there was not much fluctuation in agricultural output. Villagers continued to eat a diet of steamed bread made from maize flour (*wotou*) and rice gruel. The grain was accompanied by salted vegetables, which were usually made by each household. Since the vegetables distributed by the commune were in short supply, families began to grow them in the small gardens in front of and behind their houses. Most of the vegetables grown on collective land were sold to commune canteens or to other units, and only occasionally did villagers receive small allowances of vegetables from the collective. While food was rationed in the city, in the countryside, ration coupons were not necessary since grain was distributed to each household based on the number and ages of family members. Following the end of the Great Leap Forward, rural society was again reorganized, and the village became a production brigade of the commune. One of the big questions was how to distribute the product of collective work. At first, a decision was made to use a "360 *jin* standard for each family, whether or not it was enough." Under this standard each household received at least 360 *jin*; if the household had not expended sufficient labor to earn this much grain, they had to use work points and cash to make up the difference. The standard at the time said that shares were divided on the basis of a calculation where 70 percent of a household's grain allowance was based on the number of members of the household and 30 percent on how much they had contributed in work.[8] In calculating how to distribute grain, the brigade first deducted the amount it was required to turn over to the state and then distributed the remainder among the village households according to this standard. When there was not enough food, leaves of poplars and the Chinese scholar tree together with some edible wild herbs were eaten.

A woman with the surname Yang (fifty-two years old, a housewife; her husband is a migrant worker):

Q: What if there was not enough grain?

A: When there was not enough grain, we ate edible wild herbs, which the children gathered on their way home after school.

Q: What were the principal foods?

A: Wheat, rice, sometimes sweet potatoes. Only at Spring Festival and other holidays could we eat *baozi* (steamed stuffed bun) and *momo* (wheat flour bun).

The stuffing of *baozi* was usually made of vegetables, such as cabbages, carrots, and wild herbs.

Q: What were snacks for children?

A: Children did not have many snacks. In winter there was hawthorn fruit, and in summer they ate popsicles.

Q: How much did they cost?

A: Three cents (*fen*). Back then money was worth more.

Commune members earned work points instead of wages during the period of collective production. In Lengshuigou, men earned ten points for a day's work, and women seven to nine points. The difference in work points for women was supposed to be based on how strong a women was, but the decision was made on how strong a women looked, not on her actual work capacity. Work points were deducted for being late, although the system did make some allowances for housework and child care. The committee of the production team decided on the rules for recording work points. In addition to work points, team members got allowances of firewood, which was distributed according to the number of people in a family. If a family needed to purchase kerosene and firewood, they needed both a "kerosene certificate" and money, and there were limits on how much each household could buy. Production teams had two ways of calculating work. Members earned work points for collective physical labor, such as cultivating fields, packing straw bags, and making tiles. Those who had special skills and were assigned special tasks, like driving a car or making wine, earned both work points and some cash income, depending on the amount of skill required.

Ideological movements had a great impact on life: propaganda promoted a "radical communist spirit," egalitarianism, and everyone sharing equally. Agriculture production suffered, and this, of course, affected daily life. Under the pressure of campaigns accompanying the Great Leap Forward and the exaggeration and boasting about production that accompanied it, households were encouraged to donate their pots and pans and other iron products to the campaign for producing iron and steel. This led to even greater shortages of daily necessities. During the radical communist phase of the Great Leap Forward, everyone ate in canteens and during the first year, people were led to believe that communism was just around the corner. People were urged to eat as much as they wanted: as a result, the grain that would normally have been set aside as seed was consumed, leaving the village short of seed for the spring planting. This was followed by the three years of natural disasters. Lengshuigou had always had relatively high grain output, and in comparison with nearby villages, it suffered less from the great famine. Only three people died of starvation. Following the three years of natural disasters, the government adjusted policy, and villagers were able to return to normal agricultural production.

At the national level at this time, rural communities all over China were urged to study the example of a model commune in Shanxi province called Dazhai. Lengshuigou began to copy the Dazhai model, reorganizing the original nineteen production teams into twenty-one. The standard for distribution of output was also changed from "30 percent according to household population and 70 percent according to labor" to "70 percent according to household population and 30 percent according to labor." Even with this change, however, some widows still could not support themselves, not to mention that most of them had to help raise grandchildren.

Under the planned economy there were constant shortages of daily necessities ranging from grains, oil, meat, and cloth to cigarettes and soap, and ration coupons were needed to purchase these items. People who lived through that era said: "At that time, people were either short of money or coupons. Whenever we had both money and coupons, we would rush to make purchases."

Before 1949, peasants planted cotton, spun the yarn, and wove cloth for family use. After 1949, they began to purchase yarn for weaving or to purchase cloth. Clothes not only protected the body from cold, they also had social significance, symbolizing social status and age. Young single women preferred colorful cloth, while married women tended to choose darker colors. With the exception of students, men in the village usually wore dark clothes, while students wore shirts, "Mao jackets,"[9] and pants. Villagers wore clothes made of a variety of materials including homespun, machine-manufactured cotton cloth, and synthetic cloth, and the most common colors were black, blue, and floral patterns (red, green, and purple flowers). People went to the cooperative store to buy cloth and make clothes. Cloth purchases required both cash and ration coupons, which were distributed by the village according to the number of people in a household. Each person received coupons for 6 *zhang* (3.3 meters) a year. A grandmother surnamed Li remembered:

> At that time whoever planned to get married had to borrow ration coupons from relatives and neighbors. Some families saved coupons in advance for years for the marriage of their daughter. If it was still not enough they had to borrow or exchange grain coupons for cloth coupons.

The most popular style for men was the Mao suit, which men in ordinary families saved for formal occasions. In spring and autumn, men wore long jackets and in winter, just a cotton-padded jacket with nothing under it. For formal occasions, women liked to wear jackets with a square collar, and for daily use, they wore simple jackets (photo 4.2). A headscarf, about one square

Photo 4.2. Two sisters in Lengshuigou, circa 1960s
Village materials

meter when unfolded, was usually worn as a neckerchief, but it could also be used to cover the head when there was a strong wind. The most popular colors for the scarves were deep blue, brown, and orange.

The price for cloth, mostly blue coarse cloth, was 0.3–0.4 *yuan* per foot (*chi*) if one purchased with a ration coupon; cotton cloth and Dacron drill cloth were the first choices. If one had no coupons for cloth, purchases could only be made—at double the price—if the cooperative store still had cloth in stock. However, in most years it was impossible to purchase cloth without coupons.

During the Cultural Revolution, villagers were expected to participate in political activities and struggle sessions in addition to their regular work assignments. Broadcast stations were set up in the village and speakers were installed in every household. During the Culture Revolution, propaganda campaigns attacked the "four olds" (old customs, culture, habits, ideas) and called for replacing them with "four news." Red Guard groups were organized to support the struggle, and the brigade committee was replaced with a revolutionary committee. Most young people in Lengshuigou joined the Red Guards, and wearing a red armband on the left arm soon became fashionable. We might say that during the Cultural Revolution, ordinary peasants were changed into part-time politicians. This was especially true among the young, who exchanged their old habit of working in the fields or learning a trade for a new habit of political activism, which focused on pasting posters on walls and participating in political struggles.

During this period, villagers traveled mostly on foot. People dreamed of owning a bicycle, but it was difficult to buy one. To buy a bicycle you not only had to have money and a ration ticket, you also had to use social connections to get to the head of the line to make the purchase. Bicycles cost 200 *yuan*, which was a significant sum for a rural family. Bicycle owners were happy to show off their purchases, and some young women demanded a bicycle as a betrothal gift. The most popular bicycle brands were *Feige* ("Flying Pigeon," manufactured in Tianjin) and *Fenghuang* ("Phoenix," manufactured in Shanghai). Another status symbol in the village was the old-style treadle sewing machine. Some wealthy families owned machines, which were status symbols much like the automobile is today.

Electricity had the greatest impact on peasants' social life. The village was first linked to electricity lines in 1956, but it was only in the 1970s that villagers began to replace old-style kerosene lamps with electric lights. School children were very happy with the change since it made it easier to study at home at night. The collective era also brought changes in housing. After 1949, the collective owned all the land in the village, and peasants no longer had to purchase land to build housing. Villagers strove to acquire more land for housing, pursuing the dreams of housing that were common in traditional society. During this period, the average courtyard now had five rooms. As peasants became better off, the government found it necessary to limit the expansion of the area of land devoted to housing, with each household allotted a 150-square-meter lot. Fees were charged for land taken over for housing, with the household paying three *yuan* a year for what was formerly nonfarmland, and six *yuan* for former farmland. New housing was often built in the traditional quadrangle style of North China, with buildings on three sides of the courtyard.

Before the 1970s, there were more adobe houses than brick houses. Doors were usually wood: while some wealthy families would carve patterns on the door, the majority were just wood panels. In this age of material shortages, glass was a luxury, so average villagers just stuck newspaper to window frames to keep the wind out. In 1978, the village invested funds to set up a system of running water, and from that time on, villagers had access to clean running water.

In a word, after 1949 and especially during the collective period, there were great changes in life compared to traditional rural society. Politics came to play a central role in life, and people's lives were strongly incorporated into collective units. Although there was significant improvement in living standards, the influence of leftist thought had created a system with low levels of production efficiency. People were still living at a subsistence level with shortages of daily necessities.

New Changes in Social Life after the Reform and Opening Up Policy

Rural reforms in the late 1970s and early 1980s greatly changed rural areas, opening a new phase in village life. The introduction of the household responsibility system created new incentives for work, and peasants responded enthusiastically. Work points no longer determined income; rather, under the new policy, once the household had turned over to the collective the amount of output stipulated under the contract, everything else belonged to the family.

The first years after the launching of the reforms were a transitional phase from the planned economy to the market economy. The transition triggered the growth of a commodity economy in rural areas, leading to a decline in the number of people engaged exclusively in agriculture. Many villagers chose to do business or breed animals, and some workers chose to look for work outside the village. Although the gap between rural and urban life styles was narrowing, there were still significant differences.

One of the big changes came with the advent of television in the 1970s. At first, only two households owned black-and-white TV sets, and every evening, villagers, including some from neighboring villages, crowded into those two households to watch TV. Marriage customs became more elaborate, and when young people married, there were new material standards for essential purchases. In the early reform period, the common standard was expressed in the phrase "three running items and one carrying item," which referred to a bicycle (*Fenghuang*, *Yongjiu*, or *Feige* brand), a sewing machine (*Hudie* or *Mifeng* brand, both from Shanghai), a watch (*Meihua* or *Beijing* brand), and a portable radio (*Haiyan* brand made in Shanghai). Villagers with a monthly salary of little more than ten *yuan* had to save for years to buy these items, every one of which was worth hundreds of *yuan*. Even with ration tickets, they had to wait in line. One can still find some of these items in Lengshuigou households as a kind of nostalgic reminder of those times.

In the 1980s, radios and cameras made their appearance, and young people began to pursue fashion. For example, hair fashions began to change. Fashionable young women went to beauty shops in Jinan to get a permanent in the popular "curled bang" style. Men's hairstyles also changed from closely cropped hair to the more popular slicked-back hairstyle, usually matched with sunglasses. Bell-bottom trousers were another mark of fashion for the young. An ideal date might consist of a meal in a downtown restaurant and later a walk in the park. Due to the popularization of TV, people watched soap operas and listened to radio, picking up tips on the latest fashion trends. Not only did the TV improve villagers' sense of fashion, it also drew people away from chats at street corners after meals and children from their games of *Qiaobang*.[10]

In this transitional period, villagers were greatly influenced by various outside factors, including state policy, changing levels of technology, and especially advancement in the media for cultural transmission and transportation, which exerted a huge impact on reorganization of regional groups. Comic books affected children, radios and TVs affected adults, and radio broadcasts enriched the cultural life in rural areas. Improvements in means of transportation increased communication between the villages and cities, and accelerated the urbanization and modernization of Lengshuigou. Before 1978, there were no asphalt or gravel roads in Lengshuigou, only dirt paths that were very dusty on sunny days and muddy on rainy days. Heavy rain could bring transportation to a halt. In 1978, the people's commune provided materials, and the production brigades provided laborers and land for a joint effort to build Baixin Road (currently known as Baicai Road). The road ran through Lengshuigou and connected to Gongye North Road in the east and the west. Between 1983 and 1985, the village invested another 250,000 *yuan* to improve transportation conditions by tarring 70 percent of the roads in the village. However, due to a lack of auxiliary facilities, drainage sewers were not included, and as a result, on rainy days water flooded the streets. With the exception of the central street, there was no regular cleaning of *hutong* and by-lanes, and as a result they were dusty on sunny days and muddy on rainy days.

As the village moved into the 1990s, the social atmosphere became more open, and people came to hold more diverse attitudes and opinions. Villagers came to value both material and spiritual comforts. With development of the market economy, villagers were increasingly inclined to purchase clothes and food instead of producing them, including items such as rice, flour, vegetables, fruit, and even salted vegetables. When inviting someone to have a meal, people tended to eat in nice restaurants since this was seen as classy and elegant. With the development of cement roads in the village, transportation became more diversified. Cars came to replace traveling on foot and by bicycle. Later, the electric bicycle became a household necessity, and some wealthy families started to purchase private cars. Going into Jinan city was no longer a big deal; about 40 percent of the young people worked in Jinan. They went to work in the morning and came home in the evening, and very few villagers considered this to be a long-distance trip.

Attire also became more diversified. There was a great proliferation in materials, colors, and styles, and style differences between rural and urban women narrowed. Colorful styles were popular with both, and fashionable rural women traveled by car downtown to shop for clothes. Middle-aged women still dressed in dark colors and purchased fewer clothes than the young. There were also improvements in male attire. Young men owned both suits and casual clothes, and jeans were necessary; middle-aged and elder men preferred leisurewear and Chinese Mao suits, mostly in dark colors.

In the 1990s, political factors played little role in daily life, while economic factors became increasingly important. Urbanization and internationalization had a growing impact on villagers' lives, and there was little difference between the modern lifestyles of urban and rural dwellers. This was true not only in the case of fashion, but also housing. An increasing number of villagers built new houses using reinforced concrete, and decorating standards reflected modern standards.

In the 1990s, most villagers in Lengshuigou built brick houses, but only four families built two-story houses. House patterns were comparatively simple, overlaying one floor on the other. Color TVs, refrigerators, and washing machines entered Lengshuigou households in the latter half of the 1980s. In the 1990s, per-household consumption of electric appliances had risen. A survey showed that 7.96 percent of families owned color TVs, 2.09 percent owned refrigerators, 19.58 percent owned washing machines, 36.36 percent owned tape recorders, and 83.92 percent electric fans. Furniture had also become more elaborate, and most families had clothes closets, high and low cabinets, old-style square tables for eight people, writing desks, several old-style wooden beds (there were only a few Western-style beds with mattresses, and some beds were built with bricks), several sofas, chairs, and stools. In recent years, almost every household has added a computer, and interior decorations are almost the same as those in the cities. Two-story houses have become more common, and many of them have Western-style beds, refrigerators, and air-conditioners.

Photo 4.3. New family residences in the twenty-first century

Since the Reform and Opening Up Policy, entertainment has changed in both range and type. Villagers are no longer confined to the boundaries of the village and can enjoy the attractions of cities, other provinces, and even other nations through travel and the Internet. Nowadays, the young prefer the Web, computer games, extreme sports, and nightclubs, while the middle-aged prefer watching TV, and the elderly are enthusiastic players of poker and *majiang*. Elderly clubs and recreation centers where art performances are held, enriching villagers' lives, have been built.

Life has continued to change for Lengshuigou villagers in the twenty-first century. Income has increased, and people enjoy higher living standards. According to our survey, village households with an annual income of 10,000–19,000 *yuan* constituted the largest proportion of the population (table 4.4).

Rising economic levels have been accompanied by improvements in social life, so villagers have come to value material comforts and the freedom and diversity of spiritual life. Advancement in information-communication technology makes it possible to combine material and spiritual comfort; the most prominent expression of this is the popularity of the Internet; 49.6 percent of the surveyed villagers had one, or more than one, computer in their household. During interviews, some villagers reported that "it is very convenient to

Table 4.4. Annual household income (yuan), Lengshuigou, 2010

Income	*Frequency*	*(%)*
Under 5 thousand	24	4.5
5–9 thousand	31	5.7
10–19 thousand	150	27.8
20–29 thousand	140	25.9
30–39 thousand	105	19.4
40–49 thousand	35	6.5
50 thousand or more	47	8.7
Unclear	8	1.5
Total	540	100.0

Source: Shandong University Survey, 2010.

find information from the internet" and "family members don't have to fight for the television." Purchase of a computer has become essential for young people contemplating marriage, since it has become essential for everyday life. It is fashionable for the young to go online for news, chatting, watching movies, and writing blogs, while for the middle-aged, the major recreation is playing poker and watching TV.

Landline phones and cell phones are no longer considered luxuries, and people choose full-function cell phones so they can text, make calls, and go online to watch television programs. Washing machines, refrigerators, microwave ovens, electric baking pans, and electric rice cookers have become common items, and many families have installed air-conditioners. Transportation is diversified and modern. Besides bicycles and motorcycles, more and more families purchase electric bicycles, minivans, and cars. Our survey showed that about 10.2 percent of families have one, or more than one, minivan and 11.3 percent have one, or more than one, car.

Villagers are very pleased with changes in their after-work recreation but there is still a gap between recreation in cities and villages, and people hope that improvements will be made. Our survey on leisure activities showed that among 540 villagers surveyed, only 11.9 percent thought that they had a rich and colorful after-work recreational life, 26.9 percent thought the opposite, and only 2.2 percent had no recreation at all. From this, we can see that villagers in Lengshuigou are not fully satisfied with the current situation.

The development of industrial parks on village land has increased the village's collective income, and the money is being used to improve the living environment. Leisure squares, cultural activity centers, and other recreational places have been built to provide spaces for villagers to spend their spare time. In the "three months of winter," when villagers used to have a great deal of spare time, they did not have many recreational outlets. Now, with the improvement of living standards, villagers not only have free time in the real sense but also more interesting and diversified recreational options. Apart from customary activities such as watching TV, chatting with others, and playing chess or poker, villagers have begun to explore new interests and participate voluntarily in all kind of communal cultural and athletic activities. Surfing the Internet and traveling have also become a new style of relaxation. The new trend for traveling on holidays has been accepted as a form of cultural life. According to our survey, 27.6 percent of villagers had traveled at least once in the most recent year. Liu Chuncai, the Party secretary of Lengshuigou, gave the following account:

> The income the village receives from what are called "returned rates" [a kind of land rent payment] from the enterprises is distributed between ordinary villagers and the village, which on one hand strengthens villager collective economy and on the other hand pays for daily expenses of the village. Money spent to build public facilities, pay pensions, and NCMS (new rural cooperative medical system) subsidies all come from returned rates. For example, the leisure square built by the village in 2003 is funded by the returned rates. In the evening older women dance and have exercise on the square. Villagers go to work during the day and can take a walk on the square after work. It is a place for relaxation. We also built a cultural activity center and have held exhibitions of painting and calligraphy, allowing people of all ages to participate. Plus, the committee for the elderly and expenses for schools are all covered by the returned rates. Our village invested in building the primary school, with a cost of tens of thousands each year. The elderly over 70 can get a monthly subsidy, 5 yuan at first, then increased to 50 yuan with the development of the village collective economy. The guarantee for this subsidy is a steady income. As for NCMS, every villager pays 10 yuan in order to enjoy coverage up to a maximum of 20,000 RMB for major diseases. For two years the 10 yuan for every villager was paid by the village committee so villagers could save their own money. I consider the cooperative medical care a good thing. But if the village takes care of the fee every time, villagers will never have a sense of the costs of medical care. So during NPC and CPPCC we decided to let every villager pay 5 yuan and the village pay for the rest. If a person refuses to pay, then the village would decline his NCMS. Our aim with this measure was to arouse the sense of interest in medical care for every villager. In order to keep our environment tidy and clean, we hired a cleaning crew, whose salaries also come from the returned rates. It is also used to give economic support to poor households and newborns.

In a word, since the Reform and Opening Up Policy, social life has gone through a series of great changes. Improvements in material life and enrichment of spiritual life have given birth to a group of new-era villagers who know technology and value comforts in life. They stand between urban citizens and traditional peasants, and share the characteristics of contemporary life styles. They are different from traditional peasants in life style and much more open and fashionable.

If we look back over the three eras considered in this book, we see that Lengshuigou villagers have experienced great transformation. The major factors shaping the changes have been state policies, along with advances in science and technology. Where villagers once shared a simple and homogeneous cultural world, life is now much more diverse. Living standards have improved dramatically, and the modernization of communications and transportation has linked the village to the outside world. These transformations have shaped not only the material world but also the inner spiritual lives of individuals.

CHANGES IN THE SOCIAL STATUS OF RURAL WOMEN

In the last section of this chapter, we will focus on the changes in the social status of rural women. In the gender norms of late imperial and early twentieth-century Chinese society, women were subject to both the rules and limitations of the feudal order, as well as restrictions that came from a social order that stressed obedience to a patriarchal hierarchy, which was expressed in various forms. Women were expected to follow the directions of their fathers when young, their husbands after marriage, and their sons if they were widowed. Social norms called for women to be selfless, to obey the will of their mother-in-law, and to maintain chastity at all costs. Attitudes began to change slowly after the establishment of a new social and legal system after 1949. New attitudes were encoded in the Constitution of the People's Republic of China and the Marriage Law of the PRC; both documents stipulated that women and men are equals and that women enjoy the same rights as men. Women began to participate more actively in society, with slogans like "women hold up half the sky" designed to express both goals and practice.

In this section, we will look at the changes in women's status through the experiences of women in Lengshuigou. Let us begin with the experiences of one woman whose life spanned all three eras.

The focus of our case study is Ms. Xu. She was seventy-four years old at the time of our study and has four generations of descendants. Xu was born in the 1930s to a relatively well-off family; her father was the director of a factory. Her mother was from an eminent family and became a housewife after marriage. During the liberation war, her relatives all passed away. She was saved by a missionary hospital and then lived with her uncle and aunt in Yaoqiang. She once worked as a teacher of a literacy class and came to live in Lengshuigou after marriage.

The Subordinate Status of Women in Traditional Society

In traditional society, women were restricted within the household and treated as the personal property of the household. In the *Report on the Hunan Peasant Movement*, Mao Zedong noted that Chinese women were under the oppression of "political authority, lineage authority, religious authority and husbands' authority." Women had to act under the restrictions of traditional patriarch authority. For example, in Xu's case, she came from a good family, and her parents allowed her to learn to read and write but prohibited her from participating in any other social activities.

Q: Do you think that your parents were good to you?

A: My parents loved me very much and would not let me worry about anything. I just knew that there was a war, but I was not clear about the two sides at war.

Q: Did you feel anxious that you knew nothing about the situation outside?

A: No. I lived a happy life with nothing to worry about but to study and be pretty.

Before 1949, a woman's sphere of activities was restricted to the small courtyard of the household, and opportunities to participate in society were few. Thought and emotions were constructed within this narrow world and formed a "system of representation," which in turn shaped ideas and practices. A woman's status and identity were dependent on her family.

Elevation of Women's Status after 1949

The movement to liberate women in the early years of the PRC was not only the result of women's dissatisfaction with their status but also a result of the nation's effort to emancipate productive forces. Mobilizing state power, media, and laws, the state pressured women to transform themselves from being "persons within a family" to being "persons in society" and "citizens of the nation" (He 2008, 80). This movement brought about a fundamental change in the status of women, giving them the same rights as men in law, politics, and education.

When Xu lived in her uncle's household, she went to an old-style private school with her male cousins, an opportunity that was denied to her four female cousins. The fact that her cousins could not attend school was not just a reflection of their family's choices but also of the lack of educational resources in rural China in the 1950s. As for the "privilege" enjoyed by Xu, she explained:

> My uncle felt it was a shame to allow what I had already learned to be wasted, and he also did not want others to say that he did not treat me well. My uncle's family was a family of some standing in the village so a good reputation was very important.

Later, with the nation's increasing emphasis on female education, night classes were held, and Xu was invited to become a teacher for the literacy classes, which raised her status in the family. Xu was known to have very good calligraphy and was often asked to write couplets and letters for others. In the third year after Xu came to live in her uncle's household, land reform started, and her uncle was categorized as a landlord. However, due to the fact that his brother was a member of the underground Party and had progressive views, her uncle gave all the land to the poor and just ended up as a "small land lessor" with an assigned status of upper-middle peasant.

The promulgation of the Marriage Law of the PRC in 1950 initiated major changes: the act attacked the traditional marital system, abolishing arranged marriages, polygamy, and patriarchy. This new marriage system and the legal guarantees that it provided further elevated female social status, promoting equality between men and women, daughters-in-law and mothers-in-law, and establishing free choice of marriage partners. However, in rural areas of China, the system of arranged marriages had deep roots, and it was difficult to change villagers' long-held views in a short time.

When Xu was sixteen, matchmakers began to visit her family. Nevertheless, because of the education she had received, Xu was averse to the idea of an arranged marriage but dared not speak out at that time. To her surprise, her aunt declined all of the matchmakers' proposals.

> I had a salary from teaching literacy classes of 12 yuan a month. After turning over all the land, my uncle's family gradually became poor, so I was the breadwinner of the house. If I got married and left, then there would be no income for the family. Also, my aunt knew that I was unwilling to marry then, so she declined all the matchmakers.

From the above words, we can see that Xu was given some choice with regard to her own marriage. At the age of eighteen, she married Yang in H village and then moved to Lengshuigou. Within the traditional family, a daughter-in-law was expected to be filial to her mother-in-law and father-in-law. These traditional views clashed with the new egalitarian values expressed in the Marriage Law, and so it was natural for conflicts to occur when a conservative mother-in-law and a new-age daughter-in-law lived together. Xu's mother-in-law had many complaints and after living together for more than a year, conflicts increased. Eventually, Xu's mother-in-law realized that she could not influence her son and returned to her own home.

While women in traditional society engaged in housework, they had no cash income, leaving them no choice but to rely on their husband or their father for support. During the collective era, the household lost its importance as an economic unit. Women took part in collective labor as individuals instead of following their husbands and fathers. Hence, with the powerful intervention of the state, women gained new status through their participation in collective labor and political movements.

The elevation of female social status was made possible by support from the new political system, reorganization of society, and women's demands for emancipation. Changes in Xu's family and social status are an example of the general trends.

STRONG WOMEN DURING THE REFORM ERA AND THOSE WHO VOLUNTARILY GAVE UP THEIR RIGHTS

After the Reform and Opening Up Policy, a new female image of "strong women" emerged and gained social acceptance. However, not all women wanted to be "strong women"; some women longed to quit their jobs and be housewives, to be "a wife and a mother," raising children and caring for their husbands. Within the family, the relationship between mothers-in-law and daughters-in-law has gone through a process of slow but steady change. We can see this reflected in Xu's life:

> In the past I was badly bullied by my mother-in-law, and I hoped that one day when I became a mother-in-law, I could get rid of this situation. But the young nowadays are quite unlike what we used to be. Who can go against their will?

Women's status is determined by the authority and rights that they enjoy in a lineage and family. In Xu's family and her lineage, Xu was regarded as family head, and people in the lineage consulted her about many things. Even in the village, Xu's words had some influence, affecting some public decisions. Xu's daughters-in-law gradually grew used to her personality and authority. They reported that Xu was nice to them, and Xu believed they were satisfied with her as a mother-in-law.

As we can see in the Xu's case, a woman's status was increasingly determined by the social resources she could mobilize. Women with more social resources were able to control discourse and make decisions. Women have gradually come to see themselves as equals with men. However, any judgments about elevation or improvement of status are made in comparison with men, so they are relative and not absolute. When Xu reached old age, she transferred her power within the family to her sons and grandsons instead of to her daughters-in-law and granddaughters-in-law, the intention being to protect her own kin. Xu claims that her daughters-in-law and granddaughters-in-law agreed with this decision since they think that men should be dominant in the household. After "turning over the power," Xu switched her attention from the household to affairs in the village, at times taking part in some formal activities but mostly joining informal voluntary activities.

From this accounting of Xu's experiences, we can see that women's status changed with the trends of the times. In her life, we can clearly see the transition from the closed and conservative world of traditional society to the collective era's promotion of "women hold up half the sky" and to the new century where women enjoy higher levels of social participation and higher status in both the household and society.

NOTES

1. The standard used for classifying strata here is different from the standard that is usually used by Chinese scholars.
2. The classification took into account the total amount of land owned, but also how it was managed. Households that hired significant amounts of labor to assist with farm work were classified as *rich peasants*, those that lived off of the income from rent without working the land themselves were classified as *landlords*, even if their total land holdings were not so large.
3. For example, Zhang Xiufeng (male, born in 1923, enrolled in the Chinese People's Volunteers and fought in Korea in 1950 and died on the battlefield in 1951); Ren Yanji (male, born in 1928, enrolled in the Chinese People's Volunteers and fought in Korea in 1950 and died on the battlefield in 1952); Gao Yanlu (male, born in 1930, enrolled in the Chinese People's Volunteers and fought in Korea in 1951 and died on the battlefield in 1953); Xie Diandong (male, born in 1930, enrolled in the Chinese People's Volunteers and fought in Korea in 1950 and died on the battlefield in 1951); Ren Yancheng (male, born in 1931, enrolled in the Chinese People's Volunteers and fought in Korea in 1950 and died on the battlefield in 1952).
4. Li Xing, male, born in 1931, graduated from the Department of Physical Education of Shandong Normal University and became a middle school senior teacher.
5. Gao Changfu, male, born in 1934, graduated from the Shandong Accountant College. He was awarded a certificate as an Honored Expert Accountant from the Treasury Department for serving for over thirty years, Advanced Worker for the Capital Iron and Steel Company.
6. Xie Baoxi, male, born in 1930, graduated from the Shandong Agriculture College, and became a researcher in animal husbandry at the veterinary institute of the Shandong Academy of Agricultural Sciences
7. The authors use the Chinese term *nongmingong* for peasant workers. This Chinese term is often translated as "migrant workers," but in our case, it refers to

village members who are working in village-owned and nearby factories, so we have translated it as "peasant workers" rather than as "migrant workers."

8. At first, most production teams adopted the distribution method of "30% according to household population and 70% according to labor"; however, the disadvantages were that many families with fewer laborers got a very small portion of grains and exhausted all of the food in the middle of the year with no other choices but to eat edible wild herbs and leaves. So reforms were carried out to change the distribution method into "70% according to household population and 30% according to labor."

9. This style of jacket in Chinese is known as a "Zhongshan" jacket, taking its name from Sun Yatsen.

10. This was a game played by children and teenagers. Players used two sticks of four centimeters. One stick was held in the hand, and the other stick was used to hit; competitors tried to see who could make the stick fly farthest.

Chapter Five

Cultural Tradition and Folk Customs

Daily life in Lengshuigou moves to various rhythms, including the annual agricultural cycle of planting and harvesting, the cycle of annual rituals beginning with the lunar New Year, and the life-cycle rituals held by families and lineages that mark significant beginnings and endings in the lives of individual village residents. This chapter will look at changes in those rhythms and their meanings over the course of the twentieth and twenty-first centuries, examining the impact of the changing social environment, political movements, and rapid urbanization on what villagers see as "traditional" practices. We will begin our exploration with a consideration of ethical values and norms and then move on to look at specific rituals and practices.

CULTURAL TRADITION

Lengshuigou is located in the middle of Shandong province, a province that takes pride in its connections to the orthodox Chinese philosophical tradition. In ancient times, this part of Shandong belonged to the state of Lu, the state that was the home of Confucius and Mencius. Shandong people take pride in this heritage and believe that Confucian ethical values are the foundation of their shared collective consciousness. Those shared village values came under attack in various ways in the twentieth century—first as part of the modernist attack launched during the May Fourth movement beginning in 1919 and after 1949 during repeated attacks on old thought and old practices. We will follow the story into the twenty-first century and the efforts of the older generation to revive some of the earlier norms and practices.

The Role of Confucian Ethical Culture

Liang Shuming, the well-known twentieth-century philosopher who developed rural reconstruction programs in Shandong in the period before the Anti-Japanese War, argued that core values in Chinese society were based on the Confucian ethical tradition, rather than on the kind of religious institutions that shaped Western societies. In Liang's view, this ethical tradition fulfilled some of the functions that religion played in other societies, exercising a decisive influence on economic organization, political structures, and political activities. Within that ethical tradition "Chinese society has always valued age hierarchy, which is the first ethical principle" (Liang 1987, 113). Over the centuries, Confucian principles came to serve as the orthodox teaching that permeated all aspects of civil life. These values included ethical principles and practices that were commonly expressed in a series of formulaic phrases including "righteousness and loyalty," and "the three principles (ruler guides subject, father guides son, and husband guides wife) and five virtues (benevolence, righteousness, propriety, wisdom, and sincerity)." In the Confucian model of the ideal society, ethics and politics are isomorphic, and family and state are regarded as sharing a similar character: the family is a miniature model of the state, and the state is an expanded version of the family. The relationship between an individual and the state is a rational extension of the relationship between an individual and his family. In rural Chinese communities like Lengshuigou in the period before the twentieth century, this culture based on ethics provided the chief support for rural social order.

Rural order relied primarily on such ethical principles, which formed the fundamental base for rural society. Patriarchal ethics were presented as an integrated system that placed filial piety at the base, out of which grew love and respect for one's elder brother, and then loyalty. Internal ethical values were expressed in outward relations and attitudes. For each person, this created a circle of relationships starting with the individual and his blood-kin and expanding out to circles of increasingly distant relationships. Fei Xiaotong, whose work we have already encountered in earlier chapters, referred to this pattern as the "differential mode of association" (Fei 1992 [1948]). Fei described the system as follows: "Social relationships in China possess a self-centered quality. Like the ripples formed from a stone thrown into a lake, each circle spreading out from the center becomes more distant and at the same time more insignificant. With this pattern we are faced with the basic characteristic of Chinese social structure." Fei Xiaotong believed that the traditional humanistic theories best explained this differential mode of association. "To me, insofar as it is used to describe Chinese social relationships, the term itself signifies the ripple-like effect created from circles of relationships that spread out from the self, an effect that produces a pattern of discrete circles" (Fei 1992 [1948]). The link between ethical principles and the social order lay in their common stress on differentiation. Beginning with the individual, ethics prescribed distinctions between superior and inferior, and these distinctions placed restrictions on the individual's choice of actions. In Lengshuigou and other traditional rural villages, this mode of association was closely tied to a political order in which ritual played a central role. The differential mode of association and the moral order it created formed the social foundation of Confucian ethics, a foundation that was constantly reinvigorated through rituals and interpersonal interactions.

"The members of the lineage community recognized their common blood relationship as well as their relative status positions, forming a closely integrated unit" (Wang 1991, 23). Individuals determined their own status and appropriate roles in the village community on the basis of these principles, with different individuals playing different functional roles. If someone in the family exceeded the boundaries of his status and role, he would be criticized and might be disciplined according to the family rules. Within the family and lineage, the paternal patriarch held the highest status and the greatest authority.

Li Xingwei (age seventy-eight, born in a scholarly family, a retired teacher, one of the compilers of the *Lengshuigou Village Records*) recalled:

> Back then, domestic discipline was very strict. Younger members of the family were not allowed to sit in the middle of the central room but only in the corners. If a younger person sat in an elder's seat, he would be reprimanded. Nowadays the young no longer worry about these things. At home we were educated in this way, and when we were outside our home, we were also told to mind our manners and behave ourselves. At that time the male patriarch had absolute authority and everyone should obey. In 1947 when I was only 15 years old, my family decided my marriage. At that time it was very common for the bride to be older than the groom. The rationale for this was pretty simple and practical. When it came to helping out with labor and increasing the number of children, marrying an older woman was very good. Back then I knew nothing about rebellion and just got married.

Ethical norms legitimized the system of distinctions between superiors and inferiors. Superiors enjoyed greater rights and were able to enforce them vis-à-vis those who were in an inferior position. Those who were in an inferior position had more obligations to those who were their superiors, especially obligations to act in an obedient and submissive way, so they were at a disadvantage with regard to rights and power (Yan 2006, 207). Proper forms of ritual behavior, what Chinese refer to with the term *li*, were commonly accepted standards of behavior in Lengshuigou. These rules for behavior were readily accepted since they were not imposed from outside but rather matched the feelings of villagers. We can see how this worked by making a brief examination of an important ritual that was held in the village in 1940, a period marked by the Japanese occupation and the tumult of a raging war. In the early summer of 1940, there was a serious drought, and crops in the fields withered. On the sixth day of the sixth month of the lunar calendar, the village head and the village councilors decided to organize a ritual to pray for rain. Despite the war conditions, the organizers carefully followed established proscriptions, including taboos about the given and personal names of men who would be chosen to participate in the ceremony. Among those rules was a stipulation that, if possible, the man who was chosen to hold the water vessel in the ritual inviting the god to intervene should have a character in his name that included the rain radical; if that was not possible, then they should at all costs avoid including a man who had a character in his name that had the same pronunciation as *han*, the word for drought.

After successful completion of the prayers for rain, the village offered a Chinese opera performance in thanks. A stage was set up to the west of the village. Enclosed structures were constructed on the right and left of the stage for women, while the men could watch the play from the area in front of the stage. This practice was a reflection of the principle that it was "improper for men and women to touch each other's hand in passing objects."

During the whole ritual, from the procession out of the village to the final stage of collecting donations of grain and money, women were not only banned from participation but were also cautioned not to watch (LCZ 2010, 146–48). This gender-based hierarchical order was commonly followed in those times. "In ancient China, local rural culture played a huge role in laying down moral restrictions and behavior norms for rural residents and also provided fundamental conditions for rural order" (Hu 2008, 49).

This system of rural ethics based on the patriarchal lineage system was able to survive for so long because of its deep cultural roots and also because the agricultural production mode created a stable environment for generation after generation of Chinese peasants. This environment created the conditions in which families could grow and expand, forming larger lineages. The family ethics based on age and gender hierarchy were a cultural weapon in the hands of the family head in controlling the family and lineage, helping to ensure harmony in the family. However, this cultural system centered on lineage ethics produced a closed society, which reproduced existing patterns but at the same time blocked innovation.

These rural ethics and cultural traditions were the core of the unwritten regulations and agreements that were shared by the villagers and are also reflected in life rituals like marriages, funerals, and ceremonies honoring and offering sacrifices to the ancestors. These unwritten village regulations and agreements, together with prescribed ritual behavior, adjusted and managed relations between individuals, between individuals and society, and between man and nature. In the early decades of the twentieth century, Lengshuigou villagers gave most attention to their own place in the hierarchies and the roles they were obligated to play and had little consciousness of themselves as individuals with individual rights. We can see this ethical culture as a kind of "collective unconscious," which not only shaped ways of thinking and behavior but also promoted forms of mutual cooperation that helped the system to survive.

Political Influence after 1949

After 1949, dramatic changes in institutions and ideology led to a dismantling of traditional rural culture and its replacement by a new politically charged cultural assemblage. During the collective era, politics came to play the central role in this new culture, with political ideology replacing traditional ethics and occupying a dominant position in consciousness.

Changes in Folk Beliefs

Attacks on traditional customs started with the May Fourth movement in 1919 and intensified after the establishment of the PRC in 1949. Popular religious customs and beliefs came to be seen as the symbols of feudal superstition, the enemies of a more scientific and enlightened modern intellectual framework. Under the politicized ideology of the time, "superstitious" elements came under intense attack. The state mobilized its political and administrative power to launch campaigns to eliminate old customs and beliefs while reforming rural politics, economy, and society. Slogans at the time called for "smashing the old and establishing the new, and transforming tradition and customs."

The revolution used various methods including study and struggle campaigns to eliminate feudalism, capitalism, and revisionism and to mold the peasant population into new socialist men and women. For example, in the early stage of the Socialist Education Movement,[1] launched in 1963, rural residents were encouraged to enthusiastically study works by Mao Zedong. In the study sessions, stress was placed on "fighting selfishness and repudiating revisionism." The movement aimed to promote socialist transformation and at the same time create new behavioral codes appropriate for the "new socialist people."

However, although there was a desire "to smash" the old, this does not mean that "the old" elements were thoroughly eliminated, nor do efforts to force a "withdrawing" imply that such elements completely disappeared. Older beliefs continued to lie hidden in people's hearts and in some cases were transformed and attached themselves to newly promoted modern forms. For example, the worship of political idols in Lengshuigou can be seen as a new form of ancestor worship, which on the surface expressed support and loyalty toward the new politics but which in practice also embodied supernatural elements. By 1968—at the high point of the Cultural Revolution—the study of Mao's works had become totally dogmatized, and Mao Zedong turned into a god, an idol worshiped by villagers. Lengshuigou was enveloped in this revolutionary culture. One of our informants named Wu remembered those days. Wu, who was sixty-five when we interviewed him, had been a bricklayer, and at the time of the interview was acting as a storekeeper for a shop his son had set up. He clearly remembered the scenes of studying quotations from Chairman Mao: "Every team had an assembly place. I belonged to the fourth team and our assembly place was at the crossroads. Every morning men and women sat around Mao's picture chanting phrases." During our interviews, many of the older residents of the village showed us how they had acted in those days, expressing a kind of nostalgia for those times. Before going to collective work, everyone recited Mao quotes, and when it came time to rest in the fields they studied together the "three constantly read articles."[2] We might say that through the storms of the Cultural Revolution,

Photo 5.1. Commune members shouting "Long live Chairman Mao"

the "Leader Spirit" replaced the ancestral spirits once worshiped by Chinese rural residents. Thus, we can see that the traditional beliefs of peasants were transformed as a result of the political situation and strong political pressure from outside the rural community.

Remolding of Values

Social norms are the external manifestation of values. After 1949, the values of peasants in Lengshuigou were remolded. Peasants who were called on to join such movements, as "in agriculture learn from Dazhai," enthusiastically participated in collective activities. Through such movements, the collective was able to mobilize all the commune members, gathering both manpower and resources to carry out large-scale construction projects, including water conservancy projects that greatly improved agricultural infrastructure. When water conservancy projects had been organized in the past, they were usually led by local gentry in collaboration with local government officials and lacked the kind of unified planning that was possible under the socialist collectives. In 1975, during the campaign to learn from Dazhai, the Lengshuigou brigade sent brigade leaders to Dazhai in Jinyang County, Shanxi, to observe and learn from the experience in water conversancy there. The lessons learned were put into practice at home. The ability of the collective to mobilize labor and other resources made this kind of cross-brigade, cross-commune, and even cross-county project possible. And the ability to mobilize large numbers of people meant that the projects, in effect, benefited from free labor.

One of the results of the repeated mobilization for political movements was the weakening of the family's organization and functions as a unit for economic production. As we have already seen, this loss was compounded in the cultural sphere by the weakening of lineage consciousness and lineage authority. Land reform and collectivization turned villagers from members of a lineage into members of the collective. Mutual-aid groups and cooperatives cut across the boundaries of lineage and blood ties, and within the collective, household labor was replaced by joint labor. In the period of the people's commune, secular political power influenced every aspect of production and life in Lengshuigou, lineage relations based on kinship were further restricted, and lineage authority based on patriarchy was impaired. During the Cultural Revolution, leftist thought and action had a great impact on lineage culture.

The movement to destroy what were known as the "four olds"—old ideas, old customs, old culture, and old habits—included destruction of memorial tablets for the dead and genealogy books that recorded the generations of lineage members. In 1966, many graves were destroyed, and the bricks that had been used to build them were used to build stock barns and the brigade office. Within the village, class struggle split many families, with family members joining different factions. A new politicized style of speech came to encroach on the peasants' daily lives, dominating and guiding daily conversation.

Through these transformations villagers' sense of belonging also changed. They no longer thought of themselves as members of a lineage but rather as members of the collective that provided basic life guarantees and shelter for members. When we asked our informants how they identified themselves at that time, they gave us answers like, "I was in the first team," or "I was in the third team." These answers were much more common than "I belong to the Li lineage" or "the Ren lineage." Even today, we heard comments from our informants like, "We are not of the same team. People in their team are lazy." At present, some elders and middle-aged people whose lifetime was mostly spent in the collective period still use titles such as the "fourth team" and the "fifth team" to describe their identity and affiliation when they speak with people outside of the village.

Having said this, we can still identify elements of the older village culture that survived the efforts of the state to pressure people into following this kind of revolutionary culture. What we are going to call the "revolutionary culture stage" was most obvious in political and public life. Zhang Letian, author of *Farewell to Ideals*, about the transformation of a Zhejiang village, has argued that "in a certain sense one can see village culture and the revolutionary cultural stage as two distinct layers, occupying distinct positions" (Zhang 2005, 167). Even during the Cultural Revolution, villagers still held onto some older rituals, and despite all of the movements and struggles, clashes on a personal level were relatively rare.

Li Yanzhu (brigade accountant during the collective period):

> The people who became objects of struggle during the Cultural Revolution had actually not done anything bad. Sometimes people just found someone who married two wives to struggle against. Back then if you didn't participate, you were regarded as counter-revolutionary. So it was best just to blend in. People did not cut off all contact with those who were the objects of struggle; it was just that there were no other choices. So it was better to avoid them.

Despite outward appearances, peasants who in the past had a strong affiliation with their lineages did not suddenly turn into revolutionary "political men" with high levels of class consciousness. From 1949 to 1978, the Party strove through socialist education and repeated political movements to remold the peasant society, but they were not completely successful: traditional rural culture still exercised a certain degree of influence in peasants' daily lives and thoughts.

The Reform Policies and Diversification of Rural Culture

Following the Reform and Opening Up Policies, Chinese social structure was radically changed, with large-scale industrialization and urbanization transforming rural society. In analyzing the changes, we can identify several factors that have contributed to the growing diversity in rural culture. The changes began with the shift to non-agricultural employment, which meant that more villagers were working outside the village. This resulted not only in rising living standards but also in fundamental breaks with earlier lifestyles and consumption patterns, all of which contributed to a loosening of the bonds of earlier cultural norms. As we will see in what follows, rural culture became much more diversified, with new attitudes toward work, toward filial responsibilities, toward beauty, and much else. As part of the shift, the elder generations, who had long been the chief transmitters of cultural practices and norms, were gradually displaced as voices of authority, and younger generations increasingly took the lead.

Diversification of Rural Culture

Diversification of production: Earlier chapters have analyzed the changes in employment following the initiation of the reform policies. In contemporary Lengshuigou, the number of full-time farmers has greatly decreased and many villagers are employed in the secondary and tertiary sectors, including animal husbandry, manufacturing, and commerce. Although many villagers still have farmland, most of them regard farming as a supplement to their main source of income. Our survey of attitudes showed that while in the past many believed that farming was a peasant's obligation and moreover the only way to support a family, most now believe that if one works hard he or she can have a better life. Going out of the village to find a job and earn cash income is the best way to do this.

One of the new sources of income for Lengshuigou households is rental income. The development of industrial zones on village land has attracted a large population of migrant workers, and villagers can now make money by renting out rooms. When we visited the village during our survey work, we were often approached by middle-aged women asking if we wanted to rent a room. We saw many advertisements for rooms to rent pasted on telephone poles, and many people also posted announcements on the Internet. For example, one such announcement read:

> Licheng—Wangsheren—Wangsheren Town—residential area behind Lengshuigou village committee. 3 bedrooms and 1 sitting room (130 m^2). Price: 1,350 yuan per month. Convenient transportation. Furniture available. (The price is negotiable if furniture is not needed). It's all right to rent 2 rooms.

> Broadband, cable television, cooking utensils and solar water heater are available. Rent is negotiable after viewing the house.

Shops now line the Baicai Road, which runs through the middle of Lengshuigou. The shops include: barbershops, motorcycle repair shops, shoe stalls, butcher shops, and grocery stores. In addition to these shops that provide daily necessities for the residents, there are new businesses such as shops selling safe extension cords and shops specializing in flooring materials.

Grandpa Wu (sixty-five years of age, a bricklayer when young, now a storekeeper for his son):

> My son opened this shop with others. I have nothing to do at home so I come here to watch the shop for him. We opened this shop for some simple reasons: first, my son deals in flooring wood in the market so he knows about the market for flooring materials. So people think it is safe to buy goods from him. For peasants it's best to have this kind of assurance. Second, in recent years Lengshuigou developed fast, but there are few people selling flooring materials. We grabbed this opportunity. Indeed, there are not many customers in the village. Not because they don't have the money but because they worry that there are going to be forced demolitions of housing and it would be a pity to have to tear up a new floor shortly after installation. Though business is very slow, we can make some money when a deal is closed. In these years everyone should make money, young or old.

These glimpses of life in contemporary Lengshuigou reflect major changes in attitudes. Whether they are doing odd jobs in the market, raising cows, or renting out rooms, all represent adjustments to a market economy. With the deepening of the post-reform market economy, villagers have started to pay attention to economic interests. Older ideas that placed prime value on access to farmland and agricultural production have faded, and individuals now regard earning income as the priority. Nowadays, villagers make use of all the resources they can command, engaging in diversified forms of production. Their consciousness of commodities has strengthened, and their attitudes toward productive work are much more diverse than in the past.

These changes in economic activities have had an impact on ideas, shaking people's faith in traditional attitudes, including such earlier ideas that "it is safest to follow precedent" or that "justice is more important than profit" or that "men are superior to women." New ideas that fit better with the market economy—such as the benefits of competition and notions of equality between men and women—are increasingly common. Villagers have come to value the pursuit of economic interests. While the traditional moral view argued for the "value of justice over profit [material gains]," today's villagers are more likely to place higher value on "material gains." We can see these new ideas in some of the conflicts that have arisen over construction of new housing. For villagers, constructing new housing is one of the major events during a lifetime. Conflicts triggered by "money" have led people to repeatedly adjust their actions, pursuing the utmost benefit.

Wang (fifty years of age, a storekeeper):

> When people build new housing now, they don't behave the way they did in the past. Nowadays, only money matters. When people think about offering to help, they think they will suffer financial loss if they come to help you. Our house was built a decade ago, when things were better. Relatives would come to help, bringing food. We contracted the house out because there were no laborers in the family. At present even relatives and kin in the lineage would not lend a hand as they used to. They don't have the time. Generally we contract the house out or find workers in the market. Finding workers in the labor market saves money, and you can hire only the number of workers you need. If a relative comes to help, he should also be paid for the days he works. When our relatives built their house, we couldn't help because we had a day job. So we helped by giving them some money or things. People understand that relatives cannot help. One should not delay one's own work in order to help others. The biggest concern is the fear of running out of money. With plenty of money you don't have to ask anybody for anything, including help building a house.

Since 1949, equality between men and women has become a well-accepted principle. In contemporary society women's status has risen, and women participate in many aspects of production and life. For example, when we asked our informants, "What do you think of women's status compared with men," only 11.7 percent answered, "Not as high as men," while 77.8 percent answered, "Almost the same as men," and 9.3 percent answered, "Higher than men."

Deconstruction and reconstruction of the rural filial piety culture: For centuries, ideas and practices related to filial piety were at the center of Chinese rural society. The rapid development of the market economy, changing patterns of employment, and the changes in lifestyle that have followed are changing popular practices, including those related to the core value of filial piety. Interpersonal relations have become increasingly more distant, and the logic of rural ethics, which had grown out of the acquaintance society in which individuals dealt primarily with people they already knew, is being replaced by the logics appropriate to a market-based society. Villagers' lives play out in a new world in which greater value is placed on material gain than on justice, and utilitarian behavior is beginning to subvert older values. Influenced by values based on the market economy and imported Western ideas, people's minds have become more active, and there is a greater sense of individuality. These new values are in conflict with older rural values, creating great gaps in attitudes among villagers. Ideas about filial piety are a good example of the diversity of views.

In our survey of village values, we asked informants, "What form do you think is best for caring for the elderly?" Among the respondents, 69.1 percent chose "Children should provide care," while 20.3 percent said they would prefer to look after themselves, and 5.6 percent said they wanted to be cared for by the village committee, and 5.0 percent said they would prefer going into an old people's home. Although most respondents want their children to take care of them, the percentage desiring to get along without burdening their children is also quite high. In response to another question asking whether they agreed or disagreed with the folk saying that it was important to "bring up sons to support their parents in their old age," 34.6 percent of the informants said they "totally agree," 31.7 percent answered that they "agree," but 25.2 percent answered that they "don't agree." This suggests that while the concept of "bringing up sons to support their parents in their old age" still weighs heavily on people's minds, more people, especially the young, have had a change of heart. The older generation's understanding of ethics and morals is also changing.

Wu:

> Children are too busy to stay at home and look after us. It is important to make money. Without money, nothing can be done, not to mention taking care of the old and looking after the young. My two sons both married. We live with them by turns, for a year at a time. Usually we don't ask them for money, and they don't give us any. Sons and daughters-in-law work outside and don't care about farm work. We are responsible for the two *mu* of farming land. Nothing can be done about this. In these days one cannot survive without money. We are too old to do farm work. When it is time to harvest corn, we find three or four laborers in the market, costing us two or three hundred. We live together so we have to help our children. Besides, they don't have the time or energy for such things. Might as well do some work while we still are able.

Our survey showed that in some families, parents and children live separately, with the children giving their parents some money and grain monthly. The amount of money and/or grain depended on the family's circumstances. The Chinese take pride in their practice of filial piety, and being filial was an important part of rural ethics and the moral code. However, the impact of the market economy is deconstructing this long-held value. This deconstruction can be seen from both sides of the parent-child relationship. From the side of the children, we can identify a weakening in the idea that filial piety is obligatory. We can see this in the fact that for the younger generation, busy

Photo 5.2. Women carrying presents to celebrate a birth. Photo from the *Lengshuigu Village Gazetteer.*

with jobs and other activities, taking care of their parents' economic needs through gifts of money has increasingly become the main expression of filial piety. Older norms, which assumed the younger generation would live with their parents—providing emotional as well as economic support—are gradually disappearing. The sense of respect is gone when filial piety just means financial exchange and economic provision. Though monetary support is important in supporting the old, spiritual caring is without doubt the vital core of filial piety. Let us now look from the parents' side, where we can also identify a change in attitudes among the older generation. In Lengshuigou, the older generations' attitudes about the duties and obligations between parents and children are also changing. In the contemporary village, the older generation members often serve as assistants in domestic affairs, not only caring for themselves but also for their grandchildren. For some of the elderly, this new situation has led to a clash in roles. In traditional society, village regulations and agreements and moral pressure forced the younger generation to behave in a filial way. However, in contemporary society, there are no powerful restrictions forcing children to behave in a filial way, leaving some of the elderly in a difficult position. While they want their children to be filial, they have no choice but to accept contemporary practices.

Influences from urban culture: As China has prospered, villagers have begun to pursue modern lifestyles. Attracted by the cities with their shiny new urban culture, villagers have begun to create their own versions of modern life and consumption patterns, imitating elements of urban lifestyles.

In the countryside, as in the cities, when individuals decide to redecorate their homes, they have many choices. For example, when we called on one village household, we noticed an old-style table (square with fold-down leaves that could be raised to turn it into a round dining table) sitting in the middle of the main room. Next to it was a kind of curio shelf, with many different objects that seemed to have been randomly selected. The shelf is not actually useful. The elderly owner of the house told us his son had found the shelf for him. The son thought it was very fashionable and gave the room a modern look, while his father was not impressed and thought it was useless.

Apart from household decoration, people today pay more attention to their own appearance, wearing more colorful and fashionable clothes. As people's living standards have risen and they have more time to think about enhancing personal health and beauty, cosmetics have come into everyday use. In the past, the only personal-care products in the village were laundry soap, toilet soap, shampoo, and lotion, but now villagers use a wide variety of shampoos and skin-care products. When we visited the Xiongjin Cosmetic Store in Lengshuigou, we saw many skin-care products, including lotions, body wash, and items for hand and foot care.

Owner of Xiongjin Cosmetics Store (forty years of age):

> I opened up this store because I think now people have money and want to be good looking, so business should be good. Korean cosmetics sell well because young people nowadays admire South Korea. Mostly middle-age women in the 30s or 40s come to buy cosmetics. Some young people come but not too many since most of them shop in supermarkets. Village people nowadays are different from what they used to be and everyone wants to be pretty, having her hair done, her brow trimmed and wearing jewelry. These desires have been around for some time. Even men have begun to use skin-care products, mostly young men. The major problem of opening a store in the village is that cosmetic products don't sell very well. After all this is the countryside, and people are not very wealthy. Plus there is the influence of traditional ideas, which regard the purchase of these things as a waste of money, showing off, and not a decent business. Those who are financially well off go downtown to buy cosmetic products because they don't like to shop in small stores.

Villagers' changing attitudes toward cosmetics embody many of the changes between older and newer ideas. Some of this is a reflection of the relatively closed nature of the village in the past and the role of habitual elements in village life. Generally, a new lifestyle is not created spontaneously by villagers but is brought in from the outside by a small minority of the village community that has more contact with urban lifestyles.

Wang:

> I have been curling my hair for 4 or 5 years. Now this is nothing, but in the past it was a big deal. In the past when curly hair was not so common, people gossiped when I had my hair done. So for a while I just stopped. Afterward curling hair becomes a fashion and now everyone accepts it, so I have my hair done every year. Now the young and middle-aged can accept new things. Many young people encourage their parents to have nice clothes. The elderly are more conservative and think all this indecent.

When some of the better off and more open-minded young people first try new styles, most people in the village don't accept their practices. At first, these fashion leaders are mocked by others and often forced to give up the innovations as a result of social pressure. However, the emergence of new lifestyles is inevitable, and eventually many people enjoy the innovations. The initial rejection is usually due to the influence of old ideas. When the new lifestyles are repeatedly introduced, resistance weakens, and they come to be accepted by the majority of people.

Photo 5.3. Village shops in the twenty-first century

Through this start-and-stop process, urban lifestyles are slowly penetrating rural society. The slow-paced traditional rural culture that valued favors, blood relations, and traditional ritual behavior is constantly confronted by the new urban culture. There is a kind of symbiosis between the spread of new ideas coming from the market economy and the spread of new urban lifestyles, both of which have been pushed by an increasingly utilitarian outlook. Often it seems that villagers are permanently wandering between tradition and modernity, forced to play the role of "culturally marginalized" actors. However, villagers are not completely passive; they constantly adjust their roles, and there is cultural feedback.

Changes in Cultural Transmission Patterns

Lengshuiguo is undergoing a transformation in the way culture is transmitted from an older generation to a younger generation. The young, who once played less important roles in family affairs as well as in economic activities, now have a greater role. They respond rapidly and are leaders in their families in acquiring new knowledge, information, and technology. This reversal of positions has had an impact on traditional family ethics, leading to a diminishing of parental authority and a significant increase in the space for younger people to express their own views. Where once the older generation would have rejected their ideas, now they often listen and follow their advice.

In traditional society, it was assumed that the older generation played an important role in passing down village culture. However, with the rapid development of modern means of social communication, the older generation lacks the skills to play this role. In the place of guidance from older villagers, the younger generation creates new models based on their own experiences and those of their own age cohort who serve as peer models. We might call this transition "one from an elder-generation model to a peer-group model culture." In our survey, 80 percent of the respondents said that they think peer communication is more important than advice from the older generation with regard to social experience. We also found that the older generation relies on the younger generation with regard to scientific knowledge, modern ideas, entertainment, and consumption.[3] At first, this led to the transmission of scientific knowledge and new attitudes. The older generation in Lengshuigou farmed most of their lives, while younger villagers have followed very different occupational paths. Their work experience has brought them into contact with new knowledge and technology, which they share with the older generation. This has allowed the younger generation to assist the older generation in keeping up with a rapidly changing world. This includes information on leisure and consumption, which is one of the chief spheres in which the younger generation influences the older generation. In transmitting knowledge of brands, products, and costs, the younger generation is not only sharing information on consumption but also introducing new consumption patterns and new attitudes toward consumption.

As we can see from this, the knowledge and attitudes that the younger generation share with the older generation cover a very wide sphere and sometimes lead the younger generation to "lecture" their parents on what they ought to do. However, in most cases, the knowledge they share is of use to the older generation and also helps the older generation acquire the skills to deal with rapidly changing Chinese society.

The changes we have described so far are among the many transformations as a result of the shift to a market economy and the rapid industrialization and urbanization that have followed over the last several decades. Folk beliefs have changed or been transformed into new forms that better match contemporary society. One of the manifestations of these new ideas—less stress on filial piety, new family forms, new ways of interaction between generations—has been the loss of the authoritative voice of the older generation in transmitting and preserving older cultural values. Young people now pay more attention to the views of their peers than those of their elders and share their knowledge and skills with their parents. Although the influence of forces outside the village has strengthened, rural areas still move to a rhythm that follows its own logic, not in complete harmony with that of urban China. It seems, as the famous cultural anthropologist Marshall Sahlins has noted, that cultures disappear just as we were learning how to perceive them, and then reappear in ways we never imagined (Sahlins 1999, xxi).

FESTIVALS AND FOLK CUSTOMS

Lengshuigou is one of thousands of villages on the North China plains, and its festivals and folk customs are like those of many other villages, although thanks to its proximity to Jinan, customs have changed more quickly than in villages more distant from large cities. Before 1949, many of the village's festivals and customs embodied manifestations of deeply held ethical beliefs. After 1949, the village was immersed in political movements and struggles, and folk customs also became politicized. In the decades since the beginning of the reforms, new economic organizations and ideas have brought further change.

Traditional Festivals and Folk Customs

The French sociologist Émile Durkheim, in his classic work the *Elementary Forms of Religious Life*, discussed the place of customs or rituals that did not fall under the jurisdiction of any fixed religious group, commenting that they were the "jumbled survivals, the remnants of extinct religions," while other customs were formed "spontaneously under the influence of local causes" (Durkheim 2001 [1912], 34). Beliefs, which grow out of the everyday experiences of rural life, were over a long period of time transformed into festivals and customs. In this section, we will examine life-cycle rituals like weddings and funerals and annual celebrations to see how they have changed over the last one hundred years.

Festivals

Before 1949, all major village festivals followed the lunar calendar, and these annual cyclical events were among the high spots of the year for rural residents.[4] For Lengshuigou residents, as for most Chinese in the countryside as well as the city, celebration of the lunar New Year, now usually referred to in English as the Spring Festival, was the highlight of the annual cycle of festivals. Cheng Qiang, a researcher on popular literature and customs at the Chinese Academy of Social Sciences, has argued that the lunar New Year celebration can be seen as serving three different functions. "First, it satisfies the material and spiritual demands of individuals; second it harmonizes and strengthens the relations between people; and third it represents the relationship between man and heaven, that is between man and the supernatural world of spirits and ghosts" (Cheng 2006, 33). So we can say that the customs associated with the lunar New Year embody villagers' beliefs as well as deeper social and cultural meanings.

First, one major activity of the New Year celebration was preparing a variety of foods. Starting from the twenty-third day of the twelfth lunar month, people were busy slaughtering chickens and pigs and making bean curd and steamed buns. A second major activity was to clean the house in preparation for welcoming the New Year: this included cleaning inside and outside the house, cleaning the toilet, and repairing the paper on windows. Men got haircuts, and women washed their feet, got rid of the fine hair on their faces, and made new clothes. In those days, most rural people were quite poor and had few material possessions so the New Year presented an opportunity to acquire new things. Many people also bathed before the New Year, physically cleaning the body but also symbolically cleaning the soul.

Second, the New Year was an opportunity for social interaction to reinforce social relations by visiting relatives and friends. Visits reinforced the kinds of relationships that Fei Xiaotong described as characteristic of the differential mode of association. Visiting at the New Year was an important way for villagers to maintain and reinforce their relationships with others, both within their families and with those outside the family or lineage. On the first day of the lunar year, villagers paid New Year calls on relatives and neighbors, a sign that not only kin but also local place relations were important. In general, men went out earlier in the day to make New Year calls, and they also normally visited more individuals than did women. If there were new brides in the lineage, they usually received money as a New Year gift from members of the senior generation when they went to visit, a sign of the importance of marriage in rural society.

When calling on relatives, visitors were expected to bring gifts, usually food. The choice of gifts was based on what the visitor thought the host would like. Generally, the hosts would first decline the gifts while the guests insisted, so the two sides would negotiate for a long time. The hosts would then give the visitors a return gift, leading to another round of negotiation. This exchange of gifts and the initial denials that accompanied the process were well understood by all as an important ritual form in which each side expressed its respect for the other side.

Apart from the above functions, the lunar New Year celebration met people's desire for cultural and religious beliefs. New Year's Eve marked an important dividing line, seeing out the old year, and welcoming the New Year, but it also was seen as a mysterious transition with spiritual ramifications. The rituals on this day were carried out with a degree of solemnity: auspicious phrases written in nice handwriting on strips of red paper were pasted on the entrance gates and special festive lanterns were brought out. The family's *jiatang*, a scroll that listed the names of paternal ancestors, was hung, and sacrifices were made to the ancestral tablets. The spirits of the ancestors were welcomed back to spend the holidays with the living, families gathered with their neighbors in the early evening to light bonfires, and a long stick was put up to guard the gate. Family members gathered to share a feast, staying up all night talking. New Year's gifts were handed out to children. Villagers set off firecrackers, which were supposed to scare off evil spirits, and villagers also sent off the kitchen god on his return to heaven, an event referred to as "dispatching the horse (*famazi*)." Villagers believed in multiple gods, such as the Jade Emperor (*Tianyeye*), the Buddha, and the Gods of the Gates. During the New Year holidays, the villagers made offerings to a number of gods who were believed to protect the household. They offered incense and made ceremonial bows (*koutou*), worshiping heaven and earth, the ancestors, and various gods. They burned paper money at the gate, in front of the millstone, and in front of carts. They paid respects to the scroll depicting the generations of family ancestors and laid out the genealogy expressing their beliefs through these rituals.

The first day of the lunar year marks a new beginning. People put on new clothes and visit each other with great joy. Younger people paid New Year calls to seniors, bowing three times in the hall, calling out to the residents using kinship or fictive kin terms. They also paid New Year calls to elders in the lineage and to neighbors, making a bow with hands folded in front and offering auspicious greetings. In the next few days, people called on relatives and friends. The fifth day of the lunar year was traditionally called "breaking five" (*powu*), when people set off firecrackers and ate dumplings. On the evening of the sixth day, people "sent off" the spirits of the deceased ancestors who had come to visit with the family over the holidays; this ritual marked the end of the New Year celebrations.

The next major festival in the year was the Lantern Festival held on the fifteenth day of the year, when villagers prayed at the village temple to Guanyin (the Goddess of Mercy), viewed the colorful lanterns, enjoyed Chinese opera performances, and ate sweet dumplings. In those days, every village had a dragon-lantern team whose members paraded through the village streets accompanied by a deafening sound of gongs and drums. Villagers set off firecrackers when the dragon-lantern team passed their gate, and some people would bow down to *koutou*; members of the dragon-lantern team then also bowed. Some villagers engaged in other pastimes such as walking on stilts and joining a folk dance in which women danced while swinging a decorated paper boat back and forth.

Next on the annual festival calendar was the Spring Dragon Festival, which fell on the second day of the second month of the lunar calendar, at the time when peasants were getting ready for spring planting. This was followed by the Double Third Day, on the third day of the third lunar month, when people went to a local fair; the Tomb-Sweeping Day in the fourth lunar month; and the Dragon Boat Festival in the fifth lunar month, when people put up wormwood and ate glutinous rice balls known as *zongzi*. In the second half of the year, holidays included the Mid-Autumn Festival, which fell on the fifteenth of the eight month and was marked by family visits and the eating of moon cakes, and the Double Ninth Festival on the ninth day of the ninth lunar month, when people climbed mountains and admired chrysanthemum blossoms. All of these traditional festivals were celebrated according to dates on the lunar calendar, which had a close association with the natural rotation of agriculture work, heaven and earth, and the seasons. Over the centuries, these festivals had also come to be closely associated with various historical events, social customs, folklore explanations, and traditional religion. Traditional festivals expressed the close and harmonious links between human activities and the natural world, as well as providing a set of cyclical events that provided a rhythm for village life.

The majority of the festivals celebrated in Lengshuigou were similar to those of other North China villages with only minor differences based on local tradition. In an agricultural society where success in the harvest depended on weather, villagers had a great respect for nature, which was reflected in many of the practices that propitiated nature spirits. A traditional village was like a peaceful lake, with ways of production and life remaining stable for a fairly long time. Within that peaceful world, the annual cycle of festivals and practices associated with them was passed down from generation to generation of villagers.

Marital Customs

Fei Xiaotong once remarked that "as for our marriage, there is the matchmaker who connects us, there are ancestors who watch over us, and there are gods and ghosts who are witnesses. So in this way a marriage, which is intended to set up a personal relationship, is transformed into a bustling social event. A secular event, which is based on something very close to biological instinct, is transformed into a holy event connected with heaven. We have to admire the efforts exerted by the parents" (Fei 1999 [1947], 79). Marriages in Lengshuigou are not only bustling social events but also the embodiment of traditional culture.

There is a traditional saying that in earlier times, marriage partners were decided by the will of the parents and the words of the matchmaker. The union of two people was a social event featuring the family. To ensure the continuity of a lineage, stable families were necessary, and in order to assure stability in the family, people in the past used various methods, including fortune-telling, to try to assure that a proposed match was in line with the "will of Heaven." People believed that if the signs were right, the marriage would endure and produce a stable family. Once a match was proposed, the matchmakers would exchange detailed data on the birthdates of the man and woman so that they could consult with astrology experts to see if the two were regarded as a good match. If the results of the consultation were acceptable, the next step was a formal proposal of marriage from the man's family to the woman's family. If the woman's family agreed, then an engagement ceremony could be held.

In traditional society, marriage was a major event in the lineage, with great attention from everyone and many complex rituals. A fortune-teller would be asked to choose an auspicious date for the marital rituals, and then the man would present betrothal presents to the woman's family and receive her dowry. On the day of the marriage ceremony, the man would go to the woman's home to escort her to the wedding. On the way to the bride's home, a young boy would ride in the bridal sedan chair, and six other young boys accompanied the groom. Musicians accompanied the party, playing on trumpets and beating on gongs and drums. The bride was dressed in wedding finery, and two women of her family led her to the bridal chair. Once she was seated in the chair, a basin of water was splashed on the ground: this was a sign that "a married daughter was like spilled water," that is, she could not return to her former status in the family. When the sedan arrived at the groom's house, firecrackers were set off to greet the bride. On entering the gate, the bride stepped over a basin in which a fire was burning, a horse saddle, and a vase with three flowers or pine branches, all good luck symbols signifying a prosperous and safe life and a rise of three levels in social rank. The formal wedding ceremony took place in the groom's home, with the young couple performing a formal *koutou*, kneeling down three times and bowing their heads to the ground a total of nine times. After this, the bride entered the bridal chamber where she was expected to spend the whole day sitting on the bed without eating or drinking. In the evening, many people would come to *naodongfang*, which involved teasing the bride and the bridegroom.

The day after the wedding, the bride's family would send noodles called *Taitoumian* (raising the face noodles). At noon, the groom's family ate the food sent by the bride's family, and then after eating the noon meal, the bride and groom called on the bride's family. On noon of the third day, the groom came to escort the bride back to his family, and the young couple paid their respects to all the relatives and friends. On the sixth day, in a ritual known as *liutui*, the bride's family escorted their daughter home for another visit, and at noon, the groom visited the bride's family and shared a meal; the new couple returned to the groom's home later in the day. On the ninth day, the bride's family would again welcome her home, and on the eleventh, day the father of the bride would send her back. With this, the two families were truly united. On the eighteenth day, the bride would again visit her natal home, and on the day of a full month, the mother of the bride would send her back. After a whole month, the wedding ceremony was finally complete.

In those days, it was quite common for the bride to be several years older than the groom. One elderly villager, who had married at the age of fourteen or fifteen recalled:

> Back then boys got married at 14 or 15, and their wives were older than them by 2 or 3 years. In this way wives could help with work in the house. When I was married, I was too young to know what marriage involved, and I only came to truly understand what was involved when I reached 18 or 19.

Marriages in earlier times were not the result of love but of the need to continue a lineage. Families wanted to have many children. Worried about whether they would be able to secure a wife for their sons, parents tried to arrange marriages for their sons at an early age. Taking the lineage's interest into consideration, having a daughter-in-law as early as possible would guarantee the continuity of the family line and in addition add on extra labor to help with household tasks. Although a girl was raised by her parents, most of her productive work took place after marriage in her husband's household. It was because of this imbalance that the groom's family was expected to give a substantial betrothal gift to the bride's family. Weddings—especially the betrothal gifts—were expensive, and as a result, many poor families were not able to find brides for their sons.

As we can see from the above description, marriage customs were very complicated, and as Fei Xiaotong argued, parents devoted a great deal of effort to seeing that they were completed satisfactorily. The various rituals of a wedding ceremony were spread over a month-long period and involved not only the bride and groom but also all of their relatives. Through the marriage rites, the two families were able to extend their social networks. Such elaborate rituals were believed to be a guarantee of the stability of the marriage and harmony in the new family.

Funeral Customs

An individual's journey in this world was marked by a series of rituals that marked the journey from birth to death, from the world of the living to the world of the dead. Funerals were like the crowning ceremony in an individual life. The funeral can be seen to have embodied efforts to cope with sorrow for the loss of a relative as well as the ordinary individual's fear of death and what lay beyond. Chinese funereal rituals incorporated elements from multiple religious traditions: filial piety from Confucianism, ideas about reincarnation from Buddhism, as well as Daoist views on the meaning of life. At the same, time funeral rites incorporated important expressions of the lineage, joining together the living generations with those who were dead, reflecting the ideas of consanguinity and local place ties we have discussed in earlier sections of this book. We can see in the funeral ceremony a concentration of many of the elements of traditional Chinese culture, a ritual that provides an outward representation of ideas of hierarchy and the relations between the living and the dead.

People commonly believed that death marked the entrance into life in another world; to prepare for that new life, the body had to be cleaned and dressed in grave clothes and the mourners had to prepare the material goods that the deceased needed for life in the next world. Material possessions were replicated in paper models: clothes, gold ingot bars, horses and cattle, and so on. Special grave clothes were prepared; the grave clothes avoided the use of silk, since the pronunciation of the word for silk in Chinese is similar "to die without descendants." In the imagination of the living, the journey to the other world is long and dark, with hyenas emerging in the wilderness. To ensure safe passage to the other world, the deceased carried food known as "dog cake" to ward off the hyenas. An eternal fire was placed near the head of the deceased to light the road, and food was placed near the head for the deceased to eat along the way. Mourners burned paper money and incense and offered food in the morning, at noon, and in the evening for the dead. Fearing that the deceased might lose the way, a filial son burned paper at the crossroads of village streets to serve as a guide. Since the deceased would live in the coffin in the netherworld, it should be well made so the deceased would be able to live comfortably. Filial children would spare nothing in preparing a coffin of fine wood for a dead parent. Dedication to these tasks was strengthened by the belief that the spirits of the dead had the power to protect their descendants. The funeral was seen as a farewell ceremony for the dead individual, who was in the process of transition to the other world. Just as the living offered advice when they parted from friends going on a long journey, survivors offered many exhortations to the deceased, tidied up his or her clothes, checked to be certain that supplies and money for the trip were sufficient, and helped arrange living spaces in the next world. All of these acts embodied the family's compassion. The living, relying on their imagination about the other world, prayed that the deceased would be treated well in the netherworld and that the deceased would offer supernatural protection to his or her descendants.

Photo 5.4. Old graves in Lengshuigou

Photo 5.5. New graves in Lengshuigou

The climax of this cultural ritual is the funeral procession on the third day after death. In old times the body was kept in the house for two days, and ceremonies leading to burial began on noon of the third day. Generally the placing in the coffin began at 10 a.m. The chief mourner, who was usually the eldest son, bowed four times before the deceased. Male descendants lined up outside the house while female members of the family remained inside, crying in mourning. The funeral procession began after guests paid their respects to the deceased. First, homage should be paid in front of the coffin, and then people lifted up the coffin while the bereaved son smashed a bowl or a pot and cried. As the procession proceeded through the village to the burial site, villagers consoled the bereaved son. When the procession arrived at the burial site, the coffin was buried. Favorite possessions of the deceased were placed in the tomb along with an eternal fire. After burial, the bereaved son was expected to *koutou* to express his gratitude to those who helped in the funeral. The next morning, the son would visit the grave and "open the door" for the deceased. Three days later, the son would add some soil to the tomb, which was called "completing the tomb." Although some of the complex rituals may seem to have little function—and in some cases villagers cannot explain why they do certain things—taken as a whole, they represent social practices that had developed over a long period of time and that had come to form village traditions that were passed down from generation to generation.

The funeral ritual is a way of expressing respect for the life of the deceased, and all of the ceremonies—the numerous *koutou*, the ritual expressions of homage, the ritual crying in mourning, the carrying of a photo of the deceased, the banners, and the spirit tablets—are parts of rituals designed to show that death is not just a physical phenomenon but also a cultural phenomenon. While some of the rituals may have been developed to ward off fears of death, they have also become expressions of culture. Buddhist ideas of reincarnation provide comfort with their promises that death is not the end of life, but a turning point. The Daoist view assures us that aging and passing away are natural processes, helping people achieve an attitude of peaceful acceptance toward the death of elders, so peaceful that they even refer to funerals as "the happy funeral." We can also see the influence of traditional Chinese ghost culture on the funeral ceremony. The funeral reflects humanity's ideas about life and death, about respect for the ancestors, and about the final journey that every human must make.

Folk Customs in the Republican Period

Although the new policies in the Republican period had some influence on ordinary people's lives, production, and lifestyles, the patterns of cultural transmission in rural areas were left largely unchanged. Festivals and folk customs continued to follow earlier patterns, although we cannot say that there was no influence from foreign cultural imports.

For example, beginning in the late nineteenth century, enlightened members of the elite began to promote female education and to argue for the banning of foot binding. After the 1911 revolution, the new government urged men to cut their queues—a hairstyle that had been imposed at the beginning of the Qing dynasty as a sign of submission to the Manchu rulers—and women to stop binding their feet (Qiao 1998, 554). By the 1930s, the custom of foot binding had basically disappeared in Lengshuigou. A villager (female, over fifty) told us, "Foot-binding disappeared a long time ago. Old women over 80 in the village all have natural feet." Under the influence of new ideas and a new political regime, other festivals and folk customs also began to change. Thus, it does not seem strange that foot binding, a custom that had lasted for a thousand years, disappeared within a very short time.

Western missionaries began to work in Shandong during the late Qing dynasty, and some Lengshuigou villagers became Christians; the village Christians included both Protestants and Catholics. At the end of the nineteenth century, rural Shandong had been a center for the Boxer movement, which expressed its opposition to Western religions, raising the banner of "supporting the Qing Dynasty and wiping out the foreigners." The Boxer movement drew on many local cultural traditions including martial arts, Chinese opera, and fortune-telling. At that time, practicing martial arts was popular in the village.

> Before the founding of the PRC in the Fall after the harvest, young people used to hold wrestling contests (which they called Ba Gu Lu). Men, including Zhang Fuyong from Xiao Lengshuigou, and Wang Chunxiang and Yang Qingyun from Lengshuigou practiced Qi Jie Bian, which was a kind of martial art using broadswords and spears. Zhang Fuyong was an accomplished practitioner, and many people applauded his performances. Wang Chunxiang's broadsword and Yang Qingyun's spear were praised not only in Lengshuigou but also in other villages. (HNA n.d., 81)

Practice of martial arts not only strengthened the body but also could be used to resist foreign invasion. The connection between martial arts for protection of one's family with broader national political discourses led to their rising popularity.

In addition, "since the foundation of the republic, the government spared no efforts in enlightening people, abolishing sacrifices and destroying idols" (Zhang 1982, 746). The Republican government tried to use its administrative power to promote reforms and wipe out old customs that it believed were backward. For example, the old practice of kneeling and *koutou* during the Spring Festival was replaced with the bow. A villager (female, over seventy) told us:

> We stopped the *koutou* decades ago, before the founding of the PRC. Now people just bow. People who live to the north of the Yellow river still *koutou*, but not in this village.

Since the beginning of the twentieth century, traditional customs have gradually declined, and many rituals have been simplified. However, these changes came slowly, and many traditional cultural elements persisted. This was especially true of the activities carried out by households that played a central role in village life. Without strong pressure from some external source, these customs experienced only very slow change. For example, according to the Japanese *Kankō Chōsa* survey in the 1940s, villagers said that when parents passed away, they could not have a haircut within a month and should wear white clothes, hats, and shoes until the end of funeral. The color white, which was used in China as a sign of mourning, signified returning parents' kindness. During mourning, people could wear black, gray, and blue clothes but not red or purple ones. Hats could be white or black. Those who were mourning could not drink or smoke at banquets and one could not pay New Year's calls, set off firecrackers, or put up Spring Festival couplets. If a family wanted to hang scrolls, they had to be written on blue paper with white or black ink (KC 1955, 87). These kinds of customs had endured for a long time, becoming a part of common people's basic understanding of life, and as we might imagine, such basic ideas of what was proper behavior only changed very slowly.

Festivals and Folk Customs after 1949

After 1949, powerful political influences reached rural areas and triggered great changes in rural customs and habits. Festivals and folk customs became one of the targets of political campaigns and movements. The pressure was particularly strong during the Cultural Revolution when the practice of many traditional folk customs came to a complete halt, and the whole nation followed the new rituals of "politics in command."

With the founding of the PRC in 1949, Chinese society entered an era of rapid change as land reform and new collective institutions transformed village social organization. Although festivals and folk customs had a long history, the social transformations undercut the base that had supported traditional cultural practices. As the party and local institutions embarked on campaigns to promote new socialist thought, campaigns were carried out to abolish customs that were labeled as feudal and to transform established traditions and practices. For example, an elderly informant who had been a Red Guard during the Cultural Revolution told us about his wedding ceremony:

> My wedding ceremony was quite simple and held by the Xiang government. My wife and I fell in love when free love was quite rare. We got married during the tenth lunar month. On our wedding day we did our regular work during the day and got married at night. There were no cash gifts. We invited members of the team to have a home-cooked meal and some wine and that was it.

If we compare this Cultural Revolution–era wedding with the complicated rituals we described earlier, we can see that the matchmakers, the betrothal gifts, and most of the other ceremonies were eliminated. Funeral customs met a similar fate. In 1958, the government ruled that elaborate funerals should not be held, and so funeral customs that had survived since ancient times were replaced by simple ceremonies. Some years later, the state ordered people to move from burial of bodies to cremation, which brought even greater changes to funeral customs.

Under the socialist system, holidays and customs began to take on new forms, most of which had political meanings. The state set up a series of new festivals based on the Gregorian calendar and made them important holidays, such as the Women's Day (March 8), Labor Day (May 1), Children's Day

(June 1), the CCP Founding Day (July 1), and National Day (October 1). Unlike the traditional rural holidays that had provided the rhythm for rural life, these new holidays represented an attempt by state political power to eliminate traditional rural customs and replace them with holidays that reflected a new socialist spirit.

These efforts to introduce new attitudes and a new spirit were reflected in many forms: some came as the result of organized efforts to introduce new practices, including popular cultural activities reflecting revolutionary values. These new cultural activities were designed to replace earlier rural entertainments like Chinese opera. In Lengshuigou, such popular cultural activities thrived, as we can see from the following account from *Materials on Lengshuigou Culture and Sports Development*:

> Recreational activities in the early years of the PRC were organized by village primary school teachers and young students who returned to the village during Spring Festival. . . . These kinds of recreational activities reached a peak between 1956 and 1958. Xie Sanbao was the director of the club. Following the instructions of Xing Jinliang from the county Cultural Center, we performed several Huangmei operas[5] including "Couple View of Lights," "Collection Grass for Piggy" and musicals "Ten Sisters" and "Ten Women's Praise of Their Husbands." . . . From 1964 to 1968 (from the eve of the "The Socialist Education Movement," through the movement to "eliminate the four olds" and the Cultural Revolution), we preformed Lu-style operas,[6] like "All Are Willing," "The Bride," "By the Side of Jiangan River," "Two Yuan and Six Jiao," and a musical "The Old Couple Learning Quotes from Mao Zedong." Leaders of the *pian* sub-divisions in the village organized young people in each team to learn revolutionary songs. Cultural atmosphere in the village was good, and performances won awards in the county. (HNA n.d., 57–60)

Encouraged by the state, people were organized to rehearse all sorts of revolutionary shows and hold mass recreational activities reflecting the slogans of the time, and these came to represent the spirit of a generation. As a result of participation in such activities, people's beliefs and lifestyle were changed, and many acquired new beliefs as well as a sense of belonging to collective units. One of the distinct features of this era was the unification of efforts at political mobilization, with mass beliefs coming together to form a new political culture and creating many new politicized customs.

In the period of the leftist Cultural Revolution, people all over the country were surrounded by chaotic political struggles. "Collective unconsciousness" led to a kind of mass craziness, characterized by inflated beliefs and mistaken policies that impacted a cultural heritage that had formed over many hundreds of years. Under the slogans of "elimination of the four olds," "remove superstition" and "take class struggle as the standard," people beat, smashed, and looted cultural objects in cities and in the countryside. During this cultural disaster, while there is no question that feudal ideas were resolutely attacked, many historically important sites as well as folk customs that represented Chinese traditional culture were also damaged. During this period, all traditional folk-custom activities were suspended, and political rituals took control of every aspect in social life.

Changes in Festivals and Folk Customs since the Reform and Opening Up Policies

Revival of Folk Customs and Activities

The changes in the organization of agricultural production and the revival of household-based farming since the launching of the reform policies have led to many new institutions and also brought changes in attitudes toward cultural activities. In this new social environment, many cultural activities, including festivals and life-cycle rituals, have been revived, although they now reflect the special characteristics of contemporary times. Wedding ceremonies are a good example: while traditional customs dictated a long and complicated set of rituals, in contemporary times there is much greater diversity. Some will chose to hold Western-style wedding ceremonies, while others select a more traditional style, but one that is still different in both details and spirit from the wedding ceremony of a hundred years ago.

Under the influence of the market economy and the fast pace of contemporary lifestyles, many people turn to wedding-planning companies to arrange their wedding ceremonies. Our survey showed that the majority of young people are inclined to hold wedding ceremonies in a restaurant and to receive their friends and relatives there. Because they have to do farm work or work at their jobs, they usually set their weddings for Sundays or national holidays. A dowry usually includes furniture, a television, a washing machine, and clothes, with quality and price depending on the financial situation of the bride's family. Nowadays, in place of the traditional wedding chair, a car is usually used to bring the wife from her family home, and often several other cars escort the bridal car. The wedding-planning company provides an emcee to host the ceremony, and cameras record each stage of the events; banquets are becoming more lavish.

Although the wedding ceremony has been revived, if we compare contemporary forms with the month-long rituals of the past, then we can see that it has been simplified and modernized. The guests, of course, convey their best wishes to the newlyweds, but some of the heavier "spiritual" elements of the earlier ceremony have been replaced by more joyful entertainment in the contemporary ceremony. This is one example of the way in which people's ideas have changed, and young people have chosen to incorporate "modern" and fashionable elements in their wedding ceremonies.

After the Reform and Opening Up Policies, traditional funeral customs revived to a certain extent. However, this revival has mostly involved formalistic features, with major stress on incorporating forms that reflect people's compassion for the deceased. Funeral rituals in rural areas have been greatly simplified. Generally, the mourning ceremony is held at home. Relatives and friends come to pay their respects, the names of work units and individuals that sent funeral wreaths and scrolls are announced, memorial speeches are given, and people bow three times and say a final farewell to the deceased. Finally, the funeral procession begins, and the deceased is cremated. However, those who are within the five degrees of mourning are still expected to *koutou* to the deceased.[7]

Many of the annual festivals on the lunar calendar have been revived over the last several decades, and in 2008, the state recognized Tomb-Sweeping Day, the Dragon Boat Festival, and the Mid-Autumn Festival as legal holidays. While the holidays have been revived, customs associated with each are not identical to those of the pre-PRC period. For example, on New Year's Day, people still worship heaven and earth and the ancestors, but they seldom *koutou* when paying New Year's calls. Mostly they visit others or just make a call to express their greetings. In earlier times, people spent the afternoon of New Year's Day beating drums and gongs, preparing the dragon-lantern show, and walking on stilts. What we might refer to as "freedom to enjoy the holiday" only came with the fifth day of the first month, which marked the end of prescribed rituals. However, young people today are no longer interested in such activities, and some people even have to work in factories during the Spring Festival, so they have no time to relax and play. During the Spring Festival, people still visit relatives and friends, but for some people, the holiday offers a chance to travel or to participate in other nontraditional activities.

In conclusion, while villagers still value such festivals, they are not as enthusiastic as they once were. Some of the earlier festivals—for example the Spring Dragon Festival (second day of the second month), the Dragon Boat Festival, and the Double Ninth Festival—pass with little notice, and most people just enjoy the holidays as occasions for eating certain special foods. For example, fried beanstalk for the Spring Dragon Festival, *zongzi* for the Dragon Boat Festival, and moon cakes for the Mid-Autumn Festival. Young people who are busy with their work have little interest in such festivals and pay them little heed. From our survey, we learned that half of the respondents believe that such festivals are not as important as they once were. The percentage of those with little interest in festivals was highest among the youngest cohort.

New Features of Festive Customs

Chinese society has experienced rapid transformation since the beginning of the twenty-first century. Work patterns and life styles have changed and so have popular customs. Cultural communication among peer groups has replaced the earlier pattern in which the older generation passed on cultural customs to the younger generation. In fact, we often see the reverse in which the young are providing cultural guidance to the older generation, providing information on contemporary customs and practices. Good examples of this are changes in ideas and methods for raising children that have developed since the implementation of the one child policy. Since a married couple can only raise one child, much more time and investment is put into the education of that child. One Lengshuigou villager described the situation for us:

> In the past when the baby was 12 days old, relatives and friends would come to congratulate with eggs or noodles. Now the child has even greater value since every family has only one child. Relatives come with cash gifts, some a thousand *yuan* and generally 300 or 500 *yuan*. Boys and girls are treated in the same way because girls are also precious. The family will all go to a restaurant to celebrate. When the baby is 100 days old, it will be taken to a photo studio to take pictures. When the baby is one year old we put various items out in front of the child and look to see what she or he touches first, since this is believed to indicate the child's future occupation.

As Lengshuigou has been drawn into a more modern lifestyle, villagers—especially the young—enjoy a lifestyle that is almost identical to their urban peers. The boundary between the village and the city has been blurred, and most young people in the village have spent at least some time living in a city. Most young people in the village choose their own lovers and have freedom in getting married. As we have seen, the wedding ceremony has incorporated many Western features and is very expensive. Features that were once seen as important in the wedding ceremony have become less important; the sense of ritual has weakened while the wedding as an event has come to have a higher value, and it has become an occasion for entertainment and consumption.

> In recent years, the living standard of villagers in Lengshuigou has improved, people have become wealthier, and the scale for wedding ceremonies has gotten bigger. The betrothal gift offered to the bride by the groom is usually 11,000 *yuan*, which has the meaning of "one in a million." Apart from a TV, a washing machine, and an electric bicycle, the dowry should also include "three gold items": a gold necklace, a gold ring, and gold earrings. The groom has to spend tens or even hundreds of thousands (including the furnishing of an apartment). The wedding ceremony takes only one day. Ten cars are needed for picking up

relatives. The wedding ceremony should be recorded by a camera and is usually held in restaurants, quite a scene. (HNA n.d., 32–33)

Since the initiation of the reform policies, many older customs and ceremonies are in the process of disappearing, while some new customs have appeared. For example, holidays have become occasions to travel and shop and to meet relatives and friends. People gather to dine in restaurants or to go to KTV (Karaoke) clubs, enjoying their holidays as occasions for new forms of consumption. During the Spring Festival or other holidays, people call or text each other to send their greetings. More and more people go online so they can connect to close friends or even strangers. Choices have multiplied, and individuals enjoy a much more diversified lifestyle.

Change is of course inevitable, and the kind of rapid change that China has experienced in the last several decades has radically transformed the cultural world of villages like Lengshuigou. In that process of change, contemporary society has inherited much—including cultural traditions—from the past, adding on, adapting, and transforming that past inheritance to create new rituals and festivals that meet contemporary needs.

NOTES

1. Also known as the Four Cleanups Movement.
2. The "three constantly read articles" were essays Mao had written before 1949, which urged people to selflessly work for the completion of the revolution. The three articles included "In Memory of Norman Bethune," which was written to honor the selfless spirit of a Canadian doctor who had joined the Chinese revolution; "To Serve the People," an article written to honor another revolutionary martyr; and "The Foolish Old Man Who Removed the Mountains," an article that used a Chinese folk tale to argue that difficult odds could be overcome with sufficient hard work and dedication.
3. In response to our question, 43.6 percent reported that they got scientific knowledge and modern ideas from the younger generation, and 25.3 percent reported that they relied on the younger generation for advice on consumption and entertainment.
4. A group of retired teachers has compiled a collection of materials on culture, sports, and traditional festivals that provides details on the festivals and how they were celebrated.
5. Huangmei opera is a kind of traditional rural folk opera that has been popular for two hundred years or so.
6. Another style of rural folk opera.
7. "Five degrees of mourning" refers to the Chinese system of calculating how closely related an individual is to others. Starting with the individual, those in the generation directly above are in the first degree of mourning; connections are then counted vertically (by generation) and horizontally (aunts, uncles, and cousins).

Chapter Six

Social Relationships and Network Structures

Social relationships and network structures in rural areas have changed enormously over the past hundred years. During the first half of the twentieth century, rural relationships were characterized by what the well-known anthropologist Fei Xiaotong described as the "differential mode of association" (*chaxugeju*).[1] After collectivization a new form of social relations took shape in the countryside, in which all members of rural society were incorporated as members of the lowest sub-unit of the commune, the work team. During this period, social relations in rural areas entered a period in which the work-team-defined relationships coexisted with the more traditional relationships that had been defined by kinship (*qinyuan*) and what Fei describes as "regionalism" (*diyuan*), that is, sharing of a common native place. With the implementation of the Reform and Opening Up Policies including abolition of the commune and the division of land under the household responsibility system in 1983, state power gradually retreated, and principles of the market economy penetrated all areas of rural life. As a result of this last shift, we can say that social relations are at long last making a genuine transition from traditional- to modern-style relations.

DIFFERENTIAL MODE OF ASSOCIATION

Traditional Chinese rural society is a society based on "relationships" (*guanxi*), with kinship relations serving as the most important determinant of rural social structure.

Although Lengshuigou witnessed a variety of historical changes in the first half of the twentieth century, including the fall of the Qing dynasty and the establishment of a new Republican government, war, and gradual development of the market economy, these dramatic changes did not lead to fundamental changes in the traditional social structure. If we were to sum up in a few words our impressions of Lengshuigou and its residents before 1949, we could say that the village was still quite traditional, relatively closed to the outside world, with low levels of social exchange and migration, a place in which the people were attached to their homes and reluctant to leave. Villagers were attached to, and protected, their traditions and lived a relatively self-contained life. Village social structure followed the principles that Fei Xiaotong described in his well-known essays on rural society: the most important relations were built on consanguineous ties (*xueyuan*) of family and lineage, and regional or native-place ties (*diyuan*). These relationships together created a rural society that Fei has described as an "intimate society" in which clear distinctions were drawn between members (insiders) and outsiders. As Fei noted, Chinese rural order is rooted in a sense of intimacy that comes from the fact that people stay in the same place from cradle to grave. In this society, individuals rely not only on their own experiences but also on the experiences passed down from their ancestors. From this point of view, it is possible to infer that traditional rural society rests on consanguinity (*xueyuan*) and regionalism (*diyuan*) and is regulated by the rule of rituals. "In a Confucian social structure, kinship relationships exist as a major category that, without exaggerating, lay the foundation for all types of social relations" (Fei 2009 [1948], 6–7). This kind of society is built on ascribed blood relationships and local-place relationships and relies on Confucian ethical rules to adjust resource allocation and the maintenance of social order and the social structure.

We can see these principles very clearly in a section on family in the *Kankō Chōsa* survey that recorded the participants in a village wedding ceremony in 1937. The records are for the wedding ceremony of Li Xingjun (the son of Li Yongxiang) and include a detailed list of gifts that we have reproduced in tables 6.1 and 6.2. In rural areas, weddings are one of the most important events in a person's life. As a result, the wedding ceremony is also an event that mobilizes families and the entire lineage (*jiazu*) network. Thus, an analysis of wedding participants and gifts provides a way to understand where an individual and his family stood within the hierarchical network of relationships, as well as how the networks functioned. The records show that at the time of the wedding, Li Yongxiang's family held 9.25 *mu* of land, which matched very closely the average landholdings in the village. Let us see what we can learn from an analysis of those who attended the wedding and the gifts they offered.

As we can see from table 6.1, which categorizes those who gave gifts by their general relationship to the family, there were three major groups of par-

Table 6.1. List of wedding gifts, Lengshuigou, 1940s

Type of relationship	*Quantity*	*(%)*
Neighbors	54	57
Lineage members	23	25
Relatives	16	17
Village head	1	1
Total	94	100

Source: KC 1955, 124–25.

ticipants: lineage members, relatives,[2] and neighbors. It is interesting to note that all of these are what we call "ascribed relations." Absent from the lists are individuals who might be described as "friends," a term we use to refer to those who do not fit into any of the ascribed relations described above (i.e., members of the lineage, relatives, or neighbors). We regard a friendship relation as a relationship that would have been created through the personal effort or initiative of the individual, a relationship that would have been voluntarily and mutually established by the parties to it. Neighbors form the largest group of gift givers, with 54 neighbors out of 94 listed; lineage members come in second with 23 on the list; and relatives follow in third place with 16. The final individual listed was the village head (*zhuang zhang*). The fact that the number of lineage members is relatively small is not so surprising since this category can only include those who have a common blood relationship with the family. Some lineages were large, others small, and this would influence the number of lineage members attending the wedding. While the lineage and relative groups were limited to those who shared blood or marriage relations with the family, the concept of "neighbor" might be extended to the entire village. To sum up, from the guest headcount we can roughly figure out the scale and scope of Li Yongxiang's social relationships within the village. However, it is still difficult to determine the degree of importance of each type of social relationship.

Let us now look at the record of wedding gifts (table 6.2). Three types of wedding gifts are listed, that is, cash, staple food (*mian dian*), and gifts including meat or various kinds of cloth. However, it is almost impossible to tell from the gifts how close the relationship was between the giver and the Li family. In other words, the wedding gifts reveal little about the type of social relationship, and a check of the list shows that many participants gave almost identical gifts. For example, gifts of cash ranged from five *mao* to three *yuan*; however only one person gave three *yuan*, and the average gift was one *yuan*. For those of us familiar with contemporary practice, we can see that gift-giving etiquette was quite different from our contemporary times when the size of the gift does tell us something about the closeness of the relationship. We can also say that in terms of providing support for the family during this important social ritual, the total value of gifts from larger groups—like that of neighbors—provided significant support, even more than lineage members.

Although the value of wedding gifts was relatively uniform across the different types of wedding guests, we can identify some exceptions to this rule. To summarize, we can see that (1) within each of the categories (neighbors, lineage, and relatives), there were some who were more generous than others; and (2) among those who gave the largest gifts, relatives were better represented (as shown in table 6.2). We can suggest three factors that influenced the size of gifts: first, the closeness of the relation; second, the guest's financial situation; and third, customs regarding gift giving. If we look at the list in table 6.2 with these considerations in mind, we can see that there were no small gifts from those who can be presumed to have very close relations with the family. Moreover, we can assume that Lengshuigou gift-giving etiquette was reflected in the gifts; the etiquette assumed that gift giving was reciprocal, and someone who received a gift would be expected, when it was his turn, to give back a slightly larger gift. From this we can say that the size of the gifts more or less reflected the degree to which the giver was close to the recipient. In this case, among the eight people who gave the largest gifts, five were relatives, thereby suggesting that relatives, in comparison with other categories, held a central position in Li Yongxiang's relationship network.

Table 6.2. Value of wedding gifts, Lengshuigou, 1940s

Type of relationship	*Specific relationship to Li Yongxiang*	*Quantity of gifts*
Relatives (5)	Brother-in-law	Two *yuan* in cash, one roll of cloth, and 15 *jin* of meat
	Uncle	One roll of satin and eight *jin* of meat
	Cousin	Three *yuan* in cash and one roll of cloth
	Cousin	One roll of cloth and eight *jin* of meat
	Father-in-law	Two *yuan* in cash
Member of the lineage (1)	Member of Li Yongfang's lineage (Li Quanxiao)	Two *yuan* in cash
Neighbors (2)	Neighbor (Cheng Delin)	One roll of cloth and six *jin* of pastry
	Neighbor (Xie Baochen)	One roll of cloth and eight *jin* of meat

Source: KC 1955, 124–25.

Another striking feature of Li Yongxiang's social network as reflected in the list of wedding gifts is the absence of friends among the wedding guests.[3] We think that this is a reflection of the population stability and limited migratory flows that characterized traditional rural China, as well as structural limitations that made the maintenance of friendship with outsiders nearly impossible. Villagers were born and raised within the village's boundary. They engaged in conventional agricultural production just as their ancestors did. Their lives revolved around continuing the relationships in their bloodline (*xueyuan)* and to those who shared their native place (*diyuan*). Life was about living the experiences they inherited from their father's generation. Thus, villagers did not need to develop any kind of relationship with outsiders. With the modernization brought about in the first half of the twentieth century, a few Lengshuigou villagers began to seek non-agricultural jobs outside the village's boundary. However, such jobs were usually acquired as a result of already established social networks. Moreover, although an individual might work outside the village, his income was regarded as only supplementary, and the village was still the central focus of life. In other words, the village's social orientation was inward. With this mindset, relationships with those outside the village were regarded as of lesser value, and most villagers were not motivated to develop long-term relations with those outside the village. Ascribed relationships built on consanguinity and common native place remained at the center of networks, and those with the outside world had little influence on daily life.

Although relationships beyond the village's boundary were irrelevant from the social perspective, non-kinship relations (*fei qinzu*) still existed in social relationship building. According to table 6.2 there were three essential individuals in Li Yongxiang's relationship network: Li Quanxiao, who was from the Li Yongfang lineage, and the neighbors Cheng Delin and Xie Baochen. These wedding guests gave the largest gifts. This indicates that they, among all the lineage members and neighbors, had close ties with Li Yongxiang. Such familiarity is chiefly built upon "mutual willingness" (*qingyi xiangtou*) and characterized by "affection" (*qinggan daoxiang*) rather than by Confucian ethics. The occurrence of such relationships shows that the aforementioned "mutual willingness" was not ruled by strict and rigid Confucian social norms regarding interpersonal interactions. At the same time, maintaining this kind of relationship demanded emotional effort and extra care, given its unusual nature.

According to the analysis presented above, we can delineate a general picture of Lengshuigou's social relationships and network structures: the core layer was made up of relationships among those with blood ties of some form, including lineage members, maternal relatives, and relatives by marriage; the second layer was formed by relationships with neighbors and close lineage members; the third layer refers to relationships with neighbors and lineage members; last is the layer of relationships with villagers who are not included in the first three layers. Different layers reflect different types of familiarity. Also, such relationships, which are marked by different principles and rules, have different functions. These four layers of relationships shape the villagers and their family's basic differential mode of association within the village network.

The Basic Characteristics of the Differential Mode of Association

The Confucian-based theory on rural relationships bears the fundamental attributes of particularism (*teshu zhuyi*), that is, it reflects a differential mode of association (particularistic ties), which includes being close to insiders and distant to outsiders, respecting specific hierarchies and social structures (social order), and having more obligations than rights.

In Confucian theory, social relationships are categorized in the "five cardinal" relationships: father and son, husband and wife, ruler and subject, elder and younger brothers, and friends. Each relationship is sustained by moral elements (*daode yaosu*). For instance, blood relations or consanguinity between father and son constitute a major axis for the traditional family and its affairs; the code of conduct related to father-son relationships reflects the Confucian norm regarding filial piety, which translates as "the father is kind and the son is filial" (*fu ci zi xiao*). Filial piety is a core value within Chinese traditional social relations, and it is held in great esteem as a basis for the state. Any behavior in conflict with this principle can be harshly criticized. Thus the father-son relationship is the primary axis supporting the traditional family, whereas the relationship between husband and wife becomes an auxiliary axis. The moral rules regulating the husband-wife relationship vary according to a gender-based division of labor in which men are responsible for affairs outside the home, women for those within.

The ruler-subject relationship is guided by the moral elements of "loyalty" (*zhong*) and "righteousness" (*yi*), which refer to the idea that "if the ruler reigns with the help of rites, his ministers will serve him with loyalty" (*jun shi chen yi li, chen shi jun yi zhong*). The cardinal relationship between the elder and the younger brothers serves primarily as the standard for other more general social relationships. Finally, the cardinal relationship between friends builds on "trust" (*xin*). The idea that "if the people have no faith in their rulers, there is no standing for the state" (*min wu xin bu li*) best expresses the nature of such a relationship. Although in a Confucian society, only three of the relations—that is, the husband-wife, father-son, and the elder brother–younger brother—are included within the scope of family ethics (*jiating lunli*), the other two were often discussed using familial terms. For example, once individuals established a friendship, they tended to convert that relationship into a kind of fictive kinship, referring to each other as (older or younger) brothers and sisters. Meanwhile, the ruler-subject relationship, in spite of its social and political nature, is also instilled with the spirit of family ethics. Therefore, family relationships permeate many aspects of broader social relations.

A second important characteristic of Chinese social relations is hierarchy. In rural society, individuals must behave toward others according to their place in the hierarchical status system. Hierarchical statuses are first determined within the lineage according to generation (*beifen*); in interpersonal relationships, individuals pay great attention to their generational position within the family. Seniority within the lineage is clearly stipulated, and individuals are expected to strictly follow the rituals appropriate to their position. Gender also plays a role in positioning individuals within the family hierarchy, with men enjoying a high status and women placed in a lower and subordinate position. One expression of a woman's lower status was the often-quoted statement on the "three obediences" (*san cong*), which said that a woman should obey her father before her marriage, her husband after marriage, and her sons in widowhood. Next comes the distinction between elder and younger that described appropriate behavior between those of the same generation, with special attention to distinctions regarding statuses and identities between older and younger brothers. Such hierarchical differences empowered older brothers to control the younger ones, causing the younger to submit to the elder; such differences aggravated the imbalance between the parties. Hierarchy was also a factor in other relations, for example, relations with other blood relatives, where hierarchy was determined by whether the relationship was close or distant. The same principles could be extended to frame a range of other relationships, most of which were seen as unequal. For example, these principles could be used to talk about hierarchy between sons of the wife and concubine, or master and servant relations.

Thus, strongly influenced by Confucian ethics, rural social relations were shaped by an extreme form of particularism, which constrained individuals from the time of birth in ethical and social networks, whose principles could not be violated. This inevitably led to the entrapment of the individual in a conservative network of hierarchical interpersonal relationships. Within this system, the individual became one small component of lineage and consanguinity networks.

Finally we need to consider the heavy weight of obligations (*yiwu*) and the lighter weight given to rights (*quanli*) within social relations. The system stressed the particularistic values of "favor" (*renqing*) and "face" (*mianzi*) while giving little attention to universal values. The social order and the logic of human behavior in rural China were guided by a clear moral nature, and this allows us to consider the village as a moral community. The so-called moral community describes a communal style that takes moral obligation as its core code of conduct. While it may seem that the idea of moral obligation is not entirely compulsory, in fact, under the long-term influence of traditional culture and customs, moral obligations did become completely compulsory. This concept thus contains a double meaning (Lin 2007, 209–10).

The first meaning refers to the villagers' moral obligations toward the nation: from the perspective of the relationship between nation and rural society, obligations keep the nation–villagers relation under control and within an appropriate limit. The national ideology becomes mechanically integrated into the village's quotidian ethical practices, at the same time leaving some room for choice. Conversely, villagers, in the course of a lifetime, gradually develop their own logic of moral and ethical principles. Those principles differ from the provisions of the law of the state, but they do not conflict with the state or with the authority of the state. Although the formation of a moral community within the villages seems to give the villagers some bargaining room, in fact, the villagers have been turned into "subjects" of the state.[4] In terms of their economic activities, villagers are engaged in subsistence production, and from a political perspective, they have become subjects with a servile status.

The second meaning refers to views of morality among the villagers. From the perspective of rural society, morality is an indispensable element within social interactions and a necessary condition for the maintenance of the collective security of the rural community. The absence of morality from social interactions can compromise the village's peace and order. Therefore, villagers must unconditionally abide by moral principles and comply with the corresponding moral obligations within the context of interpersonal interactions. Only in this way can villages enjoy a normal life. The villagers have developed their own "rules and customs" on the basis of accumulated experiences in life, and by relying on morality within relationships involving families, lineages, patriarchs, and neighbors, villagers ensure the order and tranquility of the village's life. Villagers who fail to appropriately carry out the related ethical obligations can be expelled from the village for betraying the community's trust. Guided by the principle of morality, villagers look out for and assist fellow villagers, making the village a large family. It is the belief in the morality of customs that binds villagers together; at the same time morality, customs, and faith provide the ties that support reciprocal forms of cooperation. These beliefs promote a strong sense of identity within the village, creating a sphere for safe activities for all villagers.

Within such a moral community, favor (*renqing*) and face (*mianzi*) become important elements binding social relations. "Favor" is an important feature regarding the handling of interpersonal relationships in traditional Chinese society; it also can be used as a gift or a resource to be given in the context of social relationships. After helping others, the individual being assisted extends favor as a resource to the counterpart who provided the assistance. And once a manifestation of favor reaches the one who provided assistance, he needs to act on it and repay the favor, causing the individual being assisted to owe the recipient again. "Once an interpersonal exchange is kick-started, the original recipient needs to continually increase the value of the returned favor, so the person providing assistance is placed again in a position of debt, thereby perpetuating the cycle. In this way the relationship is continually re-established" (Zhai 2005, 86–87). Thus, relationships among villagers gain cohesiveness. In this context, the repetitive exchange of favor reinforces the particularistic relations based on family organization and sharing of a common native place. For villagers, favor is often rewritten in line with the closeness or distance of a relationship, thus strengthening the particularistic features of relationships. So, among friends and relatives, villagers pay less attention to whether they received a gift, or the value of the gift, and much more attention to whether the exchange ritual was conducted in a meaningful way. Thus, if someone were to give a gift that was regarded as too large, the exchange would be seen as violating the established notions of favor.

The related idea of *face* also plays an important role in regulating social relations. As a unique cultural and psychological feature of Chinese society face is often regarded as a fundamental regulator of interpersonal relationships. In traditional rural societies, individuals rely on the family organization for many forms of practical support, but following on their understanding of Confucian ethics, they also give great importance to their relative positions within the family. Face plays a crucial role in social interactions, be it in settlement of civil disputes or in arranging other social activities, for example, leasing land, arranging loans, or deciding what kind of gift to give. There are numerous examples of the importance of face in various business dealings. For example, it was advantageous to find a middleman who had good face (i.e., who had a good reputation) when arranging a loan. "A prestigious figure was likely to have good relationships (*ganqing*) with a wide circle of rich people outside the village and was able to secure favorable terms. He could negotiate a lower interest rate, obtain a loan for a longer period, arrange for its extension, or get the lender to forgo part of the interests. If the middleman was very powerful, it was said that there was no need for a contract" (Duara 1988, 186). When individuals called on a middleman to mediate a dispute or a transaction, finding someone whom both parties recognized as having face was a regular rule of rural practice. It is important to note that face was recognized within a shared rural community. While the face of a person was recognized and accepted within his own village, in interactions outside this particularistic community, a person's face would be of little use.

These kinds of particularistic relationships were also a manifestation of trust. As Max Weber and others have argued, trust within traditional Chinese society is especially developed and maintained based on consanguinity and lineage ties. Moreover, individuals are commonly inclined to distrust those outside of their family and lineage networks. Thus, it is possible to understand that villagers tend to trust family members and other individuals with whom they are well acquainted while remaining suspicious of outsiders and strangers. "In rural society, trust derives from familiarity. This kind of trust has very solid foundations, for it is rooted in customary norms. [. . .] Trust in rural society is based not on the importance of contracts but, rather, on the dependability of people, people who are so enmeshed in customary norms that they cannot behave in any other way" (Fei 1992 [1948], 43). So this kind of particularistic relationship of trust is based on the fact that partners to the relationship know each other very well; thus, these relationships are ones in which trust overlaps affection. It is for this reason that we find that when individuals want to borrow money, they turn to their relatives and friends. It is important to note that this kind of trust is very different from forms of universal trust in modern societies. This latter kind of trust in modern society is grounded in contracts and laws that provide guarantees. The key to such modern notions of trust is the strict enforcement of contracts.

In short, traditional societies—which have their social relationships regulated by Confucian ethics—value relationships bonded by consanguinity; common native place, favor, and face become the primary elements binding the social order in rural society. Furthermore, these elements, favor and face, act as an essential lubricant to maintain social stability and harmony.

The Function of Relationships in Traditional Societies

Social relationships based on kinship and regionalism constitute the small world of Chinese villagers; these relationships permeate most activities carried out by villagers on a quotidian basis. In addition to serving the important purposes of resource allocation, maintenance of order, and social structuring, these relationships create the basis for the material and social existence in rural villages. According to the Chinese philosopher Liang Shuming, China is a network-based society in which relationships (family relationships) always enjoy primacy, meaning that actions are always determined by the nature of the relationship existing between the individuals. Liang stated that the ethics-centered interpersonal relationship developed by the Chinese could be summarized as "ethical orientation" (*lunli benwei*). And that such an "ethical orientation" is actually a "relationship orientation" (Liang 2005a, 95).

Social Relationships: A Key Pattern in the Distribution of Rural Resources

From the *Kankō Chōsa* survey:

> In a family it is up to the patriarch to make decisions regarding ordinary affairs, and the patriarch usually consults with other family members in case of major events. When it comes to external affairs, the opinions of most family members matter, but the patriarch has the final say.
>
> The patriarch is also in charge of the annual family income and daily expenses. The patriarch keeps the earnings of each family member for common use. In this aspect the patriarch is responsible for the family's finances (KC 1955, 63).

As we can see from this statement, the lineage or family head played a dominant role, exercising power and controlling resources that allowed him to manage the family's finances and major events, as well as make decisions regarding the allocation of resources for all of its members. Actually, in rural societies, families or lineages usually monopolized important and rare material and spiritual resources. Such resources were allocated according to the differential mode of association.

The power to allocate resources was an important first principle. In patriarchal settings, the relationship between husband and wife followed the principle that the man was superior to the woman, meaning that the family head ruled the family. Among brothers, the elder ones enjoyed more power. Regarding affairs that were external to the nuclear family, elders in the lineage had the authority to decide matters for each family in the lineage, as well as for the entire lineage. This kind of authority structure follows the same principles as the internal-external orientation that marks the hierarchical configuration of the differential mode of association. The second factor we can observe is that allocation of land and property was also strictly carried out according to blood relationships. For instance, family land and assets were divided among sons in a given lineage; women, including mothers and married daughters (sisters) did not enjoy inheritance rights. Furthermore, lineage members were given preference regarding land transactions. This, in fact, emphasizes the principles involved in the allocation of resources. Finally, the status and position of individuals also followed the configurations of the differential mode of association model. Members, depending on their life experiences and position with the lineage, were regarded as having different degrees of face, and this created the foundations for social distinctions within social networks, both inside and outside the village.

Social Relationships: The Basis of Rural Social Order

On one level, social relationships themselves are a part of the order of society. Each layer of relationships and the rules that prescribe its arrangements are part of the regulatory norms reflecting the internal village social order and its meanings. On another level, in societies marked by extremely low migration rates and high homogeneity as well as by relationships based on intimacy, individuals tend to comply with the basic regulations around social relationships. Violating such regulations means losing social support and the ability to survive in an intimacy-based society. Individuals carefully cultivate their social relationships through favor and face, among other mechanisms, thereby sustaining and reproducing the social order. From another point of view, social relationships are also an important regulatory mechanism; in traditional rural societies, social norms and customs are often more readily accepted than are formal legal codes.

Social Relationships as a Main Element of Social Support

Social relationships also function as a mechanism of social support as they control numerous facets of village production and life. According to the *Kankō Chōsa* survey, in Lengshuigou, neighbors and lineage members often shared tools (*heju*)[5] and engaged in labor exchange (*huan gong*)[6] during the busy farming season. Neighbors frequently partnered regarding agricultural production, and borrowing from other acquaintances was a quite common phenomenon. Additionally, the supporting role of social networks was especially evident during social events such as weddings, funerals, and life-cycle rituals, among other important ceremonies. For instance:

Q: Are households that share tools (*heju*) close to each other?

A: Of course, just as if they were from the same lineage (*jiazu*).

Q: Do households sharing tools (*heju*) help each other to deal with wedding and funeral ceremonies and ordinary daily routines on a daily basis?

A: Yes, they are the most active when something like that happens to the other household.

Q: In case of borrowing food, would the household they partner with be the first one they would ask for help?

A: Of course.

Q: What about money?

A: The same. They would turn to their partners for help before they reach out to lineage members, provided that such a partner is rich.

Q: Do they go to their partners for consultation if stuck in a difficult financial situation?

A: Yes.

Q: Do they do the same if they want to sell their land?

A: No, they don't. We have professional middlemen.

Q: Who are they?

A: Li Fengfu and Xie Changxiong. (KC 1955, 26)

[Mutual help]

Q: Do villagers help each other when someone is in need?

A: Yes, they do.

Q: When does this happen?

A: Usually on the occasions of wedding or funeral ceremonies, and in other events when they are shorthanded

Q: Do they help on behalf of the village?

A: Of course not. The people who come to help are mainly made up of lineage members, friends, and neighbors.

Q: Are gifts or cash presented as gifts considered aid?

A: No, they are just an expression of congratulation or condolence from friends and lineage members; they have nothing to do with aid.

Q: How do they help at a funeral?

A: By carrying the coffin, digging the grave, and hosting other guests, among other things. (KC 1955, 40)

In sum, rural relations were structured primarily around relationships based on kinship/regionalism. Social relationships abided by conventional Confucian ethical regulations, emphasized obligations, and valued friendship ties. Such relationships bore great significance regarding the maintenance of the village routine; they also constituted basic principles for guiding social actions, thereby reflecting resource allocation and the fundamental principles of social life.

REVOLUTIONARY CHANGES IN SOCIAL RELATIONSHIPS FOLLOWING THE ESTABLISHMENT OF THE PRC

After the foundation of the PRC in 1949, rural society underwent profound change. The movements that led to collective production and the People's Commune gave the new regime unprecedented control over rural society. At the same time, these changes remolded interpersonal relations in rural society, creating a system with very different characteristics from those of traditional society.

During high socialism, a new form of social relationship took shape among villagers when public ownership of the means of production replaced private ownership; welfare began to be distributed according to work; and, as the slogans of the time claimed, the people turned into masters of their own government (*renmin dangjia zuozhu*). Thus, the small peasants of a traditional society were transformed into rural workers of a socialist country where comradeship prevailed; this was a situation in which the most important relationship driving social relations was sharing of the status of commune member (*sheyuan*). Using political force, the state broke apart consanguinity-based interpersonal relationships and regrouped individuals into a mighty political organization—the People's Commune. This created a kind of socialist-style "big family" (*da jiating*) characterized by relationships involving comradeship, equality, and mutual help. As a result, a new type of social relation gradually developed across Chinese society. This differed from relationships in pre-1949 society as it transcended the consanguinity-based relationships that marked equality in traditional society. Socialist principles such as equality (*pingdeng*), mutual help (*huzhu*), selflessness (*dagong wusi*), and cherishing collectivism (*reshou jiti*) played an important role in replacing the Confucian ethical norms guiding quotidian behavior in public settings.

The national government employed a series of socialist movements to integrate villagers into the People's Commune structure, thus making them establish relationships based on the equality, mutual help, and cooperative relations that marked socialist universalism. However, although the role of kinship was under attack and greatly diminished, it was still present and active in rural relationships. These two forms of social relationships have different structural foundations, different spatial functions, and different regulatory principles. Under the socialist system, rural collective institutions like the people's communes assumed many of the functions that lineages and families had played in traditional societies as they provided villagers with many of the necessary resources for daily life. However, under the somewhat unstable political system of the time, there were still distinctions in relationships between commune members, who would identify some of their fellow members as closer than others. In fact, particularism still played an important social role within some forms of personal relationships. As the well-known American sociologist and China expert Ezra Vogel noted, "Although comrades are theoretically equal and close companions, in practice some are more close than others" (Vogel 1965, 57). As a result, we can consider this kind of comradeship (*tongzhi guanxi*) as a kind of semi-universalistic[7] social relation (Lin 2007, 83).

Production Team as the Basic Element of Commune Member Relationships

The Basic Institutional Mechanism of Commune-Based Relationships

Ren Yanting (former Lengshuigou CPC branch secretary):

> Q: Could you describe the process to establish cooperatives and people's communes in Lengshuigou?
>
> A: The village started to set up mutual-aid teams in 1954 and lower-level and higher-level cooperatives around 1954 and 1955; after 1959 the administrative structure was basically fixed. Lengshuigou's brigade had 19 production teams, and the production teams lasted until 1983 when the household contract system (*da baogan*) replaced the production team and we established the system of control under the village committee. Membership in the production teams was decided by where you lived. A large production team had from 50 to 60 households, while the small ones had from 20 to 30 households. The production teams' scale varied and so did the value of their output. At that time the value of a work point for the best team was 9.3 and for the worst team 2.3 *mao*.

Xiao Caixing (male, Lengshuigou villager, veteran):

> Q: Could you shed some light on the basic situation of the production team?
>
> A: In Lengshuigou a production team was an extended family (*kuoda jiating*) that was managed by the leader of the production team as if he was a family head. All activities were organized around the production team, including farming production, grain allocation, wedding and funeral ceremonies, and house construction. The production team had to handle personal affairs of its members, and they would take care of the production affairs in return. Even today a man over the age of 40 can tell you clearly which production team his family belonged to.

After the foundation of the PRC, Lengshuigou underwent a collectivization process and was organized in a unified manner from mutual-aid teams, to lower level and higher level cooperatives, and finally, to the production team as a basic unit of the people's commune. Just as in other rural areas throughout the country, this revolutionary change consisted essentially of a process of collectivization—a new form of organization. It also entailed a process in which public ownership of the means of production replaced private ownership. Output was divided among the members according to the amount of work members contributed to the collective, marking a sharp change from the pre-revolution economy in which differences in family income had been dependent on how much land and equipment the family owned. Under these new arrangements, communal welfare replaced consanguinity and regionalism in public governance, and socialist values stood in the place of Confucian ethics, thereby creating a new form of social organization as well as new relationship configurations that integrated the villagers into new organizational units—the production team and the people's commune. Collectivization not only created a new economic system but also a completely new form of social relationship, the one between commune members. The entire village was transformed into a highly united structure. However, since the transformation process relied primarily on external political forces, it was not completely successful in eliminating the influences of the traditional small-peasant model of social relations. Consanguinity and regionalism as sources of identity were not completely eliminated and still continued to influence the new organizational forms.

As a new type of social organization, the production team monopolized all social resources and assumed the functions that used to be under the traditional family and lineage. Thus, it became a large family marked by strong cohesion. At that time, the often-repeated socialist slogan "under the big family everyone is equal" instilled in the production team's members a sense of universalism. However, in essence, this new type of social organization was still closed. If we compare this situation with that before the foundation of the PRC, we can see that "peasants just moved from one closed configuration—based on kinship and regionalism—to another. This impeded rural relationships from further developing into true universalism" (Lin 2007, 89). As a matter of fact, the scope of associations among villagers was still further limited; the empowerment of commune-member-based relationships caused relationships that were external to the production team to be marked by strong particularism.

The Features of Commune-Member-Based Relationships

Differences within equality: The relationship between ordinary commune members was of equality. The collectivization movements and their relevant institutional arrangements, including the elimination of private land ownership and the crackdown on kinship-based organizations, eliminated the fundamental inequalities that originally marked rural society. In addition, national propaganda campaigns stressing socialist values such as equality, solidarity, and mutual help spread recognition of these values among the villagers. These values facilitated the construction of interpersonal relationships between commune members that transcended social relations based on the traditional values of consanguinity and regionalism.

Although there were imbalances in the relationship between ordinary community members and cadres from the production teams, in general the atmosphere was one of equality. On the one hand, production team cadres did not receive special treatment. Like everyone else on the team, they had to earn work points and did not benefit from higher prestige. On the other hand, the democratic election system was well implemented in Lengshuigou. This was expressed by a popular saying in Lengshuigou, "Once all the cotton plants have been cleared, cadres step down (*bawan mianhua chai, ganbu jiu xiatai*)." This referred to the fact that at the end of each agricultural year, the production team elected new leaders democratically, removing those who were incompetent and selfish. This system placed strong restraints on the development of unequal relations between the team leaders and ordinary team members.

In those days of political and class struggle, the most obvious inequality among villagers was the result of decisions on class status (*chengfen)* that had been determined at the time of land reform. Those who had the status of poor and lower-middle peasants became the leading social class in the village. Those of the five bad classes (landlords, rich peasants, counter-revolutionaries, bad elements, and rightists) were subjected to reform and criticism. There were clear distinctions between the two major classes regarding political status, daily routines, and forms of associations. Our informants reported that relentless class struggle meetings had a huge impact on interpersonal relationships. While there is no question of the impact of such movements, in comparison with other places, the struggles were relatively mild. The excerpt below expresses the village's view on the five black categories:

Wang Chunsheng (male, Lengshuigou villager, retired teacher):

Q: How were individuals classified in the five black categories treated during the Cultural Revolution period?

A: We should try to have no contact with them in the public arena. However, I, in my humble opinion, don't think they were so bad. On the contrary, I did feel sorry for them. If they ran into something big such as wedding and funeral ceremonies and house construction, the whole production team, as well as the members of their lineage, would join together to lend a hand instead of just standing by and watching.

In addition to differences in political status among commune members, there were also some marked social distinctions in everyday life. Former Party Secretary Ren Yanting recalled:

> Among members of a production team, some were close and some were not. Regarding wedding gifts, if we were from lineages with different surnames, for example, Ren and Wang, and not on good terms, five yuan was enough. However, if we were intimate and had exchanged gifts before, we would give more generously, as if the individual was a member of our own lineage.

Since the production team monopolized all resources, these distinctions were less significant than they had been in society before collectivization. Relationships, including whether or not individuals were close to each other, were increasingly based on affective ties.

Team-member-based relations and the ties within the production brigade: Lengshuigou was a relatively large village with more than seven hundred households in the 1960s. Thus, while it fit Fei Xiaotong's category of "intimate society," because of the size, we might see it more as a "semi-intimate society"; gaining village-level mutual help was not easy. Rather, the true intimate society was based on the team of thirty to sixty households that were engaged in regular interaction. The production team thus became the most important organization in terms of everyday cooperation. As a result, the nature of production teams resembled and even transcended that of the family, and team-based relationships enjoyed a more practical meaning and orientation than relationships with other lineage members and relatives in the same village. "The interests established between and within production teams were paramount, even relationships between brothers took second place to such interests," said a villager.

All production teams in Lengshuigou at that time observed an unwritten rule that whenever a member had to deal with major life events such as wedding and funeral ceremonies or house construction, the team leader and the other members would provide assistance. Such help was calculated as one day's worth of work points. However, work points would not be assigned when team members helped members of other production teams. This mechanism supported the close interrelationship of the production team members, creating an atmosphere of mutual-help-mutual-support and social support within the group. Therefore, the social ties of team-based relationships were institutionally organized around comradeship (*qingyi gongtong*) instead of around ties based on consanguinity and lineage.

The Difficulties in Moving Beyond Relationships Based on Kinship/Lineage

The Continuity of Relationships Based on Kinship/Lineage in the New System

The newly established state authority excluded and replaced traditional lineage-oriented organizations based on kinship and lineage with this new type of social organization. However, the long history of lineage-based experiences and customs made it very difficult to completely dissolve the earlier attachments, although their significance was greatly reduced. In other words, kinship-based relationships continued to play a limited but indispensable role. Older relationships based on consanguinity and lineages were not completely negated during the process of building new social institutional mechanisms and social organizations. Thus, relationships based on kinship/lineage still enjoyed space to exist.

To understand how this operated, we need to look at some specific examples. Relationships based on kinship and lineage became a kind of resource fueling the cooperative and collectivization movements. Relationships based on kinship and regionalism became tools to develop social relations based on mutual help and cooperation. This element of continuity filled the gap between the scattered patterns characteristic of the "small peasant" mentality that marked traditional rural society and the establishment of strong cooperatives driven by a collective mentality. Such continuity was especially important in Lengshuigou, a village that was relatively rich and enjoyed relatively equal distribution of land. In this kind of environment, the internal push for collectivization was relatively weak. Before the founding of the PRC, cooperative arrangements in agriculture had been limited to arrangements that were referred to as *heju*. *Heju* was a form of cooperation in which two households, usually neighbors or relatives from the same lineage, jointly farmed their land, sharing labor and tools but with each claiming control over the harvest on their own land. Mutual-aid groups of the new socialist era were built on the basis of such *heju* relationships. Thus, production teams also were constructed on the principle of spatial proximity, drawing on elements that were typical of relationships involving lineage members and neighbors. Prior to the division and organization of individuals into production teams, mutual help and assistance drew on consanguinity and regionalism. From this we can see that the newly established collective mechanisms still reflected earlier styles of relationships; and thus, consanguinity and regionalism were integrated into the new social structure.

The Role of Relationships Based on Kinship/Lineage

Affective (qinggan) support: Although production teams and their members enjoyed a relatively good atmosphere of mutual help, which satisfied most of their material needs, this was not enough to satisfy their affective (*qinggan*) needs. And even though the production teams resembled a family, they shared only its functional aspects, not its essential aspects. Comparatively speaking, production teams lacked the affective support provided by traditional relationships based on kinship and lineage relations.

Unofficial Support: Our interview data suggests that most people commonly acknowledge that although governance was democratic during the production-team period, lineage relationships still played a role in elections of team leaders. It was easy for big families, large households, to determine the new cadres and occupy the village's leadership for long periods of time. In addition, whenever there was a conflict between individuals from two different lineages that required forceful intervention, family members and relatives on both sides would rise up to help. Thus, such situations usually transcended the personal relationship between the two parties. We can see the influence of the unofficial role lineage-based relations continued to play in such incidents.

In sum, commune-member-based relationships depended on the socialist values that stressed equality and mutual help. However, such relationships were only effective within the village and were strongest among those within the village who were members of the same production team. Thus, such relationships inevitably embodied an exclusionary nature. Relationships based on kinship and regionalism continued to exist within the village. Although they were weakened under the new system, they continued to provide affective support and unofficial support to other relationships within the village.

THE NEW TRANSFORMATION OF MODERN SOCIAL RELATIONS

The dissolution of the People's Commune system and development of the market economy following the launching of the reform policies has brought further change to social relationships in Lengshuigou. These changes have been particularly strong since the 1990s. One of the hallmarks of contemporary social relationships has been the increase in relationships involving coworkers, classmates, and friends. Although many interpersonal relationships within the village still follow the principles of comradeship discussed earlier, the differential mode of association rationale (Yang and Hou 1996) has played a much more instrumental role in the forming of relationships. Moreover, in comparison with the period of high socialism, traditional forms of association play a stronger role. As a result of the relaxing of organization structures, relationships based on kinship and lineage relations have become a powerful force in efforts by the peasantry to deal with the risks of the private market economy. The incompleteness of the private-market economic system turned such relationships into a kind of social capital that has played a strong role in supporting the lives of rural people.

We can identify some special characteristics of the recent changes. In the following subsections, we will rely on a variety of survey materials to analyze the basic circumstances and primary characteristics of contemporary social networks in Lengshuigou. To conduct the survey, we used three categories reflecting the different nature of social relationships in the village—instrumental (*gongjuxing*), affective (*qingganxing*), and associative (*jiaowangxing*) (these refer to the villagers' core social networks, to the core layer of such networks, and to the networks' actual supporting role within the village). These three types of networks are both overlapping and distinct, patterns that reflect the status and characteristics of the social networks in the village from different perspectives.

On the Composition of Social Networks

Relationships or ties are one of the core contents of social networks. The distinctiveness and proportion of a given social tie shape the characteristics of a specific network. In our study, we have classified social ties in two major categories, kinship and non-kinship relationships. Kinship relationships include six sub-categories: spouses, parents, offspring, siblings, lineage members, and relatives by marriage. Non-kinship relationships include another six sub-categories: colleagues, classmates, friends, acquaintances, neighbors, and other non-relatives.

In the case of Lengshuigou, networks have relied on kinship and regionalism since time immemorial, and as we saw earlier, non-relative relationships were absent from this village's life. After entering the collectivization period, a new form of social relationship, that is, the team-member-based relationship, was forcibly created by the new state authority. However, this kind of relationship was still confined within the village's boundaries and affected by kinship and regionalism. The recent rapid development of the market economy and rapid urbanization have resulted in new configurations in occupational structure, and the overall social structure of Lengshuigou can be said to have moved from a traditional style to a modern style. One of the important features of this "modern style" social structure are social networks that have begun to move beyond the spatial limits of the village; in this new formation, a variety of non-kinship relationships have gradually become important factors in villager's overall networks.

The Structure of Instrumental Networks

Instrumental, affective, and associative social networks are created to meet differing demands of the actors who create them and reflect different patterns of the flow of resources within a network. Each network type relies on the use of different kinds of resources that are drawn together to meet the needs of the actors creating them. Thus, different networks provide different kinds of support. Generally speaking, the three types of networks cover all of the social relationships existing in Lengshuigou.

Table 6.3 shows the results of our survey with regard to instrumental networks. When asked about membership in their instrumental networks, 91.67 percent of the respondents mentioned kinship relationships, meaning that 91.67 percent of the survey participants included at least one blood-related relative in their instrumental networks. This suggests that kinship relationships still hold an important position in villagers' networks. At the same time,

Table 6.3. Instrumental networks, Lengshuigou, 2010

Type of relationship	*Percentage of respondents selecting this type of relationship (%)*	*Average share of a specific relationship type in the participant's network (%)*
Kinship (*qinyuan*)	91.67	75.86
Spouses	37.41	9.35
Parents	25.19	9.12
Offspring	33.33	17.71
Siblings	48.89	21.16
Lineage members	30.74	13.23
Relatives formed through marriage	15.56	5.29
Non-kinship (*fei qingyuan*)	50.37	24.14
Colleagues	6.48	1.58
Classmates	10.74	3.01
Friends	34.26	12.52
Acquaintances	1.85	0.52
Neighbors	14.63	6.08
Other non-relatives	1.48	0.42

Respondents were asked to name those in their networks and state their relationship with each individual in the network.

Source: Shandong University Survey, 2010.

50.37 percent of the participants also mentioned a non-relative relationship. More than a third (34.26 percent) of the respondents said that such networks include at least one friend; thus, friendships came in in the third position. From this, we can see that friendship has become typical enough to represent a non-relative relationship and has entered the village's network structure and started to play an important role.

To understand the importance of different kinds of relationships, we asked informants what percentage of the members of their networks came from people in different relationship positions. Responses showed that on average siblings came in first at 21.16 percent, followed by offspring at 17.71 percent, lineage members at 13.23 percent, friends at 12.52 percent, and spouses at 9.35 percent.

From these responses, we can see that kinship relationships still occupy an important position within instrumental networks. This is especially true for close relatives such as siblings, spouses, and offspring, who are in the center or at a critical position within the network configuration. But a few external relationships have already become part of the villagers' instrumental networks, especially friendship. It has already transcended relationships based on kinship and regionalism, such as relationships with parents, relatives by marriage, and neighbors and is now playing a central role in networks.

The Structure of Affective Networks

In answering our question about affective networks, 94.26 percent of the participants said that kinship relationships were important; this figure is higher than the response for instrumental networks (91.67 percent). At the same time, the percentage of participants selecting non-relative relationships in their affective networks was 45.37 percent, which is lower than that of non-relatives in instrumental networks (50.37 percent) by 5 percentage points. The results show that in constructing affective networks, more than half (54.63 percent) of the survey participants have networks completely formed by kinship relationships; affective networks entirely composed of non-kinship relationships account for merely 5.74 percent of the participants. Therefore, judging solely from this data, kinship relationships are much more important than non-kinship relationships in the villagers' affective networks as shown in table 6.4.

Our tally of the results of the survey shows that kinship relationships accounted, on average, for 79.23 percent of the members of affective networks; among kin relationships the highest average percentage for sub-group was for offspring (43.15 percent); the second highest was 17.69 percent for spouses, third was 17.53 percent for siblings, and the fourth was 14.7 percent for parents. The average percentages for lineage members and relatives by

Table 6.4. Affective networks, Lengshuigou, 2010

Type of relationship	*Percentage of respondents selecting this type of relationship (%)*	*Average share of a specific relationship type in the participant's network (%)*
Kinship (*qinyuan*)	94.26	79.28
Spouses	70.00	17.69
Parents	38.70	14.70
Offspring	43.15	20.97
Siblings	46.48	17.53
Lineage members	19.07	6.22
Relatives formed through marriage	7.78	2.16
Non-kinship (*fei qingyuan*)	45.37	20.72
Colleagues	6.11	1.47
Classmates	9.26	2.49
Friends	28.33	10.43
Acquaintances	2.41	0.90
Neighbors	12.22	5.07
Other non-relatives	1.48	0.36

Respondents were asked to name those in their networks and state their relationship with each individual in the network.
Source: Shandong University Survey, 2010.

marriage were much lower. Moreover, the average percentage related to non-kinship relationships within the total number of affective networks stood at 20.72 percent; within this category, friends accounted on average for 10.43 percent and the remaining non-kinship relationships account for even smaller percentages.

On the basis of this data, we can say that affective networks in Lengshuigou have the following characteristics: at the most central and important position in such a network, there are four close relationships: spouses, offspring, siblings, and parents. These relationships are undoubtedly more important than other types of relationships, both in their importance and the weight they have in an individual's relationship network. Friendships are in second place, closely followed by lineage members and neighbors who can be considered as on the periphery of traditional relationships based on consanguinity and regionalism. While the latter are on the periphery, they are still part of intimate networks. Finally, on the outer ring are relationships involving classmates, relatives by marriage, colleagues, and others.

The Structure of Associative Networks

Associative networks, unlike the two types we have looked at so far, have several quite different features, most strikingly the relatively lower weight given to kinship-based relationships. In this type of network, non-kin play the central role.

In describing the members of their associative networks (see table 6.5), 49.26 percent of the survey participants said that kinship relationships were important, while 90.37 percent selected non-kin individuals as central members of their associative networks. From this we can assume that such non-kin relationships are more important in the villagers' daily associative interactions. Neighbors—the most commonly selected type—accounted for 52.04 percent; coming next were friends, who were selected by 43.89 percent of the respondents. These two types of relationships dominate the villagers' associative-network structure. Non-kinship relationships, on average, account for 72.5 percent of the participants' associative network members while kinship relationships account for 27.49 percent. The former is double the size of the latter. Therefore, judging merely from the data, non-relative relationships constitute a major part of a villager's associative network.

Table 6.5. Associative networks, Lengshuigou, 2010

Type of relationship	*Percentage of respondents selecting this type of relationship (%)*	*Average share of a specific relationship type in the participant's network (%)*
Kinship (*qinyuan*)	49.26	27.49
Spouses	24.63	6.18
Parents	9.26	2.75
Offspring	12.96	4.62
Siblings	20.56	7.21
Lineage members	13.15	5.08
Relative formed through marriage	5.56	1.67
Non-kinship (*fei qingyuan*)	90.37	72.50
Colleagues	20.00	8.57
Classmates	17.78	5.80
Friends	43.89	20.61
Acquaintances	7.41	3.09
Neighbors	52.04	32.93
Other non-relatives	2.96	1.50

Respondents were asked to name those in their networks and state their relationship with each individual in the network.
Source: Shandong University Survey, 2010.

In summary, neighbors and friends occupy a central position in Lengshuigou villagers' associative networks. Relationships with spouses, colleagues, and siblings form the next layer, and a third layer of relationships is formed by connections with classmates, lineage members, and offspring. At the outer level of associative networks are parents, acquaintances, and relatives by marriage.

Our analysis shows that the structure of networks in Lengshuigou has the following characteristics. First, relationships based on kinship: People in these groups still hold a central position in the villagers' networks, and they are the first choice when villagers look for help and support. However, while these relationships once held an uncontested dominant position, they are now experiencing a decline in importance. This is particularly true for relationships with parents: in the past this would have been the most important relationship for most individuals. In our survey, this relationship was not the first choice in any of the three types of relationship networks. Second, there has been a steady rise in the importance of relationships with people who are not related, and these have begun to ascend to a core position. Third, the distribution of members in the networks is now much more diversified than in the past when most people's networks conformed to a common pattern. In today's Lengshuigou, individuals construct networks by choosing the members with whom they want to associate according to their own needs. Networks, thus, are becoming increasingly diversified.

On the Constitutive Principles of Social Networks

Before 1949, the differential mode of association in Lengshuigou was regulated by conventional Confucian ethics that clearly distinguished between insiders and outsiders, stressed rank and hierarchy, and gave primacy to obligations over rights. Also regulated by mechanisms such as favor and face, relationships took place within a society characterized by a friendly spirit. After the establishment of the People's Republic of China, socialist values that stressed equality and mutual help became the leading principles regulating team-membership-based relationships. However, Confucian ethics still played an important role in the villager's daily associations, and associations between villagers were still marked by an element that reflected earlier notions of neighborliness (*qingyi gongtongti*). With the end of the rural collectivization era, team-member-based relationships disappeared, and collective values gradually faded away. Under these circumstances, Confucian values have reappeared in rural China. Villagers—under the influence of a society characterized by high levels of private market competition—began to make utilitarian calculations when building their networks; they thus started to think more about the usefulness of connections and less about ideals. Overall, we can say that the networks of contemporary villagers represent a mixture of affective and rational elements.

The Principles of Instrumental Networks

Drawing on the analysis on Lengshuigou's instrumental networks presented earlier, we can outline the basic criteria guiding the villagers' decisions regarding the members of their networks. For the core layer of their instrumental networks, villagers choose according to the degree of intimacy and trust: central positions are given to siblings, spouses, and offspring, who share biological intimacy and high levels of trust. However, individual choices are not guided by a single standard. In choosing members for a network, attention is given to the resources and abilities a member will bring to the network. In constructing instrumental networks, villagers usually do not give primacy to relationships marked with strong intimacy and trust, but rather look to see what resources individuals bring to a relationship. This is one of the reasons why parents play a relatively small role in such networks. From this perspective, only members who have strong intimacy and trust, in addition to resources, join instrumental networks. Thus, we can say that villagers constructing their instrumental networks increasingly consider the benefits that they will gain by including particular individuals. Given the kind of "rational" impulses behind such choices, we can say that, of the three types of networks, instrumental networks are the most modern.

The Principles of Affective Networks

While instrumental networks are based on relatively rational calculations of benefit, villagers stress intimacy and trust when choosing members of their affective networks. For example, the relationship with parents—the most important consanguinity-based relationship—provides a natural sense of belonging that involves unconditional intimacy and trust. Although parents are no longer able to exercise the same kind of power they once held in instrumental networks, they are the primary choice when it comes to affective networks. Relationships with other members of the lineage, which are certainly consanguinity-based relationships, are located at the periphery of this layer. In other words, we might almost consider such relations as a separate layer since it is difficult for these relationships to have the same degree of intimacy as those of parents, children, and siblings or to become part of the core layer of affective networks. Having said this, affective networks are the closest to traditional networks. We can see this in the fact that within affective networks, there is a differential mode of association distinguishing between the closest relatives and others.

The Principles of Associative Networks

In comparison with instrumental and affective networks, actors select members for their associative networks relatively randomly, although this selection process is still shaped by certain rules and restrictions. One of the determining factors is that the actors involved have some common space. Meanwhile, for instrumental and affective relationships, members wanting to join the relationship need to meet specific conditions, that is, they need to be willing to help actors in solving practical or emotional problems. In contrast, membership in associative networks is now chosen with clear purposes in mind. Following these principles, neighbors, friends, and colleagues can join associative networks. Sharing the same time and space, working together or sharing leisure together is enough to produce an associative network. In other words, members of associative networks are the people with whom one shares daily life activities. Thus, associative networks are built among those who work together and interact together. Convenience and sharing of some common background conditions are the major criteria for selecting members of such networks.

Briefly, contemporary Lengshuigou villagers rely on very different standards to choose the members of their networks. As we can see from the results of the survey, motivations and standards for selecting members have become more diversified. Yet the ties and principles set by the Confucian ethics still continue to permeate the ways in which villagers design their networks. What's even more obvious is that villagers tend to increasingly incorporate their own interests and demands into their decision-making process; this has created what we might call a *rationalized* differential mode of association.

Social Relationships: Characteristics and Development Trends

Social Relationships in Today's Society: Transformation and Characteristics

The transformation of the composition and principles ruling networks in Lengshuigou reflects a change in the villagers' relationship structures from traditional to modern. These changes parallel changes in the rural social structure from a single and unified system to one that is multiple and diverse, incorporating higher degrees of mobility. Therefore, reflecting the transformation of rural society from traditional to modern, social networks in the countryside also changed from single and unified to multiple and divided.

First, social networks are no longer restricted by relationships based on consanguinity and regionalism. The composition of networks also includes non-kin such as friends and colleagues, and these individuals are gradually moving into central positions within networks in rural areas, serving important roles. In the process of constructing networks, individuals no longer confine themselves to people who live within the village's boundaries, but actively seek various external relationships. Many of the villagers have become migrant workers, taking on non-farm jobs and establishing relationships with individuals they meet in the course of their new activities. While relationships based on consanguinity and regionalism are still the most important—even if on the surface they seem to have suffered attacks—the overall trend in social relationships is a shift to networks that are more diverse, with different kinds of relationships serving different purposes.

Second, consanguinity ties are no longer a factor determining distinctions in social networks in today's rural areas. Individuals have already started to rely on different criteria to select members for their networks and determine the position that each member will occupy. According to our analysis of today's villagers' networks, the differential mode of association still exists as a kind of social fact in all sorts of networks since different members do not enjoy the same importance. Networks abide by specific principles regarding the distinct position of their members. Also, different members enjoy different positions in relation to the center of the network. From this perspective, today's networks differ greatly from traditional networks. While it may seem that on the surface there has been little change, when we look at the content, that is, the principles that determine the formation of networks, we can clearly see a clear transformation. In today's networks, ethics, affection, and interests all play important roles when an actor selects those who will be members of his or her networks.

Third, the development of social relationships in today's countryside is confronted with a new problem: a crisis in social trust. Our survey results demonstrate that when asked to compare the quality of their interpersonal relationships over time, only 11.7 percent of the participants replied that they have become closer to their counterparts. The majority (65.4 percent) answered that they have become more estranged in those relationships, while 19.6 percent of the participants reported that their relationships remained unchanged. The number of participants who have no opinion about it accounted for 3.3 percent. As for how they evaluate levels of trust within the village, only 10.4 percent of the participants said that trust levels have increased over the years. The majority, 60.7 percent, replied that they have fallen. The percentage of participants who said they thought trust levels were unchanged, or who have no opinion, accounted for 25.6 percent and 3.3 percent.

Our survey questionnaire required participants to evaluate the degree of trust they have in other individuals and organizations. We used a scale of one to ten, with *one* being the lowest degree of trust and *ten* being the highest. From the results shown in table 6.6, we can see that family members,

Table 6.6. Degree of trust, Lengshuigou, 2010

Trusted Groups	*Average trust value*	*Standard deviation*	*Sample size*
Family members	9.62	1.06	539
Relatives	8.71	1.61	540
Classmates	7.26	2.03	494
Other villagers of the same village	6.42	2.07	537
Neighbors	7.27	2.05	493
Acquaintances	6.47	2.03	537
Government	6.19	2.80	539
Village committee leaders	5.28	2.81	540
Outsiders	3.06	2.33	536
Strangers	2.23	1.98	535

Respondents were asked to rate level of trust on a scale of 1 to 10, with 10 the highest level of trust.
Source: Shandong University Survey, 2010.

relatives, and neighbors enjoy the highest degree of trust, whereas outsiders and strangers the lowest; in between them are the village leaders.

Social Relationships: Future Development Trends

In the last several decades, Lengshuigou has been transformed from a relatively closed farming village to a rapidly urbanizing suburban community. The recent decision to locate a new Jinan High-Speed Railway station near the village is likely to greatly speed up the transformative processes as more of the village's land is taken over for construction purposes, and most of the village population moves into non-agricultural employment. Thus, in the near future, Lengshuigou will disappear as a village. Accompanying the village's urbanization and modernization, villagers' relationships will also be radically transformed. These changes are likely to come from two directions: first, physical changes in occupational and residential style and, second, structural changes in the village's social organization.

First, we anticipate that the shift, which has already begun, in the relative importance of kinship-based and non-kinship relations will continue. Kinship and regionalism formed the core of traditional rural social relations in large part because of the high degree of social stability and isolation and the low degree of heterogeneity. But, following the deep changes brought by the village's urbanization, Lengshuigou's rural structures are shifting toward mobility, openness, and heterogeneity. As many villagers shift from agricultural to non-agricultural occupations, there is increasingly less space for relationships based on kinship and regionalism in their daily lives. In contrast, the number of non-kinship-based relationships such as friendship has gradually increased, and there is more space for such relations to flourish. Ultimately, these relationships will acquire the leading position within the villagers' networks.

Second, in looking at the principles ruling the composition of networks, we believe that there will be a steady increase in the weight of rational considerations and a corresponding decline in the role of emotional attachments. As the village as a community rooted in kinship relations weakens, villagers will gradually incorporate a variety of formal rules into their decision making, and rational calculation of personal interests will become the main force driving social organizations. As the consanguinity-based community weakens, the orientation of villagers' lives will shift from a focus on life within the village to a focus on relations with the outside. Under these circumstances, villagers will make more rational calculations in constructing their own social networks. While we expect that the millennial-old legacy of Confucian ethics and bonds will continue to play some role in shaping individual behavior and network building, its influence will be steadily circumscribed and limited to fixed spaces and arenas. Thus, we can expect in the long term to see the rationalization of the differential mode of association.

Third, we anticipate that over the long run, there will be a decline in the importance and instrumental roles of relationship networks. In traditional rural societies, social relationships have important meanings for villagers; they provide the basis for social actions and determine the resources and principles that individuals use in determining what action they will take. During the collectivist era, kinship-based relationships provided an important element of emotional support when conflicts arose among commune members. After the Reform and Opening Up Policies there was a revival in the role played by relationships, which was important as villagers began to deal with a society that was external to the village, especially when faced with the uncertainties that accompanied the development of the market economy. Relationships increasingly took on a more instrumental role. However, the deepening rural modernization and increasing efficiency of the market economy are strengthening the role played by formal regulations in networks; correspondently, the support function of networks may decline.

In sum, social networks in today's rural society are characterized by a multi-element structure. Relationships with unrelated individuals have gradually assumed a central position within networks, playing an increasingly important role. The principles building social networks have been gradually freed from ethical and collective or socialist values. Relationships today are characterized by a multiple of purposes, with strong elements of rational calculation. Networks are more diversified and much more open than in the past. The types of social networks are also increasingly diversified, and individuals have come to build their own distinct networks to satisfy their own distinct demands.

NOTES

1. This will be explained in greater detail below. Gary Hamilton and Wang Zheng in their introduction to a translation of Fei's well-known work *Xiangtu Zhongguo* [*From the Soil: The Foundations of Chinese Society*], after acknowledging the complexity of the concept, go on to briefly summarize the idea in the following way: "It is clear that he [Fei] uses the term to describe analytically the patterning of Chinese society through nonequivalent, ranked categories of social relationships (*shehui guanxi*)" (Fei 1992, 18).

2. The term we have translated as "relatives" (*qinshu*) refers specifically to kinship relations outside the lineage, including maternal relatives (parents, aunts, and uncles on the mother's side of the family), as well as relatives through marriage (sisters-in-law, brothers-in-law, etc.)

3. Translator's note: In Fei's understanding, the category of "neighbors" is treated as an ascribed relationship, based on the notion of local identity. The category of "friends" includes those who are not connected through ascribed relationships. Among the neighbors may have been individuals who had closer personal relations with the groom or his family, but they are counted here as neighbors.

4. "Subjects" here contrasts with the category of "citizen."

5. *Heju* also means partnership" (*hehuo*). This is one form of traditional agricultural cooperation, according to which households shared tools and livestock. In general, households possessing about 10 *mu* of land tended to engage in this kind of partnership.

6. Labor exchange refers to arrangements made during the busy agricultural season when two households combined their efforts to conduct farming work.

7. Ezra Vogel refers to it as "universalistic ethics" (Vogel 1965, 57).

Chapter Seven

Economic Structure and Development

The twentieth-century "Chinese miracle" is rooted in fundamental economic changes that transformed a poor socialist agricultural society into the "world's factory" in less than thirty years. This chapter will explore those transformations from the micro level through an examination of the changes in our village from the 1940s to the early twenty-first century. At the beginning of those seven decades, Lengshuigou was a large agriculture-centered village growing rice for the market and other grains for home use. In the 1950s, land reform was followed by collectivization that converted an agricultural economy based on private land ownership into a socialist system; the villagers became members of work teams, and land-ownership rights passed to the collective. Then beginning in the late 1970s, reforms led to the dissolution of the commune, a return to family-based responsibility for farming, and the development of village-owned small-scale industries. Freed from the obligations of compulsory labor, Lengshuigou villagers began to find jobs outside the village, and the village government began to leverage its land resources, creating a large-scale dairy farm and an industrial park.

This chapter examines changes in economic structure and development strategies through description and analysis of changes in the fundamental units of economic analysis: land, labor, and capital. The first section of the chapter looks at structural changes in the economy and the second half at new economic trends since the initiation of reforms.

CHANGES IN ECONOMIC STRUCTURE

Prewar Peasant Economy

The North China rural economy was based on a small peasant mode of production in which individual households worked their own small farms. Western economists have engaged in heated debates about the nature of that small peasant mode of production. One school, represented by the Russian economist Alexander V. Chayanov, argued for a consumption-labor balance within the family in which the aim of the peasant household's economic activities was family subsistence, not maximization of profit. This model assumes that the peasant family allocates family labor to achieve survival without regard for maximum profits. Another school, represented by the American economist Theodore W. Schultz, argued that peasants were rational economic actors who, even though they were using traditional technology, pursued profits. In Shultz's view the peasant household's allocation of essential productive inputs—including both labor and capital—followed economically rational principles (Wen 2009, 22–4).

On the basis of our study we believe that Chayanov's theory of the peasant household provides a better explanation of the Lengshuigou peasant economy. In the early twentieth century peasant households' allocations of land, labor, and capital were made with little impact from state policies, market mechanisms, or links to the urban economy. However, things were very slowly beginning to change.

Land

In the period before land reform the state's policies with regard to land were relatively stable, supporting a system of what in contemporary China is conventionally referred to as a feudal land ownership system. Under that system peasant families owned their own land and changes in land ownership were the result of sales arranged between private landowners.

In the prewar period Lengshuigou had a total of 280 hectares of land (42 *qing*), with 93.3 hectares (14 *qing*) planted in rice and 186.7 (28 *qing*) planted in dry field grain crops (KC 1955, 1). At that time there were no clear borders distinguishing land that belonged to the village of Lengshuigou from neighboring villages and there were frequent changes in ownership as a result of private sales. Some of these sales were between people from different villages and the overall trend was for land formerly owned by people of other villages to be sold to Lengshuigou villagers.

There were two reasons for this: first, Lengshuigou villagers were richer than those in neighboring villages and second, they were interested in buying land. The gap between the rich and poor in Lengshuigou was quite small and the village was relatively wealthy in comparison with its neighbors. We can see evidence of this from the *Kankō Chōsa* survey report that in 1940 Lengshuigou villagers employed 17 long-term laborers from other villages, while only three Lengshuigou men were working outside the village as long-term hired labor (KC 1955, 178).

Residents of Lengshuigou, like those in most of rural China, believed that owning farming land was the most important basis of wealth and so villagers sought to buy as much land as possible; at the time of land reform village land holdings reached more than 9000 *mu*.

One section of the *Kankō Chōsa* survey charted the customs with regard to land sales, including detailed explanations about land prices, conditions for purchase, how buyers and sellers negotiated through middlemen, and how disputes over land sales were resolved. For example, average prices for land depended on the quality of a particular field: "According to the quality of the land, land was divided into three categories of superior, medium and inferior. A *mu* of superior dry field land was worth 300 *yuan*, medium 200 *yuan* and inferior 100 *yuan*; a *mu* of superior rice paddy was worth 400 *yuan*, medium 300 *yuan* and inferior 200 *yuan*" (KC 1955, 200).

When making a deal the two parties to the sale invited the various people involved in the sale to meals. "Usually during the process of making a land sale the buyer should offer two meals. Once the draft contract was signed, he should invite the middleman, the man responsible for surveying the size of the field, the buyer's kinsmen, relatives, and friends; on the day the surveyor measured the field he should invite the seller, the middleman, the surveyor, and neighbors. In addition to the meals the middleman was paid a fee for his services" (KC 1955, 201).

Under the conditions of low labor productivity that prevailed at that time peasants believed that increasing the cultivated area through acquiring more land was the best strategy for guaranteeing the survival of future generations. Expanding of cultivated land was the first choice because strategies to raise productivity were limited by the general shortage of capital to fund regular investment in production; as a result most households preferred to expand the cultivated area rather than switching to intensive modes of production that would involve investment in both labor and other inputs.

In Lengshuigou, as Chayanov suggested, peasant households tried to produce as much grain as possible, rather than experimenting with other crops that they could market for greater income. However, families did grow vegetables and fruit for their own consumption, selling what was left over in local markets. From the above we can see that peasants spent their savings on buying land rather than in investing to increase productivity.

Labor

In the small peasant economy labor played an important role in overall agricultural productivity. If we were to rank the three important inputs—land, labor, and capital—land came first, labor second, and capital inputs third. In the early twentieth century there was a slow but steady increase in the labor supply as the result of population growth. This steady increase in rural labor supply was a result of the generally pro-natal culture of Chinese society, which was reflected in the common saying "more sons, more blessings." Records show that in 1928 Lengshuigou contained around 350 households and in 1941 the number had increased to 360 with a population of 1,800 people (Myers 1970, 89). While there was slow population growth it brought almost no change in the structure of the population since most of the population remained in the countryside with little occupational or spatial mobility. Lengshuigou was relatively wealthy and able to achieve self-sufficiency in output, so villagers were under little pressure to seek outside employment. As a result communication with other villages was relatively limited and there was little outward mobility of the labor force. Some villagers did hire day laborers to assist in the busy agricultural season but those hired were usually hired by the day from a day laborers market in a nearby village.

Capital

In this period, capital was in general in short supply and not mobile; thus it did not play a significant role in stimulating agricultural production. When a family did need to borrow money, they usually sought loans from someone in the village.

Compared with land and labor, capital's contribution to agricultural production was small. Peasants toiled in the fields to meet the consumption needs of the family rather than for sale in the market. Although some peasants did sell in the market when there was surplus grain, this was quite different from specialized production aiming to make profits. We can find further evidence for this tendency in practices related to cotton production. Peasants wove cloth using cotton yarn that they purchased in periodic markets. In an earlier day peasant women had spun their own yarn but after 1900 cotton yarn was readily available in the markets at a low price, so most families purchased yarn to weave into cloth. After 1938 the price for cotton yarn rose, forcing most peasants to weave less cloth (Myers 1970, 91).

While most households followed the patterns we have described above, there were a small number of households engaged in handicraft as a way to earn cash income. The *Kankō Chōsa* survey reported: "Peasants wove straw rope as a sideline. In idle seasons, dozens of people went out to work as coolies. . . . In the village there were 10 people who made farming tools in a blacksmith shop, 12 people who worked in a potter's workshop and 3 households who ran grocery stores" (KC 1955, 9 and 232).

According to the *Kankō Chōsa* materials few village families had been forced to take out large loans or make large repayments of debts and most credit arrangements were made within the village. As we can see from table 7.1, loans were among villagers, mostly among households of poor peasants. "Families with less land borrowed from those with a lot of land and land renters borrowed from landlords." Only a few households borrowed from the bank. Loaning money in order to make ends meet could be traced back as far as villagers could recollect.

In summary we can see that during the prewar period outside forces had little impact on the village and in general the village was relatively inward looking. There was a general shortage of capital and the limited capital resources were basically not mobile; as a result both agriculture and industry were underdeveloped. Most peasant households lived in a self-sufficient economic world where production of grain and handicrafts was primarily for family consumption. The lack of market-directed motivation to produce more played a role in limiting peasants' interactions with the market and led most households to focus on relations within the village, leading to what we might call a society in which relations took place only among those who one knew well.

In a word, during this period land, labor, and capital each operated according to its own inner logic. In the case of land we can see the concentration of land as a result of sales under the system of private landownership. Labor saw a slow expansion but little of the labor supply was mobile, with most tied to the land. As for capital there was little investment in agriculture and as a

Table 7.1. Village loans, Lengshuigou, early 1940s (unit: *yuan*)

	High-income villagers	*Middle-income villagers*	*Low-income villagers*
Total	10	78–80	270–280
Households with Loans	none	10–20	270–280
Amount of the Loan (*yuan*)		10–100	10–30
Creditor		kinsmen, relatives, friends, neighbors	kinsmen, relatives, friends, neighbors
Interest		none	none
Payment Deadline		within a month	within a month

Source: KC 1955, 218.

result productivity per land unit remained low. If we were to search for any impact of investment, we can only find evidence of a slight boost in agriculture and handicraft production. Overall we can see a cycle in which low levels of capital investment yielded low efficiency, which in turn had little impact on the existing low level of output.

Socialist Collective Economy

While state intervention in the village economy had been quite limited during the early twentieth century, this situation changed following the establishment of the PRC. As state authority began to penetrate the village, it provided concrete directions on allocation and distribution of resources; government intervention brought changes in distribution and mobilization of land, labor, and capital. These changes began with a shift from private land ownership to collective land ownership. Labor also saw major changes from a system with high levels of household independence in allocation of labor resources to a system with high levels of organized collective labor. The state came to control both occupational and regional mobility. Finally, collective production required much higher levels of investment and the rise in investment resulted in increases in agriculture output.

Land

Beginning with land reform and moving on through the movement to build cooperatives and eventually the commune, a series of changes radically altered the management of land. In the autumn of 1950 under the direction of the land reform work team of Licheng County (now Licheng District), Lengshuigou began land reform, the goal of which was "land to the tillers." As a result of land reform every peasant obtained at least a small piece of land, however, land reform did not change the system of private ownership of land. We might say that the traditional feudal system of land ownership had been replaced by a system of small peasant land ownership. Moreover, land reform did not improve the backward production conditions, leaving in place the system in which the holdings of a single peasant family were scattered among a number of small plots. To deal with those fundamental problems the state decided to move forward with rural socialist transformation and so the movement to create agricultural cooperatives was launched. This rural cooperative movement paralleled the changes that were taking place in the cities and towns where private commerce and industry were being transformed into socialist enterprises.

Changes in rural organization followed plans set out by national authorities. The first major shift in organization followed the 1952 *Resolution on*

Mutual Cooperation in Agricultural Production; under this plan 85 percent of villagers in Lengshuigou joined one of the long-term mutual-aid groups. In the winter of 1954 villagers established lower-level agricultural producer's cooperatives in which a household's land contributions to the cooperative were turned into shares in a new cooperative enterprise in which all members worked together on the land. Lengshuigou established eight lower-level agricultural cooperatives with 95 percent of village households becoming share-holding members. Under the cooperatives once the state grain tax had been paid the output was divided based on a formula that took into account a per capita allotment plus return to the shares (land) that each family had contributed to the cooperative. Later higher-level agricultural cooperatives were established with all village households joining. These higher-level cooperatives abolished the system of share holding; rights to the land were transferred to the collective, along with any formerly privately owned animals and agricultural implements. Under this system, work was done collectively and distribution followed a system in which each person obtained a minimum allotment and the remainder was divided based on work contribution. These changes followed on state directives, including Mao Zedong's July 1956 *Report on the Agricultural Cooperatives*, and Sixth Plenary Session's October 1956 *Resolution on the Problem of the Agricultural Cooperation Movement*. In 1957 Lengshuigou implemented these new directives.

Former accountant Li, 66 at the time of our interview, described changes of that time:

> The cooperative movement went through three periods beginning with mutual aid teams, then lower-level cooperatives and higher-level cooperatives. In the period of mutual aid teams land still belonged to individuals, not the collective; in the period of the lower-level cooperatives land was taken as shares, under the unified management of the cooperative; in the period of higher-level cooperatives land belonged to the cooperative. Not just land, but also cattle and other things all belonged to the cooperative, leaving nothing to individuals.

In evaluating the cooperative movement we can see that the cooperatives brought an end to the thousand-year-old agricultural production mode based on small peasant farming. Private ownership by individual peasant families came to an end, to be replaced by collective management of larger units of land. These changes laid the base for the establishment of the People's Commune system.

The Resolution on Establishing People's Communes in Rural Areas was announced in September 1958; in response to this directive, Licheng County established the Dongjiao (East Suburbs) People's Commune, which included the villages of Lengshuigou, Shuipocun, Yangjiatun and Lijiazhuang. Compared with higher-level cooperatives the people's communes were on a larger scale, with a higher level of collective activities; all means of production were put under unified management of the commune. In terms of distribution the commune stressed egalitarian distribution. By increasing the scale of production the commune aimed to remove the contradictions between agriculture and industry and to lower the transaction costs of exchange between peasant households and the state. However, as practice would later show, peasants' motivation to work was reduced by the system of public land ownership and factors of production, leading to a decline in agricultural labor productivity and agricultural yield.

Labor

In this period state policy directly influenced the allocation of labor, limiting both occupational and spatial mobility. During the early years of the PRC state planning was based on a model that called for primitive accumulation in agriculture to support rapid industrialization. To implement this policy the state established a household registration system that clearly divided individuals and households between urban and rural registration. Those with rural registration were to be tied to the land where they would provide the labor force for primitive accumulation. The result was an unbalanced deployment of labor and other productive factors between urban and rural areas.

Under the collective economy the organization and allocation of labor differed during different phases of development. In the early stages—which corresponded to the period of mutual-aid groups in the countryside—participation was voluntary. Peasants voluntarily joined together with friends and neighbors to work together for mutual benefit, forming loose cooperative arrangements; during this period the household was still the basic production unit and individual households controlled the output that was produced on their land. Under the lower-level cooperatives labor was organized according to administrative regulations, with the cooperative establishing goals and assigning tasks. The once loose mutual-aid relationship became institutionalized. The harvest, apart from paying grain tax to the state, was divided by rules that allocated 40 percent on a per capita basis, 60 percent according to contributions of land. With the shift to higher-level cooperatives labor was completely incorporated into a system of collective production. Distribution to individual households was based on a formula that allocated part (60–70 percent) on a per capita basis and the rest (30–40 percent) on the basis of labor contributions, calculated in work points. In the early stages of the commune distribution was based on the whole commune; later this shifted to a three-level system, with the fundamental calculation of distribution based on the production team, which was a sub-unit of the brigade (village).

As we can see from the above brief description the state steadily moved to incorporate rural labor into a more organized system. On the one hand this process was a response to the demands of the planned economy and on the other hand it provided the means by which to carry out primitive accumulation in the service of industrialization. However the highly centralized economic policies took away the freedom of the rural labor force to make decisions with regard to work, leaving them subordinated to cooperatives or the commune. During this period there was no freedom of movement among the labor force, no opportunities to change occupation or spatial location except as assigned by the state. "Under the strict control of the household registration system, the population could not move freely, nor could members of the labor force. The peasant was actually like a pawn on the chessboard" (Han 2008, 6). During this period labor lost both flexibility and vitality.

Capital

One of the major goals of the collective economy was to increase agriculture productivity and capital investment was given a major role. The commune created a new large-scale unit that was much better prepared to invest in production than the small, individual households of the small peasant economy.

Capital in agricultural production: In an effort to fully benefit from the economies of scale the state invested a large amount of capital, undertaking efforts to improve the variety of crops, cultivation techniques, farm implements, and irrigation and drainage facilities. Lengshuigou had for many years mainly planted crops such as rice, wheat, sorghum, millet, corn, and beans. Over time the original seed varieties had degenerated resulting in lowered yields, so one of the first forms of investment was in improved seed varieties. The first steps were taken in 1952 with the introduction of higher quality local varieties, followed in 1954 by the introduction of hybrid varieties. In 1970 irradiated seeds were introduced for the first time and by 1978 the transition to use of quality seeds had been completed. (LCZ 2010, 78).

A second aspect of investment in agriculture involved the introduction of "scientific" farming techniques. One part of this new scientific farming regime was the introduction in 1952 of chemical fertilizers, which contributed to higher yields per *mu.* Despite this good beginning there was a temporary reversal during the Great Leap Forward of 1958 when peasants were encouraged "to dig deep and plant seeds intensively," that is, to plow deeply and to plant crops very close together. As Lengshuigou villagers soon learned these practices were not based on sound scientific or economic principles and resulted in disaster. The combination of mistaken scientific principles and the three years of natural disasters produced the lowest crop yields since 1949.

Finally beginning in 1963 adjustment policies returned to more scientific principles with local areas encouraged to use techniques appropriate to their specific conditions; under these adjustment policies agriculture began to a move in a positive direction with standardized production techniques.

In this period there was significant investment in farming machinery in order to increase productive efficiency. In the pre-1949 peasant economy villagers had used low efficiency traditional farming tools pulled by cattle. New plows were introduced beginning in 1950 and from the 1970s mechanization advanced further, with the introduction of tractors, furrow-irrigation machines, and harvesters. Great efforts were also made in leveling and constructing fields and in improving irrigation. These efforts were particularly effective after the development of the higher-level cooperatives and the communes since it was easier to mobilize labor to engage in such efforts. In 1967 during the movement to "Learn from Dazhai in agricultural production" village labor was mobilized to level 400 *mu* of land on the east slope. In the spring of 1971 Dongjiao People's Commune invested a large amount of money and organized all young members of the commune to build a water pump station in the eastern part of Lengshuigou. The village then invested in constructing about 1,000 meters of pipes and 4,100 meters of channels to bring water for irrigation to the village's fields. This project led to the irrigation of an additional 2,100 *mu* of farming land, or about 70 percent of the total farmland of the village. At about the same time the village drilled 105 wells to utilize underground water resources (LCZ 2010, 76).

Capital in development of commune enterprises: Under the collective economy the state strongly encouraged the development of commerce and small-scale sideline industries. Much of the investment in these areas built on handicraft industries that had been practiced on an individual household basis under the small peasant economy. Under the new socialist economy handicrafts were organized by agricultural producers' cooperatives, becoming a part of the collective economy and incorporated in a unified accounting system. These first efforts became the base for development of Township and Village Enterprises (TVE) and as we know these became a vital force in rural industrialization. During the collective period these TVE were an important part of the village's collective capital, making significant contributions to the development of the village collective economy.

For Lengshuigou an important step was taken with the establishment of a factory processing pig bristle in 1964. This factory was a joint operation of the Lengshuigou production brigade and the Jinan Livestock Import and Export Corporation. The factory was large scale, employing at the peak of production 280 workers, with an annual turnover of 200,000 *yuan*. From the

1970s to the 1980s many other enterprises were established in the village, including a shoe manufacturing factory and a fertilizer factory. The development of these factories strengthened village collective capital and promoted the village economy.

As for service industries Lengshuigou established a branch store of the Licheng Supply and Marketing Cooperative in 1953. Supply and Marketing organizations were "cooperatives" with villagers as shareholders and 80 percent of Lengshuigou villagers held shares. This Supply and Marketing Cooperative store sold groceries as well as inputs for agricultural production and agricultural products (LCZ 2010, 83–4).

Overall we can see a major transformation in the village economy that followed on the growing role of the state in directing development. State guidelines on investment promoted development of agriculture and industrial and commercial sidelines. On one hand there was a steady increase in capital invested in agriculture, which led to steady growth in output. On the other hand the growth of TVEs led to changes in the industrial and agricultural structures.

Peasant Household Economy after the Reform and Opening Up Policies

While the collective economy began on a great wave of enthusiasm, problems with the system of collective work, especially the system of "sharing a common pot" of the People's Commune period,[1] became increasingly obvious as labor productivity fell. As people came to realize that higher levels of collective production were not necessarily good, local areas began to experiment with new forms of rural organization that are referred to under the general term "household responsibility system." Those local experiments became the base of the reform policies.

The household responsibility system established a two-tier system of management that combined household management of agriculture production with integrated activities at the village level. This new system freed rural labor power, greatly raising labor productivity. This "new style rural economic mode" gave the peasant household much higher levels of freedom in choosing how to allocate their resources, and this new flexibility increased motivation to work and led to a great increase in productivity. Under this system, the household was required to turn over a part of its output to the state and assign a part of it to the collective for collective uses. The remainder could be used as the household wished. With the increased motivation this system provided, people began to work harder, income increased, and living conditions began to improve.

During the transitional period from the collective economy to the reform era, state policy still placed some limits on mobility and distribution of economic resources. At the same time, the market came to play an increasing role in shaping economic choices, and urban influences increasingly could be seen in village life. In looking at what happened to land, labor, and capital we can see these influences at work: rural villagers began to think in new ways about the use of land, and there was an increase in the occupational and spatial mobility of labor. People also began to explore new ways of using capital in the pursuit of economic profits.

Land

One of the most important elements of the reform policies was the shift in regulations with regard to land. While land continued to be owned collectively, use rights to the land were contracted to individual households. Lengshuigou began to implement the new system in August 1983 under the regulations that had been set out in *Trial Measures for the Shandong Province Agricultural Production Responsibility System* issued in August 1982. Under this reform, the brigade (village) was taken as the basic unit, with land measured and divided among the households. Certificates, which laid out the long-term contract terms, were issued to each household.

In Lengshuigou, 3,892 *mu* of land was contracted to 1,100 households in the village. Villagers now had the freedom to make production decisions as long as they turned over the contracted amount of grain to the state. Productivity rose, peasants were much more enthusiastic about work, and every household saw an increase in output. Since peasant households were now almost all producing some surplus over their consumption needs, they became much more interested in developing links to markets. And as peasants became more involved in the market economy, the borders of the village economy became increasingly blurred.

As urban developments began to influence the village, we also can see changes in village land use. There was a shift from the exclusive use of land to grow grain to planting of a variety of commercial crops intended for the market. Land formerly used to plant grain crops for self-sufficient consumption now was planted with economic crops to meet market needs. At the same time, the state's and the collective's projects began to shift agricultural land to non-agricultural uses.

First, with Jinan's fast urbanization and expansion, more and more land in Lengshuigou was requisitioned by the state for non-agricultural purposes, such as building roads and building public facilities. We can see this in the statistics on land use: in 1974, the total amount of cultivated land was 4,601 *mu*, but by1989, it had dropped to 4,219 *mu*. Especially after 2001, the trans-

Table 7.2. Per capita land, Lengshuigou, 1974–1989 (unit: *mu*)

Year	*1974*	*1976*	*1978*	*1980*	*1982*	*1984*	*1986*	*1988*	*1989*
Land	4,601	4,505	4,415	4,402	4,402	4,279	4,279	4,231	4,219
Per Person	1.39	1.33	1.28	1.27	1.25	1.20	1.22	1.22	1.20
Per Household	6.54	5.95	5.20	5.20	4.75	4.45	4.38	4.14	3.83

Source: Xu and Yang 1994, 70.

fer of formerly cultivable land to other uses became particularly noticeable as we can see in tables 7.2 and 7.3.

Second, the rural economy came increasingly under the influence of the market, which stimulated peasant household production. It also changed the ways in which rural villagers regarded the land: this can be seen as more villagers adjusted production to market demand, decreasing the amount of land they planted in grain and increasing the amount of land planted in commercial crops. Table 7.4 shows that the grain yield per *mu* increased from 4,640 kilograms per hectare (*gongqing*) in 2001 to 5,142 kilograms per hectare in 2004; however, while output per unit of land rose, because of the decrease in planted area, the total output fell from 1,763 tons in 2001 to 1,703 tons in 2004.

We can also see changes in fruit and vegetable crops in the early twenty-first century in response to growing urban demand. Jinan provides a very large market for fruit and vegetables. As living standards in the city rose, demand increased, and local farmers began to produce more, as we can see from table 7.4. The table also shows a sharp drop in the production of vegetables and fruit in 2010. This is a reflection of the total decline of agricultural land as a result of the village's decision to convert a large part of its land area into an industrial park.

Over three decades of the reform era, we can see dramatic changes in the use of village land—from collective production to the household responsibility system with its improved incentives and involvement in the market, and finally to the transfer of land from agricultural to industrial use.

Labor

The household responsibility system freed labor from the collective economy, allowing families to choose how to allocate their labor, increasing the possibility for mobility. At the same time, urbanization and the development of the market economy began to impact labor allocation.

At the beginning of the reform period, there were many concerns with regard to labor. The collective system was plagued by problems, including lack of enthusiasm, slackness at work, and low labor productivity. The shift to the

Table 7.3. Loss of agricultural land, Lengshuigou, 1997–2005 (unit: hectare)

	1997		*2001*		*2005*	
Project	*Wangsheren*	*Lengshuigou*	*Wangsheren*	*Lengshuigou*	*Wangsheren*	*Lengshuigou*
Farming Land at the End of Year	2,497	265	2,451	260	1,824	160
Paddy Field	540	13.34	244.5	0	115	0
(1) Land Occupied by National Infrastructure	76.8	—	—	117	216	—
(2) Land Occupied by the Village Collective	6.1	1.7	2	—	—	—

Source: Statistical table about the conditions of rural economy in Lengshuigou (internal material).

Table 7.4. Lengshuigou crop yields, 2001, 2004, and 2010

	2001			2004			2010		
Project	*Seeded area (hectare)*	*Total yield (ton)*	*Per unit area yield (kilogram)*	*Seeded area (hectare)*	*Total yield (ton)*	*Per unit area yield (kilogram)*	*Seeded area (hectare)*	*Total yield (ton)*	*Per unit area yield (kilogram)*
Seeded area (hectare)	450	—	—	393	—	—	173	—	—
1. **grain**	380	1,763	4,640	328	1,703	5,142	157	2,002	6,375
1.1 summer harvest	193	870	4,500	154	920	5,974	157	1,060	6,750
1.2 autumn harvest	187	893	4,770	174	783	4,500	157	942	6,000
2. **vegetables and fruits**	62	1,240	20,000	65	1,300	20,000	1 2	—	3,500

Source: Crops in Lengshuigou (internal material).

household responsibility system freed labor from collective responsibilities and led to a more efficient allocation of labor within the market economy. In thinking about the problems of labor under the collective system, we can see that although the system promised egalitarianism under a legally sanctioned distribution system, it actually involved a form of what we might call "legalized exploitation." It was this exploitation that caused the problems with labor motivation, which the household responsibility system was able to reverse.

Second, as the market economy developed, new ideas spread among the peasantry, introducing them to ideas of profit and of equality. This led to sharp increases in the mobility of labor out of agriculture and into higher profit non-agricultural industries. As we can see from table 7.5, the percentage of the Lengshuigou labor force involved in agriculture dropped from close to 90 percent in the early 1980s to 27.9 percent in 1989.

Since the 1990s, the acceleration of urbanization, development of rural reforms, and loosening of the household registration system have created a large supply of surplus rural labor. These individuals, now commonly referred to as "rural migrant workers" (*nongmingong*), have flowed in large numbers into the cities. They are an important reflection of the sharp contrasts, administratively, in China's dual system that divides individuals into those with urban and those with rural household registrations. Although similar phenomena exist in other countries, the term "rural migrant workers" has a special meaning in Chinese society. Despite the fact that such workers are engaged in relatively stable as well as unstable non-agricultural jobs in the city, they are still identified as "peasants," a category that is difficult to explain when we take occupation as the central factor in analyzing social structure. They are a group with a special identity formed in the transfer of rural labor into non-agricultural occupations during a transitional period. They form a large and awkward group, located in a space between peasants and urban citizens. Those classified in this way have an identity and status that it is difficult to escape.

Table 7.5. Decline in agricultural labor force, Lengshuigou, 1980s

Year	*1982*	*1983*	*1985*	*1986*	*1987*	*1988*	*1989*
Laborers (individuals)	1,767	1,775	1,800	1,750	1,790	1,800	1,810
Number of Laborers in agriculture, forestry, fishing, and hunting	1,590	1,290	853	680	600	500	505
Percentage (%)	89.98	72.67	47.39	38.86	33.52	27.78	27.90

Source: Xu and Yang 1994, 64.

Capital

In the new-style rural economy under the household responsibility system, peasants became involved in the market economy, spending more time on producing agricultural and sideline products that would produce maximum profits. Capital investment came to play an increasingly important role in production. However, unlike investment under the collective, individuals made investment decisions voluntarily. Let us look at two aspects of this new style of investment, first as seen in agricultural production and then as seen in the development of sidelines and industry.

As we have seen in the section on land use, there has been a sharp decline in agricultural land as a result of road building and using land for non-agricultural purposes. Given the shortage of land, the extensive production mode used during the collective period, which relied on increasing the cultivable land and increasing labor, is no longer possible. Thus, Lengshuigou peasants have turned to intensive modes of agricultural production, which require intensive and meticulous farming. One of the signs of this is a change in the ratio of capital to labor, which is a reflection of the gradual replacement of labor with capital, as seen in the mechanization of agricultural production.

Capital investment in agriculture has led to higher labor productivity and a greater variety of crops. As the variety of products has increased, links to the broader market are very important, and peasants can no longer limit their sphere of activities to the village. Peasants have thus voluntarily become integrated into the market. Apart from increasing capital investment in agricultural production, peasants also have invested in various enterprises in response to a state policy for support of township enterprises, and the economic benefits of this can be very clearly seen. These investments of capital, machinery, and technology have stimulated the development of village commerce and industry and boosted villagers' income.

Ren Yanting (former Party branch secretary of the village):

> In the 1980s Provincial leaders sent out directives to encourage the development of township enterprises. Provinces and cities assigned quotas to towns, counties, and villages. In that intense political situation, without deliberating on feasibility, we set up several enterprises, mostly joint-equity enterprises. The earliest was a bristle processing factory, which was built jointly by the village, and a production and processing plant.

Overall, we can see that under the reform policies, capital has come to play a more important role than land and labor in village development. Agricultural economic patterns have changed from the old extensive cultivation pattern to the intensive cultivation pattern, which is dependent on capital investment. With more capital investment, agricultural productivity has risen, and the range for production and exchange of agricultural products has expanded. As for industrial sidelines, with the nation making great efforts to promote township enterprises, the amount of capital invested has increased and started to play a bigger role.

While the household responsibility system emancipated rural productive forces, it also gave rise to a new set of problems. On the plus side, we have seen how allowing the peasant household to operate as an independent agent has increased production. On the negative side, peasant household units farm on a very small scale and are unable to carry out large-scale operations; thus, they are not able to make the most productive use of all factors of production. Moreover, individual peasant households have little power to deal with the risks in the market economy. Thus, when we think of the future, it would seem that the current small-scale household-based production is not going to be able to meet the needs of future society.

In a word, since the 1980s, under the influence of the household responsibility system, economic development in Lengshuigou has entered a new era. As we have seen, during this transitional period, the pressures of urbanization and introduction of market mechanisms have had a major impact on the village economy. As for land, we can identify the beginning of two trends, which have developed more in the twenty-first century: first, the shifting of land to non-agricultural use (such as the building of industrial parks and real estate development) and second, the beginnings of scale farming (such as the building of the dairy farm). As for labor and capital, labor mobility has increased, and non-agricultural urban capital has started to enter the village, leading to a new direction for development of the rural economy.

NEW TRENDS IN ECONOMIC DEVELOPMENT

In the twenty-first century, urbanization has accelerated, and there has been a deepening of the influence of the market mechanism, resulting in a great increase in the use of land for non-agricultural purposes. On the labor front, we now see greater diversity in both occupational and spatial mobility of the labor force, while rising levels of urban capital investment in the village have made clear the importance of capital in contemporary rural development.

New Changes in Land Use

In the twenty-first century, the city of Jinan has grown rapidly, and its eastern suburbs will soon encroach on the village of Lengshuigou. As a rural area in the outer suburbs of a large city, Lengshuigou has felt the strong impact of urbanization, which has presented many opportunities for more profitable use of its land. This section will look at two trends in land use: first, the conversion of formerly agricultural land to non-agricultural uses and, second, the development of large-scale production on land that is still used for agricultural activities.

A Chinese village is both a place of residence and a place of production, and as population increased, the amount of land occupied by residences tended to increase. We learned from village informants that Lengshuigou officials have tried to stop the expansion of land occupied by residences and that no new applications for housing plots have been approved since 1993. Rather, the village has decided on a development plan in which all new land allotted for housing is used for construction of apartment buildings. In 2002, the village committee constructed two commercial apartment buildings with a gross floor area of 15,000 square meters; villagers could purchase flats in the buildings at a price of 1,300 *yuan* per square meter. In the end, many of the apartments were purchased by nonnatives who were working on the industrial estate or by people with urban household registrations who were attracted by the relatively low price. Records show that some 130 non-village households bought apartments in the two buildings. The development of real estate has pushed the village to create the kind of living environment characteristic of an urban neighborhood.

Liu Chuncai, the village Party secretary gave us this account of the apartment construction:

> We first built a new office building for the village committee. Construction was started in April 2002 and finished in October, costing a total of 700,000 *yuan*. Later, the village contacted a real estate agency to build two commercial apartment buildings of 15,000 square meters in total. We wanted to build apartment buildings as a way to save land. For decades the village secretary had not approved a single request for new house plots, but villagers need new houses when they decide to divide their families, or because of the birth of a new generation. The amount of land in the village was limited. If we allotted the same amount of land for single-family dwellings, we would only be able to house ten households, but with apartment buildings, the same amount of land could provide apartments for more than 110 households. We put out a notice for public bidding on the project and selected a company with abundant funds. Then the village committee and the real estate agency signed a contract according to which we paid construction costs in stages, for example so much money when you finished the construction of three floors.
>
> The real estate company set up a sales center and used our village broadcast system to advertise the sale of apartments to villagers. Villagers who wanted to buy an apartment at the price of 1,300 *yuan* per square meter should hurry and

sign up; discounts were offered to those who signed up first. Those who wanted to buy an apartment had to make a down payment of 50 percent of the purchase price. More than four million *yuan* was gathered from more than 30 households. These down payments served as capital for the construction company to begin construction of the two buildings. As construction continued, the buyers made additional payments with 90 percent of the purchase price due by the time construction reached the final stages. After selling apartments within the village, the remainder were sold to people outside at the slightly higher price of 1,350 *yuan* per square meter, which means that an extra 50 *yuan* was needed per square meter compared with the sales price within the village. Using this system of down payments and follow-up payments as the work progressed, the construction company was able to complete the construction tasks. When we did a final settling of accounts, we learned that the construction for the apartments averaged 680 *yuan* per square meter. Using this method, villagers were able to obtain new housing, the real estate investor was able to make a profit, and the village collective got rich. In various projects to transform the older parts of the village, the village committee invested 8 million *yuan* and earned a profit of 70 million.

From this, we can say the direction for village development is quite clear, which is the gradual conversion of the village into an urban-style neighborhood through the construction of more high-rise buildings. In this process the villagers' household registrations will be converted from agricultural (*nongye hukou*) to urban registrations (*chengshi hukou*). The district government wants to reorganize all of the village land into urban-style neighborhoods as a way of making money. But villagers also have demands of their own. For example, each household should have a minimum of 60 square meters of housing space. In addition, separate buildings should be constructed as rental properties. In the foreseeable future, villagers in Lengshuigou will be very wealthy because of the village's suburban location. With acceleration of urbanization of Jinan land in Lengshuigou, it will become very valuable.

As we can see from Secretary Liu's explanation, land utilization plans for Lengshuigou take advantage of the village's location to develop non-agriculture uses of the land. This has brought many new residents into the village, adding significantly to the resources the village committee can use for collective investment.

In addition to building apartments, Lengshuigou has rented some land out to industrial parks. In May 2005, the town of Wangsheren built an 8,000 *mu* industrial park near Lengshuigou, named the Xingfuliu Industrial Development Zone. Construction of the industrial park was part of a town development strategy that planned to use the industrial park to bring investment in enterprises that would lead regional development. Lengshuigou seized the opportunity and decided to rent 1,000 *mu* of its land to the industrial park scheme.

Party Secretary Liu Chuncai explained the reasoning behind the plan:

In 2002 the government began to advocate for the development of industrial parks, and this was a great opportunity for us. The town government of Wangsheren designated 8,000 *mu* of land from the junction of Gongye Bei road and Kaiyuan road to the north for construction of industrial parks. However, they had difficulty implementing the scheme because of the different demands from nearby villages. Some demanded high prices, and as a result they could not reach agreements. Our village was at the north end of this area. For us, it was a good thing. At the very least we would be able to develop the land without going through the onerous procedures usually required to convert agriculture land to other uses. We had a lot of land, but how to make use of this advantage? Cultivating the land will not make us rich. With land distributed to every household, peasants have control of the land. They work hard and toil all year long but still can't make much money. Besides, some land in our village is waterlogged lowland, hard to cultivate and very dependent on weather, with a low yield. So we thought about first renting out this kind of land and keeping the good land, since land quality doesn't matter in constructing industrial parks. After everything was settled, we used all kinds of methods to attract enterprises—we advertised, we called on connections, villagers talked to relatives with connections, etc. In order to make arrangements so that both sides would profit, we lowered the threshold for enterprises and were open to negotiations. We are responsible for constructing roads and providing water and electricity, and the government agreed not to collect taxes for three years. After considering the conditions of the village and the enterprise, agreements were reached and contracts were signed. Enterprises settled in the industrial park also invited other enterprises to join them, and thus our village's industrial park came into being.

We hoped that the construction of the industrial park would promote village development in three ways. The first was to find a way to get the most out of our land and its good location near Jinan. By setting up the industrial park at our own initiative, we hoped to preserve our village's control over the land and block efforts by the state to commandeer it. The second consideration was that setting up the industrial park would allow villagers to increase their income. After toiling in the fields for so many years, people just managed to support themselves, and the sole purpose for working in the field was to get food. It is hard for people to make money with just one *mu* of land, when you take into account the investment they have to make in seeds, fertilizer, pesticide, and irrigation. Profits are really low. For each *mu* of land that was occupied by the industrial park, a household would get 850 *yuan* rent, which was sufficient to make ends meet. If you were to farm the same one *mu* of land, by the time you subtracted all of the investment costs from income, you would not be able to make 850 *yuan*. And furthermore, one never knew how the weather would influence output. The third aim was to enhance our collective economy. Let me explain how it worked. When enterprises want to invest here, we contract land out to them

> on a thirty-year lease and they construct the facilities they need, thus saving us time and energy. Contracts are usually for 30 years with rental fees rising every five years according to a scale that measures the growth rate of society and price inflation. When the contract expires after 30 years, everything on the surface of the land will belong to the collective. Needless to say, there is no point in the firms tearing down the buildings at the end of their contracts. But if enterprises want to pull down the buildings, there is binding contract which stipulates ownership of everything on the land goes to us. All of our contracts with the enterprises follow this model. The industrial park has attracted investment worth 300,000,000, so after 30 years, we will be in possession of real estate worth this amount. In this way, our collective economy is enhanced and land preserved.

In 2002, Hongteng Industrial Company, Ltd., invested 30 million *yuan* to build Hongteng Science and Technology Industrial Park, of 80,000 square meters. This park is bordered by Gongye Bei road on the south and Happy Willow Square to the west; the park covers more than 500 *mu* with factories, administrative offices, science and technology labs, and all the necessary supporting infrastructure. The environment is nice, with a green area of 40 percent. Because of the nice location, environment, services, and functions, some fifty enterprises, including Xingquan and Yongjun have set up businesses in the park. Development of such industrial parks has played a major role in stimulating industrialization in rural areas and has played a vital part in the development of Lengshuigou.

Photo 7.1. Hongteng Hotel in the Hongteng Industrial Park

Secretary Liu Chuncai commented:

> As for attracting enterprises, we took the initiative and got hold of a key person, Cheng Kehong, the director of Hongteng, who was from our village and whose mother still lived in the most luxurious 3-story-house in the village. He often came back to visit his mother, and he had warm feelings toward the village. We approached him first, but naturally he would not choose our location if there were no profits. So after some discussion, we offered him a rental price of 1,000 *yuan* per mu when it was 3,000 or 4,000 per *mu* in other villages. Finally he decided to acquire use rights to 400 *mu* at a price of 1,000 *yuan/mu* and so the industrial park was constructed. Cheng Kehong was a member of the Association of Industry and Commerce, and had many close acquaintances with other entrepreneurs. With his introduction, many enterprises came to settle down in Lengshuigou.

From the account of the secretary, we can see that that the leaders of Lengshuigou have played an aggressive role in promoting industrial parks. The village was particularly happy with the Hongteng Company, which is a large-scale privately operated enterprise that does business in a number of industries, including catering, furniture manufacturing, real estate, and many other fields. It has business offices in Wangsheren and Jinan, and as we have seen, its owner was a native of Lengshuigou. Drawn by the offer of unusually low rent, Hongteng decided to enter the Kaiyuan Road industrial park. The company divided the industrial park into four relatively independent areas—areas A, B, C, and D—and then constructed factories and infrastructure and improved the overall environment under a unified plan. Because of its business association with other enterprises, Hongteng was able to use its social networks to attract many other companies to come to this industrial park. In this way, Hongteng was able to earn significant profits from leasing factories and equipment to other companies. Both the company and the village prospered.

Since the beginning of the early twenty-first century, the amount of farmland has sharply contracted as the village made arrangements to lease land for the construction of industrial parks, and most village families came to depend on non-farm employment for a significant portion of their income. To measure how villagers felt about these changes, we conducted a survey of attitudes toward work and learned that more than half (58.6 percent) replied that although you could not earn much from cultivating the land, it was good to have it as insurance for survival. An additional 9.6 percent of the respondents agreed with the statement "farm work is a peasant's duty" (table 7.6).

This means that when villagers worry about survival in times of crisis, they still see tilling the land as a kind of guarantee of survival. "For a peasant, whether he is engaged in other lines of work and regardless of how wealthy

Table 7.6. Villagers' attitudes toward farming, Lengshuigou, 2010

Attitude toward farming	*Frequency*	*(%)*
Not profitable but a life guarantee	316	58.6
No prospect at all	115	21.3
A peasant's duty	52	9.6
A higher income can be guaranteed by intensive production and growing of specialized crops	49	9.1
Other	7	1.3
Total	539	100.0

Source: Shandong University Survey, 2010.

he is, farmland is still the most reliable social guarantee. Farmland can provide people with the most basic living conditions" (Xu and Yang 1994, 78). So for peasants, farmland's function as a social guarantee is still important. However, when we consider the age distribution of respondents, we see that while the older villagers still saw land as providing a guarantee, younger villagers thought there was little future in farming.

Changes in Labor

There were major changes in the organization and mobility of labor as a result of the high-speed growth of the Chinese economy. The number of Lengshuigou villagers working in industrial and service sector jobs greatly increased. The village's industrial parks offered new employment opportunities to those in the village community and also attracted many migrant workers from other places. As the number of migrant workers increased, this also stimulated the development of the catering and service industries, increasing the opportunities for employment in the service sector. Party Secretary Liu explained the changes in the following way:

Liu Chuncai:

> When the village decided to invest in the industrial parks, we decided to lower the rental fees for land to 1,000 *yuan/mu* since we were located some distance from existing centers. At that time land use fees for land north of the Gongye Bei road were set at 3–4,000 per *mu*. Because of the low price, many enterprises chose to settle in Lengshuigou. Most of the firms that came to the industrial park just built factories, although a few enterprises also built living areas for their staff, but this was not so common. So, most enterprise staff had to rent housing in the village. As for Lengshuigou natives, at least 500 found jobs in the firms in the industrial park. In addition, regular labor enterprises also needed personnel with higher-level skills, including engineers and managerial staff. Most of these

were hired from outside the village. Since it was more convenient to commute to work, many of these people chose to live in the village, which brought in rent, stimulated consumption, and provided information and technology as well. Some shops in the service industry such as barbershops and restaurants were doing very well, including motorcycle taxis that park along the road waiting for customers. In this way villagers got rich, and the village collective also got rich. It's just like the traditional Chinese saying: "The big river can be full only when the small streams are running."

Another village cadre gave us a similar account.
Zhang Yuanxiu (head of the Lengshuigou Women's Association):

The industrial park promotes employment in our village and neighboring villages. Another thing is that some migrant workers who have a job in the industrial park rent houses in our village, which brings rent and increases villagers' income. They also bring information and promote consumption. People from outside the village live, eat, and spend money here. There are about 2–3,000 people who work for Hongteng who live, eat, and spend money here. To spend is to invest, pushing development of the catering industry, commerce, service industry, and other tertiary industries. The number of restaurants and shops has increased, and none of the village restaurants have closed down. Transportation is also promoted because enterprises have to go out to do business. There are many motorcycle taxis here. They would not be here if they could not make money. This is an economic chain. There are many shops and barbershops in our village, none of which has closed down, because there are more customers flocking to them. In the past there were not so many shops, barbershops, and restaurants. All these are brought by the industrial park. Commerce has developed as a result of the industrial park.

Mobility of labor has also increased. Our villagers have gradually accepted the new-style economic order. From an objective point of view, they had no choice but to change: farming land has decreased as land was converted to other uses, and at the same time, agricultural mechanization decreased the demand for field labor. As a result, more and more villagers have left the village to look for non-agricultural jobs. Now more villagers focus on finding employment in the secondary and tertiary sectors of industry and services.

There has been a steady increase in the percentage of the labor force that has left the village: the figure stood at 50.7 percent in 1999, 56.7 percent in 2000, 59.2 percent in 2001, 62.7 percent in 2002, 60 percent in 2003, 63.4 percent in 2005, and 62.7 percent in 2006. As we can see, over half of all workers now work outside the village. As to where they go, most workers find jobs in Jinan or in the rapidly developing coastal regions of Shandong province. As for what they do, we can find them working in industrial enterprises, commerce, factories, and mines in the suburbs; some have also started their own businesses in such fields as commerce, construction, and transportation.

Among the respondents to our questionnaire, 69.8 percent had experience working outside the village, and more than half had worked outside for more than six years. When asked about the "major source of family income," 70.6 percent of the respondents chose "doing migrant work" and only 6.7 percent answered "agricultural production." When asked about "the number of migrant workers in the family," only 15.5 percent answered "none," while 61 percent of the respondents had two or more migrant workers in the family. When asked, "Is doing migrant work helpful to the family financially?" 93.9 percent answered "helpful." From this we can see that working outside the village is now a very common experience and that most villagers look positively on leaving the village to hunt for jobs.

Changes in Capital

Capital investment has been a crucial factor in the transformation of Lengshuigou. More than one hundred enterprises have entered the village, beginning with the development of the Kaiyuan Road industrial park. The enterprises are engaged in a wide variety of activities, including food processing, commerce and trade, decorative sculpture, logistics, radiator processing, paper manufacture, energy technology, furniture manufacturing, rubber products manufacturing, and many more. These labor-intensive enterprises have pushed social and economic development in Lengshuigou and surrounding villages, and most importantly, they have provided employment opportunities for villagers.

As we have seen in the section on labor, the industrial park has provided employment for more than five hundred Lengshuigou residents. Some enterprises, particularly assembly plants, had a high demand for female labor. However, the male-to-female ratio in the labor force is 1.4 to 1, and as a result, there is not sufficient female labor to meet the needs of companies that want to hire young female labor. Thus, firms have had to seek workers from other villages and areas.

One of the consequences of the high demand for labor has been in-migration of workers from many other areas, and this has stimulated the development of the service industries. Although the industrial development is what a visitor would immediately notice, there has also been a rapid development of agriculture and sideline industries. The village has developed a very prosperous dairy industry, and many villagers have become wealthy through their involvement in this industry. Many villagers became wealthy through livestock breeding. Table 7.7 provides statistics on income from different sectors, and as we can see, animal husbandry is one of the pillars of the local economy.

Table 7.7. Wangsheren income by sector, 1999, 2000, 2002, 2003, 2005, and 2006 (unit: ten thousand *yuan*)

Year	*1999*	*2000*	*2002*	*2003*	*2005*	*2006*
Total Income	4,772	3,695	3,518	3,861	4,900	4,930
1. Agriculture	480	359	300	300	290	300
2. Forestry	3	2	—	1	0	0
3. Animal Husbandry	700	700	830	1,000	1,200	1,210
4. Fishery	15	5	—	—	0	0
5. Industry	860	730	650	585	670	670
6. Construction	670	400	600	650	750	750
7. Transportation	510	400	300	350	380	380
8. Catering Industry	960	450	410	460	650	660
9. Service Industry	70	40	40	40	80	80
10. Other Incomes	504	405	280	505	880	880

Source: Wangsheren's internal materials.

The dairy industry traces its origins to 1983, when some village households began to raise dairy cows. At that time, a single dairy cow could produce an annual profit of about 1,000 *yuan*. In 1986, one of the dairy companies set up a milk collection center in the village, and by 1988 the number of dairy farmers had grown to 30, with over 150 cows, and annual profits had risen to 3,000 *yuan* per cow. By 1999, there were 80 households with more than 400 cows. In response to the development of the dairy industry, in June of 1999, the village committee decided to set up a dairy farm covering 80 *mu* with unified planning, management, sales, and water and electricity supply. In 1999, 18 dairy farmers with 235 cows moved to the new village farm, and the farm produced a daily milk yield of 2 tons. In 2001, the dairy farm was expanded to 300 *mu* and given a new name: the Lengshuigou Demonstration Dairy Farm. Forty cow breeders joined the new base with a total of 600 cows; the daily milk yield rose to 9.5 tons and, farmers were earning a profit of 5,000 *yuan* per cow. Lengshuigou's dairy farm is one of the top 100 dairy farms in China and the largest in Jinan. It has modern facilities including seven mechanized milking halls, a total of 7,200 cows, a daily milk yield of over 30 tons, and yearly sales of 55 billion *yuan* (LCZ 2010, 84).

The village secretary, Liu Chuncai, who was among the first to raise cows, gave us an account of the reasons for building the cow-breeding base:

> In 1993 I took on the duty of village Party secretary and have held this position for 17 years (2010). I was among the first to breed cows in the village and it was financially rewarding then for the price for milk was 4 *mao* per *jin*, so I was making more money than workers at the Jinan Iron Company. I gradually became rich, built a house, and bought furniture, motorcycles, refrigerators, ice

Photo 7.2. Lengshuigou Dairy Farm

lockers, and other modern electric appliances. People in the village started to follow my way to breed cows, and gradually it became a business of some scale with a milk collecting center set up in the village.

Back then each household raised its own cows. Later people found that profits were low when cows were raised by the household. We also learned that this method of relying on individual households was too inefficient and we could not benefit from the reduced costs that come from scale. Overall our methods could not stand up to the intense competition in the market and needed to be changed. So villagers were willing to let the collective organize all the scattered dairy farmers, acting in unison to cope with the market. With this will and through my own investigation, I thought it was feasible to build a cow farm to raise all the cows together. It was easy to manage this way and could reduce dairy farmers' labor. At that time (the 1990s), the nation also advocated industrialized operation, and many villages built greenhouses to raise vegetables. But in our village, we decided that it made more sense to set up a dairy farm. Afterwards many greenhouses could no longer deliver profit, while the dairy farm in our village has flourished.

From the above interview, we can see that by following the example of the village secretary, who got rich first by breeding cows, more and more households in the village stepped into this business, changing breeding methods from household-based small-scale production to the development of a modern collective dairy farm.

Nowadays villagers' commercial awareness has greatly increased, and more and more people have gotten involved in non-agricultural production. As a result, there are many privately owned shops in the village, and living standards have continued to rise. The Lengshuigou of today, with its dairy farm and industrial parks, apartment complexes and service industries, is a long way from the inward-looking village of the 1940s. We can imagine that the development of a new railroad station nearby will mark the beginning of the next stage of the village's transition and that in ten or fifteen years the village will be fully integrated into the city of Jinan.

NOTE

1. "Sharing a common pot" refers to the system under the People's Commune in which food and other necessities were supplied to everyone, whether or not they worked hard. This term is now used to refer to the problems of extreme egalitarianism under the commune, which is commonly thought to have led to a great decline in the motivation to work, leading to low levels of efficiency.

Chapter Eight

Transformation and Future of the Village

Over the last three decades, Lengshuigou society has experienced rapid transformation that reflects the broader changes in Chinese society. In this concluding chapter, we review those changes, offering our analysis of the dynamics that have created contemporary village society and our speculation on future development trends.

Social change is a dialectical process that involves both differentiation and integration, each of which is influenced by various internal and external factors. Social change and social order can be analyzed from the micro level, looking at the social integration of individuals, and from the macro level, focusing on integration of the whole system. Analysis of the social order from the angle of individual social integration focuses on the interaction among actors in the course of daily life as well as the nature of their relationships; analysis of the social order focuses on the nature of the aggregate social system. Taken together, the two provide the kind of comprehensive assessment of social change that we have pursued in this volume.

REVIEW OF A CENTURY OF CHANGE

From Traditional and Closed to Relatively Open

Our study began from the *Kankō Chōsa* reports, using those early 1940s survey materials to describe what we have for convenience referred to as "traditional" Chinese society, a society that was based on a relatively self-sufficient agrarian regime: economically, it was rooted in a self-sufficient smallholder economy; politically it was characterized by a "double-track" system of control, which saw a separation between autocratic imperial power at the national level and independent self-governance at the grassroots level; and culturally, it was shaped by a Confucian culture that emphasized blood relationships. Although we can distinguish the three layers of economics, politics, and culture, the three shared a number of common principles that tied them together in an interrelated organic whole (Qiu 2008, 27). Throughout this book, we have referred to this "traditional" China as a patriarchal society. We chose this expression to stress the integration of the political institutions based on a legal framework shaped by Confucian ethics and an economic system that supported family-based economic activities. In the period before the founding of the PRC, state control over the countryside was weak and depended on village lineages and local gentry elite, who were the central figures in exercising local political control. In this society, traditional morality and customs served as the main mechanisms for mediating interpersonal interaction, and family and lineage exercised strong control and influence over the actions of individuals.

In Chinese traditional society, the state played little role in bringing about rural social integration, a situation that was reflected in the common saying that "state power goes no farther than the walls of the county town."

> Patriarchal power based on consanguinity and the power of the local gentry served as forces driving integration of rural society and successfully maintained control for thousands of years with the support of Confucian ethics and the feudal land system. This kind of society operated in a slow and persistent manner. The patriarchal lineage worked together with the local gentry and a weak state to maintain order in an integrated rural society. (Wang and Li 2010, 17)

As we saw in chapter 2, under the Guomindang government efforts were made to increase the state's control over rural society. GMD efforts to construct more effective institutions at the county level were based on a policy adopted at the Second National Policy Conference in December 1932, which declared that "improvement of county administration shall be the top priority for now." However, GMD efforts did not lead to effective rule.

> On the surface it seemed that the Nationalist Party government established a relatively complete administrative system at the grass-roots level and strengthened political control over rural areas through the county administration, but the Nationalist Party was not able to effectively implement its own policies. There were many problems including a failure to create the full-range of institutions or assign appropriate personnel. National authority was weakened and decrees were not enforced and as a result national authority at the grass roots level was, as before, very weak. (Liu 2003, 29)

In spite of the efforts of the GMD to set up a new system of rural administration that reached into the villages, the patriarchal lineage continued to exercise great influence over all aspects of rural society, acting as an important pillar maintaining social order in rural areas.

During the years of the Anti-Japanese War, state efforts to integrate rural society were influenced by wartime conditions, and the state made little headway in integrating rural society in villages like Lengshuigou. In fact, it seemed as though the state was absent, and the lineage and local-relations-based system continued to play a dominant role in maintaining public order. As we have seen, Lengshuigou, as a relatively prosperous village, was also relatively closed to outside contacts, and this also played a role in its ability to maintain existing systems of local control. Most of the village residents devoted most of their time to farming, and human relations continued to follow established patterns. In dealing with their fellow villagers, people in Lengshuigou turned to traditional ideas about human sentiment and duty. Their daily life followed customary habits and moved to the rhythm of the agricultural and ritual festival calendars. Traditional logics dominated the operation of all forms of capital, economic, social, and cultural life. Values and customs handed down from senior generations provided the logic and served as the key standards and justification for actions in everyday life. They were also the standard for social integration.

Having said this, we also must add that villages like Lengshuigou were not completely cut off from the dramatic changes of the first half of the twentieth century. In the cities, heated contests raged between the advocates of "tradition" and "modernity," "East" and "West." Ideas promoted by members of the May Fourth generation had a major impact on plans for rural reform and played a central role in shaping the efforts to deal with all of the problems that arose from the crisis in the existing system of rural life and political control.

Constantly Changing Villages

From the Founding of the PRC to the Reform and Opening Up Policies: Collectivized Villages under the Absolute Control of the State

The establishment of the PRC and its extension of control over rural areas marked the beginning of a cycle of revolutionary change in village society. The Chinese government launched a series of major movements designed to deal with the country's relatively backward economy: at the top of the list was creation of a socialist economy, which in the countryside led to the establishment of a system of public ownership of the means of production. After creating administrative units to guide the planned economy, priority was given to a policy centered on heavy industrialization. To realize this goal, institutions were set up to centralize control over all economic resources. As a result, collectivization proceeded in the countryside, and rural production was incorporated into the state's macro-economic system of control.

As we have seen in the experiences of Lengshuigou, the rural revolution began with land reform: within the space of a few years, the thousand-year-old system of feudal land ownership was destroyed, replaced by a system of private ownership. As part of this campaign, lineage land, which had been the base of the lineage's power, was confiscated and redistributed to poor peasants. This removed the physical base of lineage power in the village.

Following land reform, new types of rural organization promoted by the socialist ideology began to play an increasingly important role. Step by step, new organizations were created in the countryside—mutual-aid groups, lower level cooperatives, higher level cooperatives, and finally the people's communes. The communes joined administrative and economic organization in one institution, lasting for more than twenty years until their dissolution in 1984 when the household responsibility system returned control over farming to individual households.

We have identified three major stages in rural organization after the establishment of the PRC. The first stage was the movement for agricultural cooperation between 1949 and 1957. During that stage, tenant farmers gained land, creating a new society in which every village family owned at least a small amount of land. As the process of collectivization advanced, the small-landholding peasants were turned into farm laborers, working together on land that came to be publicly owned. During the second stage of the People's Commune (from 1958 to 1984), a new system of organization was created based on public ownership of land and other means of production. From a sociological perspective we have seen that the shift to the people's communes represented not just a change in economic organization but also impacted all aspects of daily life, including family life, labor style, reproduction, child-raising methods, and attitudes toward and enjoyment of leisure time. The third stage covers the period since the breakup of the communes in 1984, a stage that has been characterized by a gradual transformation to a new lifestyle in which village families make their own economic decisions in a system shaped by the market economy.

As we saw in the descriptions in this book, one of the chief characteristics of this process was the creation of new levels of political authority that reached down into the village, cutting across the earlier patterns of organization based on family and lineage. These new organizations served multiple functions. They were administrative units, but also the fundamental building blocks of the system of economic organization. They were also official units in the national political system, responsible for organizing production and for managing and integrating all aspects of society. A variety of institutional arrangements, including the household registration system, were created to guarantee that the new rural organizations would be able to fulfill their tasks. Together these various institutions produced a dual economic structure, with the state-owned industrial economy as one dimension and the people's commune-controlled agricultural economy as the second dimension. This total system produced profound changes in the relationship between Chinese villages and the national state. The PRC state, much more powerful than its imperial and Republican predecessors, had gained control over rural society. During this period, social order in the countryside was based on an integrated system that had become highly politicized, built on the bases of the dual economy and a social system rooted in a hierarchy of politically determined class statuses.

China's rural areas, under the conditions outlined above, became a test site subjected to comprehensive and profound influence and control from the national government in pursuit of a national development strategy focusing on heavy industrialization. The patterns of action of rural dwellers came to reflect a new set of values as villagers were persuaded to view their own interests as directly subordinate to the interests of the state, with interests of the state elevated to an almost sacred position. What we see in Lengshuigou matches very well with Tang Kuiyu's suggestion that "under certain social historical conditions, an ideology will inevitably lead to a way of life, and an absolute ideology can lead to an extreme way of life" (Tang 2008, 83).

The changes we have seen in Lengshuigou were similar to those experienced by villages all over China. Collective forms of organization replaced family- and lineage-based social organization, and state-directed forms of public life replaced earlier patterns of thought and lifestyle. The traditional forces that had earlier driven social integration in the village suffered a heavy blow, people came to identify in a relatively extreme way with national interests, and those new ideas became the foundation for personal interaction and social relations. However, in spite of the heavy pressure of the state ideology, there were still remnants of former patterns of action based on consanguinity and regional ties, values that would reassert themselves after the launching of the reforms and the dissolution of the commune and its patterns of collective labor.

After the Reform and Opening Up: Villages under Weakened State Control

The rural areas were the first area for experimentation in the nationwide reform policies, which were officially launched in late 1978. The reforms brought the dissolution of the people's communes, which were a key pillar of the existing dual economic system. Although the people's communes which had been the main institution supporting the agrarian sector of the dual economy were dissolved, this did not bring an end to a dual economic structure:

rather, the dual economic structure based on a sharp distinction between the industrial and agricultural economies was replaced by a new dual economic structure based on distinctions between urban and rural areas.

The household responsibility system, which was the core institutional innovation in the rural reforms, represented a new form of economic management in which land was still owned by the collective while the collective contracted responsibility for production to the household and also gave the household the right to determine how to use its own labor resources. This reform established a new relationship with regard to rights and obligations among the state, the collective, and farmers. The state no longer used plans as a way to intervene in agricultural production. The reforms thus marked a major retreat by the state from direct involvement in controlling agricultural production, and by raising the incentives to individual households, not only maximized the incentives in agricultural production but also opened the door for rural dwellers to participate in non-agricultural sectors. The reforms thus highlighted the important role of the household in agricultural production, encouraging individual workers and entrepreneurs to pursue their own interests. Family-based operation became the new model for economic development in rural areas, and family-based rural enterprises were a crucial embodiment of this pattern.

One of the most important results of the reforms was in breaking down the barriers between urban and rural areas. When we trace the causal chains that led to this result, we can see that the changes began with the freeing of rural labor, which provided strong incentives and stimulated the creativity of those in farming communities. This touched off a process of differentiation among former commune members: many former rural dwellers sought work in urban society. At the same time, there was a boom in the development of TVEs in the countryside and a heightened pace of development in the cities. Together these changes created a new stratum of workers who had rural-residence status but were engaged in industrial production. As these changes proceeded, economic logics increasingly penetrated all aspects of life. One of the important results of the household responsibility system, which can be viewed as a kind of second land reform that returned control over land and labor use to the household, was a change in rural attitudes. Ideological mobilization during the collective period had led commune members to identify their own interests with those of the state. The reforms reversed that process, and rural dwellers came to focus on their own interests. As a new behavioral logic based on commodified relations spread in the villages, it became a major factor in family calculations and came to influence all aspects of daily life. Rural behavior began to reflect the characteristics of instrumental rationality. "Instrumental rationality" as we use it here refers to a situation in which individual behavior is driven by the pursuit of material gain; the individual makes rational choices in pursuit of his or her goals, considering only how to maximize the desired outcome with little concern for people's emotional and spiritual values. In short, economic logics become the leading factor in systemic integration in rural areas. The "national logic" of the collective period has been replaced by a new logic in which not only things but also human relations have been commodified.

In Lengshuigou, one of the biggest changes during the reform era has been the revival of some pre-collective patterns of interaction. We can see these changes in the agricultural sector where intensive patterns of cultivation are replacing the extensive mode that was common in earlier periods. The shift to intensive forms of cultivation has resulted in much closer links between household production and the market. As rural producers are increasingly confronted with the challenges of an unpredictable market economy, villagers have rediscovered the importance of family and lineage ties as a basis for cooperation. These kinds of personal ties known as "*guanxi*"—personal relationships modeled on Fei Xiaotong's differential mode of association—have become an important form of social capital, which can be drawn upon as a support in daily activities.

Villages in the Process of Rural-Urban Transformation

As China entered the twenty-first century, the national government began to focus attention on the "three rural" problem—a formulation that summed up the inequalities that had been created by national development strategies that had stressed rapid industrialization. Rural areas had fallen increasingly behind urban regions in average income, in social infrastructure, in education, and in the extent of the social net to support the aged and the poor. Rapid development following the initiation of the economic reform policies had exacerbated the problem in many areas as migrant workers flowed out of rural areas seeking jobs in the city, leaving behind elderly parents and young children. The Chinese Communist Party's answer to the challenges posed by growing inequality was a call to all levels of government to put greater stress on rural development, including a program to build "new socialist villages." The new-socialist-village agenda included improving rural infrastructure and narrowing the gap between urban and rural living conditions. Government leaders at all levels were told to put aside older ways of thinking, which had been based on "different policies respectively for urban and rural areas, and which had stressed growth in urban areas while restraining rural areas." The new policies called for reversing the order, giving priority to rural areas to help them catch up (Su, Lin, and Xie 2009, 83). The overall plans called for a more equal new socialist countryside; to achieve that goal, policies would be designed to promote rural growth not only economically in the form of agricultural modernization but also to promote a new spiritual culture.

While the new-socialist-village plan called for an integration of urban and rural areas and a gradual shrinking of the gaps in income and lifestyles between the two areas, the Chinese economic and social structures in the twenty-first century are still characterized by a dual structure, with major inequality between the two zones. While the gap in income between urban and rural areas shrank in the early years of the reform period, it had begun to rise again by the early 1990s and continued to rise for more than a decade. Statistical records for the national economy show an urban-to-rural ratio of disposable income at 2.6 to 1 in 1976. By 1981, that ratio had fallen to 1.8 to 1 but then rose again, reaching 2.2 to 1 in 1990, 2.7 to 1 in 1995, 2.8 to 1 in 2000, 3.2 to 1 in 2005, and 3.3 to 1 in 2009, before falling slightly in 2010, the year of our survey work, to 3.2 to 1 (CSB 2011).

Lengshuigou's location in the outer suburbs of the growing city of Jinan is a major factor in its fate, and the village has been relatively successful in leveraging its location. Ties with organizations in Jinan led to the construction of TVEs during the collective period that provided jobs as well as a venue for the development of familiarity with industrial production and the development of entrepreneurial talent. The village's most successful venture has been its large dairy farm, which is one of the major suppliers of milk to the Jinan market and which brings significant income to some of the village residents. The conversion of village land into an industrial park brought rent income to the village and provided non-agricultural jobs for many village residents; and the use of village land to construct commercial housing has brought new residents into the village. In the twenty-first century, most village families earn a significant portion of their income from employment in non-agricultural endeavors. The planned construction of a new high-speed rail station near the village is likely to speed up the process of transition of the village, and we can imagine that within a decade, Lengshuigou will disappear as a rural community.

Brief Conclusion

On the basis of our study of Lengshuigou across almost a century, we have drawn a number of general conclusions about Chinese rural development.

First, rural development has been shaped by a combination of endogenous and exogenous factors. The most important exogenous factor is state policy, which has strongly shaped the environment and provided the deep logic of development. The most important endogenous factor is the consciousness of the villagers and their leaders in understanding, responding to, and taking advantage of opportunities offered by changing state initiatives. State policies are designed to motivate rural change, but there is no question that rural responses have varied: some villages have been better able to respond and take advantage of state-policy changes than others.

Second, state policies take as their fundamental principle development of the agrarian economy, and the major lines of development are promoting industrialized agriculture and intensive cultivation. We have seen both of these processes at work in Lengshuigou, with the development of the large-scale dairy farm and the conversion of village land to industrial parks. While the industrial parks have brought temporary gains to village residents through jobs and land rents, we believe that developing industrial-style agriculture—in forms like the dairy farm—is a better long-term strategy for stable rural development.

Third, we believe that developing a more effective system of rural self-government is also essential for continued development. We have seen through the Lengshuigou experience various efforts to implement forms of rural governance: a "traditional style" based on family and lineage before 1949, a system of direct state control from the 1950s to the reform era, and a system based on the village committee since the beginning of the reforms. Lengshuigou, like other villages, now faces the challenge of finding a way to improve the system of local self-governance in ways that truly reflect the views of its residents. One important step to achieving this is the cultivation of local elites who can earn the trust of those in the community. There is no question that rural residents have been a relatively vulnerable group and that their views are not fully reflected in development policies. Moreover, as the reforms have proceeded and rural residents have had more economic choices, there has been a tendency for individuals and families to pursue personal goals, putting little time or effort into participating in public activities in the village. How to get greater involvement in public affairs is still an open question, and yet, increasing participation and organization is key to effective self-government,

In developing structures for rural self-governance, it is important to draw clear distinctions between the institutions that work for self-governance in urban settings and those that are needed in the countryside. For urban residents, there is a clear separation between the workplace and the neighborhood where one lives, and neighborhood self-governance organizations need only consider issues related to daily life. In the countryside, the village collective still controls the contracts for land and so the village is both a place for work and for daily livelihood. Self-governance organizations must be designed to deal with both. Although individual households have gained control over the management of their allotted farm land and use of family labor, they are still weak in the face of market risks, and they have little power to resist the attempts of capital that run counter to their own interests. While rural dwellers need the support of local organizations to defend their interests with regard to production, when it comes to dealing with daily life, there is less of a gap with urban dwellers. As villages are transformed, simply copying urban institutions for neighborhood self-governance will not serve the interests of the village communities.

Finally, we want to comment on the process of "modernization" and its relationship to existing patterns of life. Modernization is a double-edged sword, bringing improved living standards but at the same time weakening ideas and relationships that have supported rural society until now. Finding ways to keep the best of the past and blending those ideas and institutions with new forms will be a continuing challenge for rural communities. For example, ways must be found to achieve industrialization without harming the environment and without bringing an end to the beauties of the rural countryside. We should learn from the experience of foreign countries whose development took place at the expense of the environment and should study new technologies that will allow us to mitigate the bad effects of industrialization on the environment.

Another major concern is identity. As modernization proceeds, an increasingly large percentage of the population is living in urban areas. China was until very recently a nation of peasants, but the peasantry is now shrinking. One of the major questions is about what happens to the subjective identity of those who remain in rural areas and continue to engage in agriculture. The transition to a modern society challenges earlier values and identities and leaves us with the question of the nature of new identities forged by rural dwellers. From the current perspective, it seems that instrumental rationality has become a dominating force in rural life and that earlier styles of human interaction as well as the traditions of mutual aid have been sharply attacked. How will Chinese rural communities craft new forms of identity that can, as Habermas suggested, make use of new forms of communicative rationality to avoid the pitfalls of too great a reliance on instrumental rationality? This remains a challenge not only for China's rural communities but for all of Chinese society.

Epilogue

A Century of Change in a Chinese Village was published in 2013. In the years since then, we have continued to pursue our goal of "recording major contemporary changes and following closely village life" by paying close attention to developments in Lengshuigou. Every year, we have visited the village to assess recent changes. While no major changes have occurred in the last few years, the villagers are now on the eve of the biggest change of all—the disappearance of their village. Needless to say, Lengshuigou residents are deeply concerned about their future.

The village's disappearance is one of the results of the government decision to construct a new East Jinan passenger terminal. Construction began in 2015, and some of the village's land has already been requisitioned. But that was only the first stage. This rail station, which is slated for completion in 2018, will be the biggest integrated transit hub in Shandong Province. The plans call for the construction of an enormous commercial complex, as well as schools, hospitals, and other public facilities, all of which will make the district a new satellite hub of Jinan. Lengshuigou and other nearby villages are all scheduled for demolition within the next year. The villagers will be moved into a new high-density apartment complex, and the village will cease to exist.

Needless to say, contemporary Lengshuigou is currently facing great uncertainties: on the one hand, rapid urbanization will end its existence. The village, which has hundreds of years of history, will disappear as an independent rural community. On the other hand, as our study has documented, villagers' lifestyles and attitudes, indeed, the very nature of the community, had already experienced far-reaching changes in recent decades. The one certainty is that what lies ahead will introduce yet more drastic disruptions as the community is incorporated within Shandong's, and China's relentless urbanization.

While individuals and families in the village are deeply concerned about the future in light of these drastic changes, the organizations that have held village life together also face great uncertainty as Lengshuigou disappears as a distinct political unit. Soon its residents will no longer be registered as peasants, but will gain much-coveted urban registration; that is, they will be classified as city dwellers, more fully incorporated in a larger all-encompassing urban community as they exchange village homes for new apartments. How will the ties of Lengshuigou's people to their ancestors alter as the physical world they have known disappears, and the graves that bound past and present are displaced?

Lengshuigou is now at a turning point: the traditional rural lifestyle is coming to an end, and a new urban lifestyle, which will offer many opportunities to the younger generation, is beginning. Most of the younger generation are looking forward to this new stage in their lives, even though it is going to take some time for them to become accustomed to the different pace and customs of urban life. In the years ahead, we plan to continue to follow their lives as they experience this confrontation between "traditional" and "modern" ways of being, grasp new opportunities, and meet these new challenges.

Lin Juren
September 2017

References

BSJ/NBS. 2011. *Jinan Statistical Yearbook* [济南统计年鉴]. 北京: 中国统计出版社.

BSL. 2009. *1999–2009 Licheng Yearbook* [历城年鉴]. Edited by Bureau of Statistics of Licheng District (济南市历城区统计局).

Cao, Jinqing 曹锦清. 2000. *Along the Yellow River: Reflections on China's Rural Society* [黄河边的中国——一个学者对乡村社会的观察与思考]. 上海: 上海文艺出版社.

Chan, Anita, Richard Madsen, and Jonathan Unger. 1984. *Chen Village: The Recent History of a Peasant Community in Mao's China*. Berkeley: University of California Press.

———. 1992. *Chen Village under Mao and Deng*. Berkeley: University of California Press.

Cheng, Qiang 程蔷. 2006. "Inheritance and Evolvement of Folk Festivals" [民俗节日的继承和演变]. 上海大学学报 (社会科学版) 第13卷 (第4期): 31–40.

Chow, Yung-Teh. 1966. *Social Mobility in China: Status Careers among the Gentry in a Chinese Community*. New York: Atherton Press.

Cong, Hanxiang 从翰香, ed. 1995. *Rural Hebei-Shandong-Henan in Modern Times* [近代冀鲁豫乡村]. 北京: 中国社会科学出版社.

Constitution of the People's Republic of China. 1982, December 4. Edited by National People's Congress—Fifth National People's Congress.

Crook, Isabel, and David Crook. 1959. *Ten Mile Inn: Revolution in a Chinese Village*. London: Routledge & Kegan Paul.

———. 1979. *Ten Mile Inn: Mass Movement in a Chinese Village*. London: Routledge & Kegan Paul.

CSB. 2011. *China Statistical Yearbook 2011* [中国统计年鉴]. 北京: 中国统计出版社.

Deng, Dacai 邓大才. 2010. "Four Paradigms beyond the Village: Methodology Perspective: Freedman, Huang, Skinner, and Duara" [超越村庄的四种范式: 方

法论视角——以施坚雅、弗里德曼、黄宗智、杜赞奇为例]. 社会科学研究 (第2期): 130–36.

Deng, Hongxun 邓鸿勋, and Baipu Lu 陆百莆, eds. 2006. *Out of the Dual Structure—Migrant Workers, Urbanization and Construction of New Rural Area* [走出二元结构——农民工、城镇化与新农村建设]. 北京: 中国发展出版社.

Du, Runsheng 杜润生. 2003. *Institutional Changes in Rural China* [中国农村制度变迁]. 成都: 四川人民出版社.

Duara, Prasenjit. 1988. *Culture, Power, and the State: Rural North China, 1900–1942*. Stanford: Stanford University Press.

Durkheim, Émile. 2001 [1912]. *The Elementary Forms of the Religious Life*. London: Oxford University Press.

Encyclopedia of China, The. 1991. *The Encyclopedia of China* [中国大百科全书]. Edited by Encyclopedia Editorial [大百科全书编辑部]. 北京: 中国大百科全书出版社.

Fei, Xiaotong [Fei, Hsiao't'ung]. 1980. *Peasant Life in China: A Field Study of Country Life in the Yangtze Valley*. London: Routledge and Kegan Paul.

Fei, Xiaotong 费孝通. 1986 [1939]. *Jiangcun Economy: Peasant Life in China* [江村经济一中国农民的生活]. 南京: 江苏人民出版社.

———. 1992 [1948]. *From the Soil: The Foundations of Chinese Society*. Berkeley: University of California Press.

———. 1999 [1947]. *The Institutions for Reproduction (生育制度)*. 北京: 商务印书馆.

———. 2009 [1948]. "Rural Recovery" [乡土重建]. In *Fei Xiaotong Complete Works* [费孝通全集]. 呼和浩特: 内蒙古人民出版社.

Fei, Xiaotong, and Zhiyi Zhang. 1945. *Earthbound China: A Study of Rural Economy in Yunnan*. New York: University of Chicago Press.

———. 1990. *Earthbound China: A Study of Rural Economy in Yunnan* [云南三村]. 天津: 天津人民出版社.

Feng, Erkang 冯尔康, ed. 1994. *Chinese Social Structure and Its Changes* [中国社会结构的演变]. 郑州: 河南人民出版社.

Freedman, Maurice. 1963. "A Chinese Phase in Social Anthropology." *British Journal of Sociology* 14 (1): 1–19.

———. 1979. *The Study of Chinese Society: Essays by Maurice Freedman (Selected and Introduced by G. W. Skinner)*. Stanford: Stanford University Press.

Friedman, Edward, Paul Pickowicz, and Mark Selden. 1991. *Chinese Village, Socialist State*. New Haven, CT: Yale University Press.

Gamble, Sidney D. 1933. *How Chinese Families Live in Peiping*. London: Funk and Wagnall.

———. 1963. *North China Villages: Social, Political, and Economic Activities before 1933*. Berkeley: University of California Press.

———. 1968. *Ting Hsien: A North China Rural Community*. Stanford: Stanford University Press.

———. 2011 [1921]. *Peking: A Social Survey, Global Oriental Classic Reprints*. Folkestone, UK: Global Oriental.

Gao, Hongbo 高洪波, Chaoqun Li李超群, and Qingwu Qin秦庆武. 2009. *Reflection on the Historic Leap: Practice and Exploration of Rural Reformation Development in Recent 30 Years in Shandong* [历史跨越的审视——山东农村改革发展*30*年实践与探索]. 济南: 山东人民出版社.

Ge, Jianhong 葛剑雄, and Yangfang Hou 侯杨方, eds. 2001. *History of China's Population* [中国人口史]. 第6卷. 上海: 复旦大学出版社.

Grove, Linda. 2006. *A Chinese Economic Revolution: Rural Entrepreneurship in the Twentieth Century.* New York: Rowman & Littlefield.

———. 2014. "Revisiting the *Kankō Chōsa* Villages: A Review of Chinese and Japanese Studies of North China Rural Society." *International Journal of Asian Studies* 11 (1): 77–98.

Guo, Yuhua 郭于华. 2002. "Moral Economy or Rational Peasant" [道义经济还是理性小农]. 读书 (第5期): 104–10.

Han, Jun 韩俊. 2008. *Solving Issues Concerning Agriculture, Countryside and Farmers in China: Rural Reform and Development in 30 Years* [破解三农难题——*30*年农村改革与发展]. 北京: 中国发展出版社.

Han, Min. 2001. *Social Change and Continuity in a Village in Northern Anhui, China: A Response to Revolution and Reform, Senri Ethnological Studies*, 58. Osaka: National Museum of Ethnology.

He, Ping 何平. 2008. "The State's Promotion of Female Status: One Example of Female Liberation from the Liberation Period" [国家在场下的妇女地位提升——以建国初期的妇女解放为例]. 宁波党校学报 (第2期): 80–83.

He, Xuefeng 贺雪峰, ed. 2009. *Village Governance: Some Case Studies* [村治模式：若干案例研究], (中国村治模式实证研究丛书). 济南: 山东人民出版社.

———. 2012. "Discussions on Village Morphology and Village Social Structure—From a Rural Survey of Yingshan Village in Hubei" [村庄形态与村庄社会结构散论——湖北英山农村调查随笔之一]. 华中科技大学 中国乡村治理研究中心. Accessed December 9, 2015. http://www.snzg.cn/article/2008/0203/article_9061.html.

He, Xuefeng 贺雪峰, and Zhihui Tong 仝志辉. 2002. "On Rural Social Relations" [论村庄社会关联]. 中国社会科学 (第3期): 124–34.

———. 2002. *Social Connections between Villages—the Social Base of Village Order* [论村庄社会关联——兼论村庄秩序的社会基础]. 北京: 中国社会科学.

HNA. n.d. *Development of Education in Lengshuigou Village: An Overview* [冷水沟教育发展概况 by 冷水沟村华年联谊会编]. Edited by Huanian Association [华年联谊会编].

Hsu, Francis L. K. 1948. *Under the Ancestors' Shadow: Chinese Culture and Personality*. New York: Columbia University Press.

Hu, Biliang 胡必亮. 2005. *Guanxi Community* [关系共同体]. 北京: 人民出版社.

Hu, Haipeng 扈海鹏. 2008. "Rural Order and Rural Culture in a Changing Society" [变化社会中的乡村秩序与乡村文化]. 唯实 (第12期): 48–53.

Huang, Philip C. 1985. *The Peasant Economy and Social Change in North China.* Stanford: Stanford University Press.

Huang, Shumin 黄树民. 2002 [1989]. *The Spiral Road: Change in a Chinese Village through the Eyes of a Communist Party Leader* [林村的故事*: 1949* 年后的中国农村变革]. 北京: 三联书店.

Jiang, Pei 江沛. 1998. "Structural Change of Northern Rural Society in the Period of the Republic of China (1912–1949)" [民国时期华北农村社会结构的变迁]. 南开学报 (第4期): 18–23.

Jin, Guantao 金观涛, and Qingfeng Liu刘青峰. 2010. *The Transformation of Chinese Society (1840–1956): The Fate of Its Ultrastable Structure in Modern Times* [开放中的变迁——再论中国社会超稳定结构]. 北京: 法律出版社.

Jinan Licheng District Chronicles Office, 济南市历城区史志办公室编, ed. 2007. *Licheng District: The Most Important Events in the Last 20 Years* [历城建区20年大事记] 北京: 中央文献出版社.

KC. 1955. *Survey of Chinese Village Customs* [中國農村慣行調查 / *Chūgoku Nōson Kankō Chōsa*]. Edited by the Editorial Committee for Chinese Village Social Customs [*Chūgoku Nōson Kankō Chōsa Kankokai* (中国農村調査刊行会)]. 東京: 岩波書店.

Kipnis, Andrew B. 1997. *Producing Guanxi: Sentiment, Self, and Subculture in a North China Village*. Durham, NC: Duke University Press.

Kipnis, Andrew B., Luigi Tomba, and Jonathan Unger, eds. 2009. *Contemporary Chinese Society and Politics*. Vol. 4. London; New York: Routledge.

Kulp, Daniel Harrison. 1925. *Country Life in South China: The Sociology of Familism. Volume I. Phenix Village, Kwantung, China*. New York: Columbia University Press.

Lan, Linyou 兰林友. 2007. *No Temples to Be Found: A Re-study on South Manchurian Railways Co. Villages in Northern China* [庙无寻处——华北满铁调查村落的人类学再研究]. 哈尔滨: 黑龙江人民出版社.

———. 2012. *Lian Hua Luo: An Anthropological Re-study on South Manchurian Railways Co. Villages in Northern China* [莲花落——华北满铁调查村落的人类学再研究]. 北京: 社会科学文献出版社.

Lan, Yuyun 蓝宇蕴. 2005. *Village in a City: A Field Study on a "New Village Community"* [都市里的村庄：一个"新村社共同体"的实地研究]. 北京: 三联书店.

LCZ, ed. 2010. *Lengshuigou Village Gazetteer* [冷水沟村志]. Edited by Lengshuigou Village Chronicles Committee; principal editor: Li Tingfu [冷水沟村志编撰委员会编李廷夫主编]. 济南: 年济南海东文化发展有限公司印刷.

Lei, Jieqiong 雷洁琼. 1994. *Marriage and Family Transformation in Rural China Post-Economic Reform* [改革以来中国农村婚姻家庭的新变化]. 北京: 北京大学出版社.

Li, Huaiyin. 2005. *Village Governance in North China, 1875–1936*. Stanford: Stanford University Press.

———. 2009. *Village China under Socialism and Reform: A Micro History, 1948–2008*. Stanford: Stanford University Press.

Li, Jinghan 李景汉. 2005. *Survey of the Social Situation of Ding County* (定县社会概况调查). 上海: 上海人民出版社.

Li, Keqiang 李克强. 2010. "Several Problems Concerning Adjustment of Economic Structure to Promote Sustainable Development" [关于调整经济结构促进持续发展的几个问题]. 求是杂志 (第11期): 3–15.

Li, Peilin 李培林. 2004. "Social Logic in the Final Ending of a Village—Story of Yang Cheng Village" [村落终结的社会逻辑——羊城村的故事]. 江苏社会科学 (第1期): 1–10.

———, ed. 2010. *Contemporary Chinese People's Livelihood* [当代中国民生]. 北京: 社会科学文献出版社.

Li, Shanfeng 李善峰. 2004. "Chinese Village Study in the Twentieth Century—A Discussion Based on a Work as a Clue" [20世纪的中国村落研究: 一个以著作为线索的讨论]. 民俗研究 (第3期): 25–39.

Li, Tingfu 李廷夫, ed. 2011. *Celebrated People and Events in Lengshuigou* [冷水沟村名人轶事].

Li, Yining 厉以宁. 2008. "On the Reform of the Urban-Rural Dual System" [论城乡二元体制的改革]. 北京大学学报 *(哲社版)* 第45卷 (第2期): 5–11.

Liang, Shuming 梁漱溟. 1987. *Essence of Chinese Culture* [中国文化要义]. 上海: 学林出版社.

———. 2005a. *General Idea on Rural Construction* [乡村建设理论]. Second edition. 第2卷, *Complete Works of Liang Shuming* [梁漱溟全集]. 济南: 山东人民出版社.

———. 2005b. *Complete Works of Liang Shuming* [梁漱溟全集]. Second edition. 第3卷. 济南: 山东人民出版社.

Licheng County Goverment. 2012. "Licheng County Government." [济南市历城区政府]. Accessed December 9, 2015. http://www.licheng.gov.cn/tabid/105/Default.aspx.

Licheng County Records. 2012. "Licheng County Records." Accessed May 15, 2012. http://www.lcqq.gov.cn/show.asp?newsid=2257&sortid=2&typeid=104&pid=3.

Lin, Juren 林聚任. 2007. *Reconstruction of Social Trust and Capital: Research on Current Social Relations in Rural China* [社会信任和社会资本重建——当前乡村社会关系研究]. 济南: 山东人民出版社.

Lin, Yaohua 林耀华. 1948. *The Golden Wing: A Sociological Study of Chinese Familism*. New York: Oxford University Press.

———. 2000 [1935]. *The Yi of Liangshan* [义序的宗族研究]. 北京: 三联书店.

Lipton, Michael. 1977. *Why Poor People Stay Poor: A Study of Urban Bias in World Development*. London: Temple Smith.

Liu, Chun 刘椿. 2003. "Discussion about Reform on County-Level Administration Actualized by Government of Nationalist Party" [论国民党政府农村县制改革]. 深圳大学学报 *(人文社会科学版)* (第4期): 27–31.

Lu, Xueyi 陆学艺, ed. 2001. *Self-Created Villages* [内发的村庄：行仁村]. 北京: 社会科学文献出版社.

———. 2002. *Three Rural Theory: Contemporary China's Agriculture, Village, and Peasant Research* [三农论：当代中国农业、农村、农民研究]. 北京: 社会科学文献出版社.

Lu, Yao 路遥 and Mamoru Sasaki 佐々木衞. 1993. *Chinese Family, Village, and Gods: Modern Rural Society in North China* [中国の家•村•神々——近代華北農村社会]. 東京：東方書店.

Mao, Dan 毛丹. 2000. *Transition of a Rural Community—Observations and Analysis about the Unitization of Jianshanxia Village* [一个村落共同体的变迁——关于尖山下村的单位化的观察与阐释]. 上海: 学林出版社.

———. 2010. "The Contemporary Fate of the Village Community: Observations from Four Dimensions" [村落共同体的当代命运：四个观察维度]. 社会学研究 (第1期): 1–33.

Mao, Zedong 毛泽东. 1991. *Mao Zedong Selected Works* [毛泽东选集]. Vol. 第1卷. 北京: 人民出版社.

Mendras, Henri. 1970. *La Fin des Paysans*. Paris: A. Colin.

Mitani, Takashi 三谷孝. 1999. *Rural Change in China—Family, Village, and State* [中国農村変革と家族•村落/国家. 東京：汲古書院].

———. 2000. *Rural Change in China—Family, Village and State*, vol. 2 [中国農村変革と家族•村落/国家. 東京：汲古書院].

Mitani, Takashi 三谷孝 et al. 2000. *Reading China from the Villages: A Fifty-Year History of Rural North China* [村から中国を読む——華北農村五十年史]. 東京：青木書店.

Myers, Ramon Hawley. 1970. *The Chinese Peasant Economy: Agricultural Development in Hopei and Shantung, 1890–1949*. Cambridge, MA: Harvard University Press.

Myrdal, Jan. 1965. *Report from a Chinese Village*. New York: Pantheon Books.

Nakao, Katsumi. 1990. *The Structure of Power and Social Change in a Chinese Village* [中国村落の権力構造と社会変化]. Tokyo: Ajia Seikei Gakkai.

Nee, Victor, and David Stark, eds. *Remaking the Economic Institutions of Socialism: China and Eastern Europe*. Stanford: Stanford University Press.

Oi, Jean C. 1991. *State and Peasant in Contemporary China: The Political Economy of Village Government*. Berkeley: University of California Press.

———. 1999. *Rural China Takes Off: Institutional Foundations of Economic Reform*. Berkeley: University of California Press.

Parish, William L., ed. 1985. *Chinese Rural Development: The Great Transformation*. New York; Armonk, NY: M. E. Sharpe.

Parish, William L., and Martin King Whyte. 1978. *Village and Family in Contemporary China*. Chicago: University of Chicago Press.

Qiao, Zhiqiang 乔志强, ed. 1998. *Transformation of the Rural Society in Northern China in Modern Times* [近代华北农村社会变迁]. 北京: 人民出版社.

Qiu, Menghua 邱梦华. 2008. "The Role of Cooperation among Farmers in Village Order during the Transition Period: A Study Based on Two Villages in Southeast Zhejiang Province" [社会变迁中的农民合作与村庄秩序——以浙东南两个村为例]. 博士学位, 社会学, 上海大学.

Sahlins, Marshall. 1999. "What Is Anthropological Enlightenment? Some Lessons of the Twentieth-Century." *Annual Review of Anthropology* 28 (1): i–xxiii.

SHZ. 1989. *Compilation on Shandong's Cooperative Movement* [山东省农业合作化史料汇编]. 下册. 济南: 山东人民出版社.

Siu, Helen F. 1989. *Agents and Victims in South China—Accomplices in Rural Revolution*. New Haven, CT: Yale University Press.

Skinner, G. William. 1964. "Marketing and Social Structure in Rural China: Part I." *Journal of Asian Studies* 24 (1): 3–43.

———. 1965. "Marketing and Social Structure in Rural China: Part II." *Journal of Asian Studies* 24 (2): 195–228.

———. 1965. "Marketing and Social Structure in Rural China: Part III." *Journal of Asian Studies* 24 (3): 363–99.

SSY. 2011. *Shandong Statistical Yearbook 2011* [山东统计年鉴*2011*]. Edited by Shandong Statistics Bureau [山东省统计局]. 北京: 中国统计出版社.

Su, Hailing 苏海玲, Juren Lin 林聚任, and Yuxi Xie 解玉喜. 2009. "The Role of Internal Factors in the Supply of Public Goods in Rural Villages." [论村庄内部因素在公共物品供给中的作用及实现机]. 社会科学 (第10期): 77–83.

Sun, Taoxia 孙兆霞. 2005. *Tun Pu Folk Society: Jiuxi Village* [屯堡乡民社：九溪村]. 北京: 社会科学文献出版社.

SZ. 1994. *Shandong Gazetteer—Population Gazetteer* [山东省志•人口志, *by* 山东省地方史志编纂委员会]. 济南: 齐鲁书社.

Sztompka, Piotr. 2003. *The Sociology of Social Change*. Oxford: Blackwell.

Tang, Kuiyu 唐魁玉. 2008. "Life Style Based on 'Ideology'—General Characteristics of Life History in Chinese Society from 1949 to 1978" [作为"意识形态"化的生活方式——1949年到1978年中国社会生活史的总体特征]. 理论界 (3月):80–83.

Unger, Jonathan. 2002. *The Transformation of Rural China*. New York; Armonk, NY: M. E. Sharpe.

Vogel, Ezra F. 1965. "From Friendship to Comradeship: The Change in Personal Relations in Communist China." *The China Quarterly* (21): 46–60.

Walder, Andrew, ed. 1998. *Zouping in Transition: The Process of Reform in Rural North China*. Cambridge, MA: Harvard University Press.

Wang, Huning 王沪宁. 1991. *Contemporary Chinese Village Family Culture: Modernization of Chinese Society* [当代中国村落家族文化：对中国社会现代化的一项探索]. 上海: 上海人民出版社.

Wang, Mengkui 王梦奎, ed. 2004. *Urbanization with Chinese Characteristics* [中国特色城镇化道路]. 北京: 中国发展出版社.

Wang, Mingming 王铭铭. 1997. *Community Development: A Case Study of a Han Family in Xi Village* [社区的历程：溪村汉人家庭的个案研究]. 天津: 天津人民出版社.

———. 1997. "A Small Place and a Huge Society" [小地方与大社会——中国社会的社区观察]. 社会学研究 (第1期): 86–96.

———. 2005. "Inheritance and Reflection—'Re-studies' on Three Anthropological Field Investigation Points in Yunnan" [继承与反思——记云南三个人类学田野工作地点的'再研究']. 社会学研究 (第2期): 132–54.

Wang, Xiaorong 王晓荣, and Li Bin 李斌. 2010. "Changing Models for Social Integration since the Founding of the PRC: Experiences and Inspirations." [建国以来农村社会整合模式的历史变迁及经验启示]. 东南学术 (第1期): 16–21.

Wang, Yanyan 王艳艳. 2008. "Urbanization and Modernization in a Suburban District Impacted by Changes in both Rural and Urban Society—Based on a Case Study of Lengshuigou" [城乡互动作用下发达地区城郊村的城市化与现代化发展——以济南市王舍人镇冷水沟村为个案]. 学硕士学位, 社会学系, 山东大学.

Wang, Ying 王颖. 2002. "Empirical Research on Shanghai Urban Community—the Community Type, the Location Structure and Changing Trend" [上海城市社区实证研究——社区类型、区位结构及变化趋势]. 城市规划汇刊 (第6期): 33–40.

Wang, Yuesheng 王跃生. 2006. *Social Transformation and Changes in Marriage and Family: Rural South Hebei from the 1930s to the 1990s* [中国当代家庭结构变动分析——立足于社会变革时代的农村]. 北京: 北京:三联书店.

Wang, Zhaocheng 王兆成, ed. 2008. *Change in Rural China: American Scholars' Social Research in Zouping County Shandong* [乡土中国的变迁：美国学者在山东邹平的社会研究]. 济南: 山东人民出版社.

Wei, Yani 魏娅妮. 2009. "The Impact of the Industrial Park on Village Changes—a Case Study of Lengshuigou Village in Jinan" [探析工业园区对村落变迁的影响——以济南市冷水沟村为例]. 硕士学位, 社会学系, 山东大学.

Wen, Tiejun 温铁军. 2009. *Rural Issues & Institutional Evolution* [*"*三农*"*问题与制度变迁]. 北京: 中国经济出版社.

Whyte, Martin King, ed. 2010. *One Country, Two Societies: Rural-Urban Inequality in Contemporary China*, Harvard Contemporary China Series: 16. Cambridge, MA: Harvard University Press.

Wu, Yi 吴毅. 2002. *Authority and Order in Village Governance: Expressions from Chuan Dong Shuang Village in the 20th Century* [村治变迁中的权威与秩序: *20*世纪川东双村的表达]. 北京: 中国社会科学出版社.

Xie, Yong 谢泳. 1998. *Southwest Association and Modern Chinese Intellectuals* [魁阁——中国现代学术集团的雏形]. 长沙: 湖南文艺出版社.

Xie, Zhikui 谢志岿. 2005. *The Transition from Village to Urban Community—A Study of Institutions, Policies as Seen in the Phenomenon of "Villages within the City"* [村落向城市社区的转型——制度、政策与中国城市化进程中城中村问题研究]. 北京: 中国社会科学出版社.

Xu, Bin 许斌, and Hongbao Hu胡鸿保. 2005. "The Pursuit of Villages—Reflections on Two Different Anthropological Field Investigations" [追寻村落——对两种不同的人类学田野研究的省思]. 思想战线 (第3期): 42–45.

Xu, Jingze 徐经泽, and Shanmin Yang 杨善民. 1994. *Modernization: Village's Choice* [现代化: 乡村的选择]. 济南: 山东大学出版社.

Xu, Yong 徐勇. 2006. "Reflection on the Methodology of Contemporary Rural China" [当前中国农村研究方法论问题的反思]. 河北学刊 (第2期): 55–60.

Yan, Yunxiang 阎云翔. 1996. *The Flow of Gifts: Reciprocity and Social Networks in a Chinese Village*. Stanford: Stanford University Press.

———. 2003. *Private Life under Socialism: Love, Intimacy, and Family Change in a Chinese Village, 1949–1999*. Stanford: Stanford University Press.

———. 2006. "The 'Differential Mode of Association' and Hierarchy in Chinese Culture" [差序格局与中国文化的等级观]. 社会学研究 (第4期): 201–13.

Yang, C. K. 1959. *Chinese Communist Society: The Family and the Village*. Cambridge, MA: MIT Press.

———. 1959. *A Chinese Village in Early Communist Transition*. Cambridge, MA: MIT Press.

———. 1965 [1959]. *Chinese Communist Society: The Family and the Village*. Cambridge, MA: MIT Press.

Yang, Martin C. 1945. *A Chinese Village: Taitou, Shantung Province*. New York: Columbia University Press.

Yang, Shanhua 杨善华, and Hongrui Hou 侯红蕊. 1996. "Kin and Marriage Relations, Affection and Material Advantage: Rationalization of the 'Differential Mode of Association' in Contemporary Chinese Society" [血缘、姻缘、亲情与利益——现阶段中国农村社会中"差序格局"的"理性化"趋势]. 宁夏社会科学 (第6期): 51–58.

Yu, Jianrong 于建嵘. 2001. *Politics in Yue Village: Study of a Changing Village Political Structure* [岳村政治——转型期中国乡村政治结构研究]. 北京: 商务印书馆.

Zhai, Xuewei 翟学伟. 2005. *The Production of Human Relations, Face, and Power* [人情、面子与权力的再生产]. 北京: 北京大学出版社.

Zhang, Letian 张乐天. 2005. *Farewell to Ideals—Studies of People's Commune* [告别理想——人民公社制度研究]. 上海: 上海人民出版社.

Zhang, Si 张思. 2005. *Contemporary Changes in Rural Community in Northern China: A Historical Anthropological Research on Agriculture and Customs* [近代华北村落共同体的变迁——农耕结合习惯的历史人类学考察]. 北京: 商务印书馆.

Zhang, Xueqiang 张学强。2006. *Village Transition and Peasant Memory: A Case Study of Land Reform in the Shandong Base Area*, 1941–1951 [乡村变迁与农民记忆：山东老区土地改革，1941-1951].北京: 社会科学文献出版社.

Zhang, Yufa 张玉法. 1982. *Studies on Modernized Areas in China, Shandong, 1860–1916* [中国现代化的区域研究 山东省，*1860–1916*]. 台北: 中央研究院近代史研究所.

Zhe, Xiaoye 折晓叶. 1997. *Reconstructing a Village: Changes in a "Super Village"* 村庄的再造：一个"超级村庄"的社会变迁. 北京: 中国社会科学出版社.

Zhe, Xiaoye 折晓叶, and Yingying Chen 陈婴婴. 2000. *Practice in the Community: Development of "Super Villages"* [社区的实践: "超级村庄"的发展历程]. 杭州: 浙江人民出版社.

Zheng, Haolan 郑浩澜. 2006. "'Village Community' and Village Reforms—A Review on Japanese Studies on Rural China" ["村落共同体"与乡村变革——日本学界中国农村研究述评] In *Discussion on Rural China* [乡村中国评论 by 吴毅], edited by Yi Wu. 桂林: 广西师范大学出版社.

Zheng, Mengxuan 郑孟煊, ed. 2006. *The Urbanization of Shipai Village* [城市化中的石牌村]. 北京: 社会科学文献出版社.

Zhou, Daming 周大鸣. 2002. *Lineage and Society in Contemporary Southern China* [当代华南的宗族与社会]. 哈尔滨: 黑龙江人民出版社.

———. 2006. *Transitions in Feng Huang Village: Follow-Up Studies on Rural Life in Southeast China* [凤凰村的变迁: <华南的乡村生活>追踪研究]. 北京: 社会科学文献出版社.

Zhu, Wei 朱炜. 2009. "A Geographer's Perspective on the Arrangement of Living Space in Northern Zhejiang Villages" [基于地理学视角的浙北乡村聚落空间研究]. 博士学位, 建筑学系, 浙江大学.

Zhuang, Kongshao 庄孔韶. 2000. *The Silver Wing—Local Social and Cultural Change: 1920–1990* [银翅: 中国的地方社会与文化变迁]. 北京: 三联书店.

———, ed. 2004. *Travel in Time and Space: Looking Back at a Century of Chinese Rural Anthropology* [时空穿行: 中国乡村人类学世纪回访]. 北京: 中国人民大学出版社.

———. 2007. "'Locust' Method and 'Mole Method'—Comments on the Research Orientation of Anthropology and Other Related Disciplines" ["蝗虫"法与"鼹鼠"法——人类学及其相关学科的研究取向评论]. 开放时代 (第3期): 131–50.

Index

About the Editors

Lin Juren is professor of sociology and chair of the department of sociology in the School of Philosophy and Social Development at Shandong University. He received his PhD from Nankai University and was a visiting scholar at the Harvard Yenching Institute in 2001–2002 and at York University in 2005–2006. His research interests include rural sociology, development sociology, and the sociology of science.

Linda Grove is professor emerita at Sophia University in Tokyo, where she taught Chinese history and served as dean of the Faculty of Comparative Culture and vice president for academic exchange. Her research interests are in modern Chinese social and economic history, and she has done extensive fieldwork in rural North China.

ASIA/PACIFIC/PERSPECTIVES

Series Editor: Mark Selden

Crime, Punishment, and Policing in China
edited by Børge Bakken

Woman, Man, Bangkok: Love, Sex, and Popular Culture in Thailand
by Scot Barmé

Making the Foreign Serve China: Managing Foreigners in the People's Republic
by Anne-Marie Brady

Marketing Dictatorship: Propaganda and Thought Work in China
by Anne-Marie Brady

Collaborative Nationalism: The Politics of Friendship on China's Mongolian Frontier
by Uradyn E. Bulag

The Mongols at China's Edge: History and the Politics of National Unity
by Uradyn E. Bulag

Transforming Asian Socialism: China and Vietnam Compared
edited by Anita Chan, Benedict J. Tria Kerkvliet, and Jonathan Unger

Bound to Emancipate: Working Women and Urban Citizenship in Early Twentieth-Century China
by Angelina Chin

The Search for the Beautiful Woman: A Cultural History of Japanese and Chinese Beauty
by Cho Kyo, translated by Kyoko Iriye Selden

China's Great Proletarian Cultural Revolution: Master Narratives and Post-Mao Counternarratives
edited by Woei Lien Chong

North China at War: The Social Ecology of Revolution, 1937–1945
edited by Feng Chongyi and David S. G. Goodman

The People between the Rivers: The Rise and Fall of a Bronze Drum Culture, 200–750 CE
by Catherine Churchman

Prosperity's Predicament: Identity, Reform, and Resistance in Rural Wartime China
by Isabel Brown Crook and Christina Kelley Gilmartin with Yu Xiji, edited by Gail Hershatter and Emily Honig

Little Friends: Children's Film and Media Culture in China
by Stephanie Hemelryk Donald

Beachheads: War, Peace, and Tourism in Postwar Okinawa
by Gerald Figal

Gender in Motion: Divisions of Labor and Cultural Change in Late Imperial and Modern China
edited by Bryna Goodman and Wendy Larson
Social and Political Change in Revolutionary China: The Taihang Base Area in the War of Resistance to Japan, 1937–1945
by David S. G. Goodman
A Century of Change in a Chinese Village: The Crisis of the Countryside
edited by Linda Grove
Rice Wars in Colonial Vietnam: The Great Famine and the Viet Minh Road to Power
by Geoffrey C. Gunn
Islands of Discontent: Okinawan Responses to Japanese and American Power
edited by Laura Hein and Mark Selden
Masculinities in Chinese History
by Bret Hinsch
The Rise of Tea Culture in China: The Invention of the Individual
by Bret Hinsch
Women in Early Imperial China, Second Edition
by Bret Hinsch
Chinese Civil Justice, Past and Present
by Philip C. C. Huang
Local Democracy and Development: The Kerala People's Campaign for Decentralized Planning
by T. M. Thomas Isaac with Richard W. Franke
Hidden Treasures: Lives of First-Generation Korean Women in Japan
by Jackie J. Kim with Sonia Ryang
North Korea: Beyond Charismatic Politics
by Heonik Kwon and Byung-Ho Chung
Postwar Vietnam: Dynamics of a Transforming Society
edited by Hy V. Luong
From Silicon Valley to Shenzhen: Global Production and Work in the IT Industry
by Boy Lüthje, Stefanie Hürtgen, Peter Pawlicki, and Martina Sproll
Resistant Islands: Okinawa Confronts Japan and the United States
by Gavan McCormack and Satoko Oka Norimatsu
The Indonesian Presidency: The Shift from Personal towards Constitutional Rule
by Angus McIntyre
Nationalisms of Japan: Managing and Mystifying Identity
by Brian J. McVeigh

The Korean War: A Hidden History
edited by Tessa Morris-Suzuki
To the Diamond Mountains: A Hundred-Year Journey through China and Korea
by Tessa Morris-Suzuki
To Hell and Back: The Last Train from Hiroshima
by Charles Pellegrino
From Underground to Independent: Alternative Film Culture in Contemporary China
edited by Paul G. Pickowicz and Yingjin Zhang
Wife or Worker? Asian Women and Migration
edited by Nicola Piper and Mina Roces
Social Movements in India: Poverty, Power, and Politics
edited by Raka Ray and Mary Fainsod Katzenstein
Pan-Asianism: A Documentary History, Volume 1, 1850–1920
edited by Sven Saaler and Christopher W. A. Szpilman
Pan-Asianism: A Documentary History, Volume 2, 1920–Present
edited by Sven Saaler and Christopher W. A. Szpilman
Biology and Revolution in Twentieth-Century China
by Laurence Schneider
Contentious Kwangju: The May 18th Uprising in Korea's Past and Present
edited by Gi-Wook Shin and Kyong Moon Hwang
Thought Reform and China's Dangerous Classes: Reeducation, Resistance, and the People
by Aminda M. Smith
When the Earth Roars: Lessons from the History of Earthquakes in Japan
by Gregory Smits
Subaltern China: Rural Migrants, Media, and Cultural Practices
by Wanning Sun
Japan's New Middle Class, Third Edition
by Ezra F. Vogel with a chapter by Suzanne Hall Vogel, foreword by William W. Kelly
The Japanese Family in Transition: From the Professional Housewife Ideal to the Dilemmas of Choice
by Suzanne Hall Vogel with Steven K. Vogel
The Korean War: An International History
by Wada Haruki
The United States and China: A History from the Eighteenth Century to the Present
by Dong Wang
The Inside Story of China's High-Tech Industry: Making Silicon Valley in Beijing
by Yu Zhou

www.ingramcontent.com/pod-product-compliance
Lightning Source LLC
Chambersburg PA
CBHW060147280326
41932CB00012B/1668